2A

Math in Focus®

Singapore Math®
by Marshall Cavendish

Reteach

Author
Dr. Fong Ho Kheong

Marshall Cavendish Education

U.S. Distributor
Houghton
Mifflin
Harcourt

Published by Marshall Cavendish Education
An imprint of Marshall Cavendish Education Pte Ltd
Times Centre, 1 New Industrial Road, Singapore 536196
Customer Service Hotline: (65) 6213 9444
US Office Tel: (1-914) 332 8888 Fax: (1-914) 332 8882
E-mail: tmesales@mceducation.com
Website: www.mceducation.com

Distributed by
Houghton Mifflin Harcourt
222 Berkeley Street
Boston, MA 02116
Tel: 617-351-5000
Website: www.hmheducation.com/mathinfocus

First published 2015

Math in Focus® Reteach 2A
ISBN 978-0-544-19249-2

Printed in Singapore

2 3 4 5 6 7 8 20 19 18 17 16 15
4500495934 1401 A B C D E

Contents

CHAPTER 4 Using Bar Models: Addition and Subtraction

CHAPTER 5 Multiplication and Division

CHAPTER 6 Multiplication Tables of 2, 5, and 10

Chapter 7 Metric Measurement of Length

Chapter 8 Mass

Chapter 9 Volume

Introducing

Math in Focus®

Reteach

Reteach 2A and *2B*, written to complement *Math in Focus®: Singapore Math®* by Marshall Cavendish Grade 2, offer a second opportunity to practice skills and concepts at the entry level. Key vocabulary terms are explained in context, complemented by sample problems with clearly worked solutions.

Not all children are able to master a new concept or skill after the first practice. A second opportunity to practice at the same level before moving on can be key to long-term success.

Monitor students' levels of understanding during daily instruction and as they work on Practice exercises. Provide *Reteach* worksheets for extra support to students who would benefit from further practice at a basic level.

Name: ______________________ Date: ______________

CHAPTER 1 Numbers to 1,000

Worksheet 1 Counting

What is the number shown by the base-ten blocks?
Write the number in words.

1.

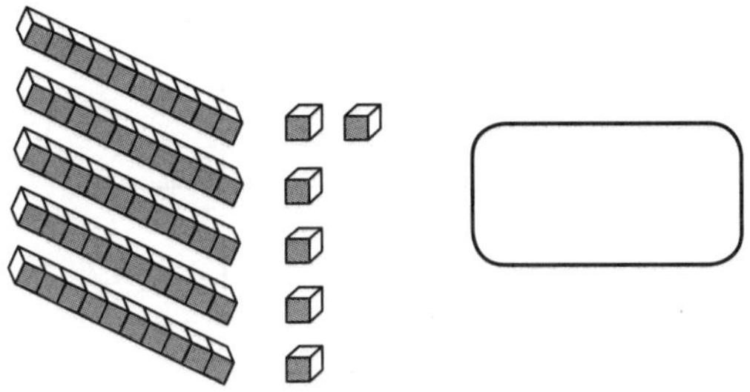

____

Count on by ones.
Use base-ten blocks to help you.

2. 28, 29, ________, 31, ________, ________

Count on by tens.
Use base-ten blocks to help you.

3. 22, 32, ________, ________, 62, ________

Name: ______________________ Date: ______________

Write the numbers shown by the base-ten blocks.

Example

Thousand	Hundreds	Tens	Ones
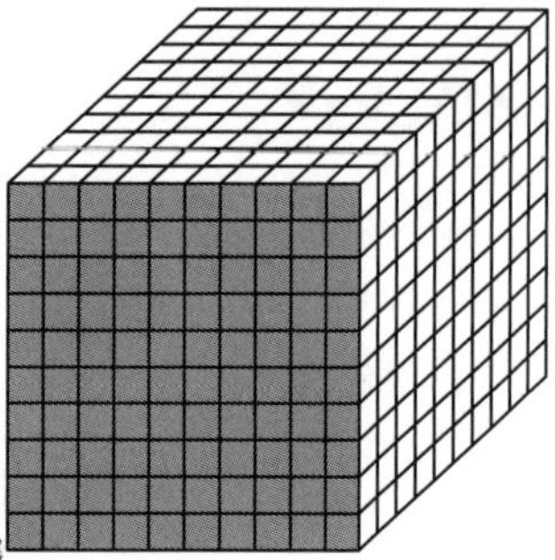			
1	0	0	0

one **thousand**

1,000

4.

Hundreds	Tens	Ones
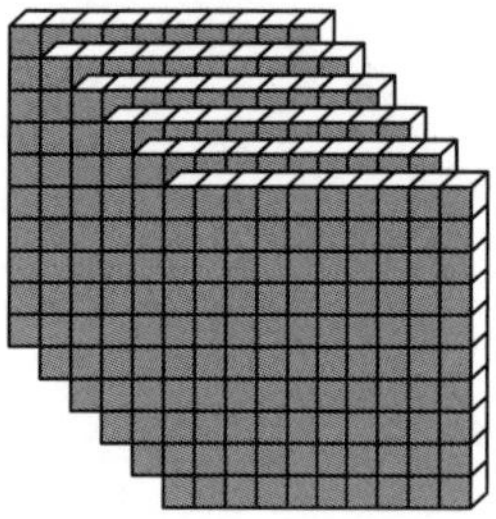	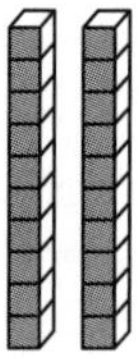	

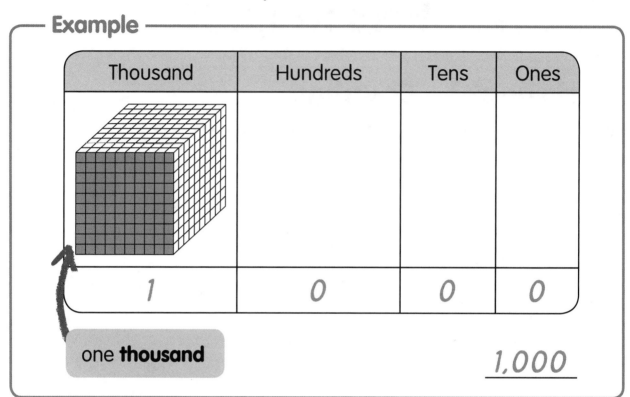

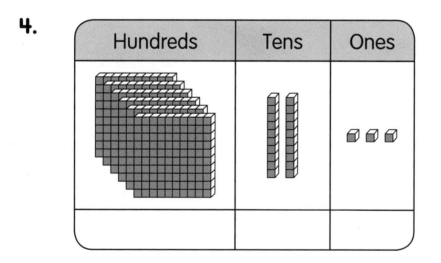

______

Name: ______________________ Date: ______________

5.

Hundreds	Tens	Ones
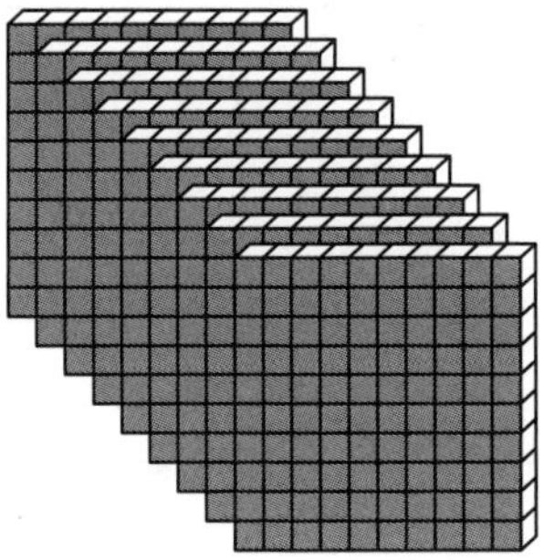	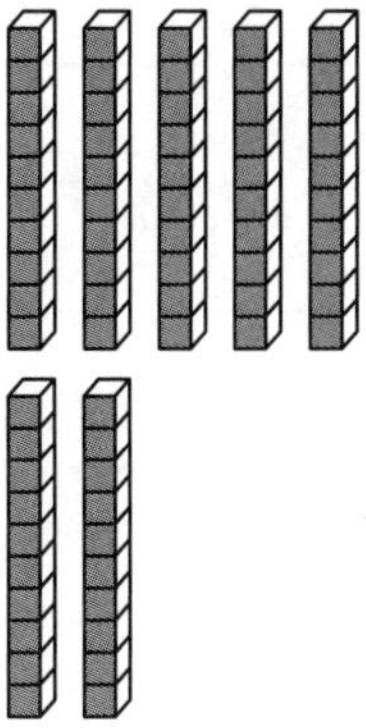	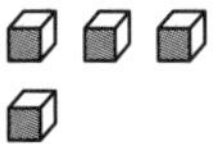

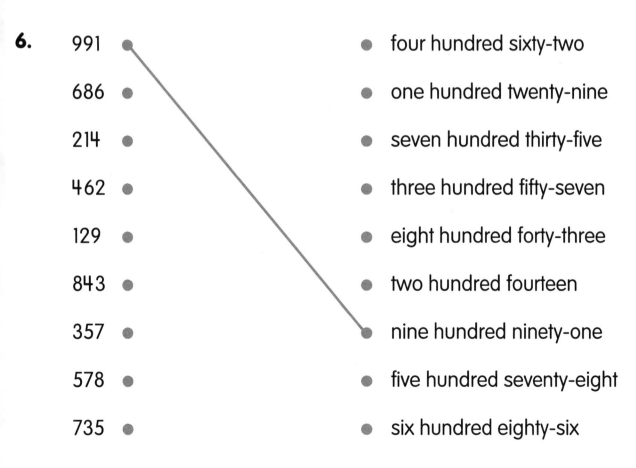

______

Match.

6.

991 •	• four hundred sixty-two
686 •	• one hundred twenty-nine
214 •	• seven hundred thirty-five
462 •	• three hundred fifty-seven
129 •	• eight hundred forty-three
843 •	• two hundred fourteen
357 •	• nine hundred ninety-one
578 •	• five hundred seventy-eight
735 •	• six hundred eighty-six

Name: ______________________ Date: ______________

Write the numbers in words.

Example

534	*five hundred thirty-four*

7.

759	

8.

845	

9.

372	

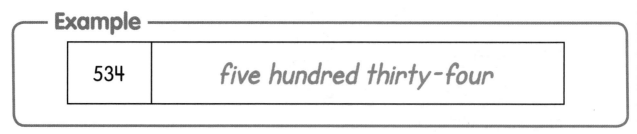

Name: ______________________ Date: ____________

Count by ones.
Find the missing numbers.

Example

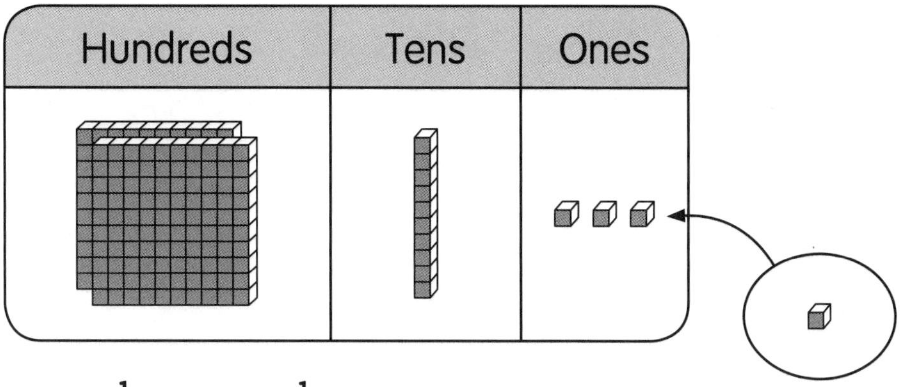

+ 1 + 1

213, 214, 215, 216, 217

10.

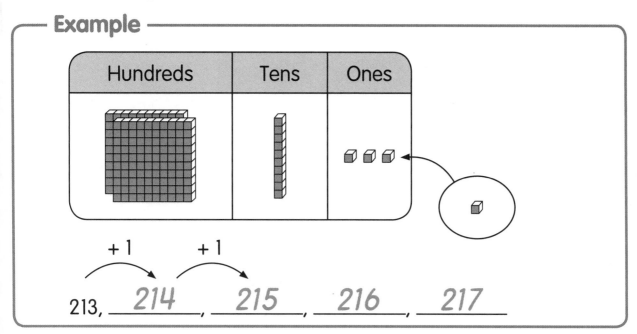

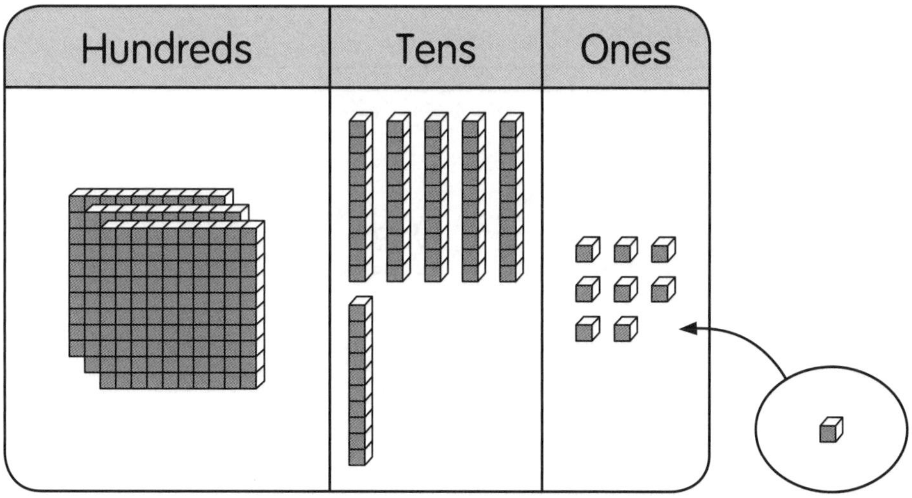

368, ________, ________, ________, ________

11. 821, ________, 823, ________, ________

Name: ______________________ Date: ______________

Count by tens.
Find the missing numbers.

Example

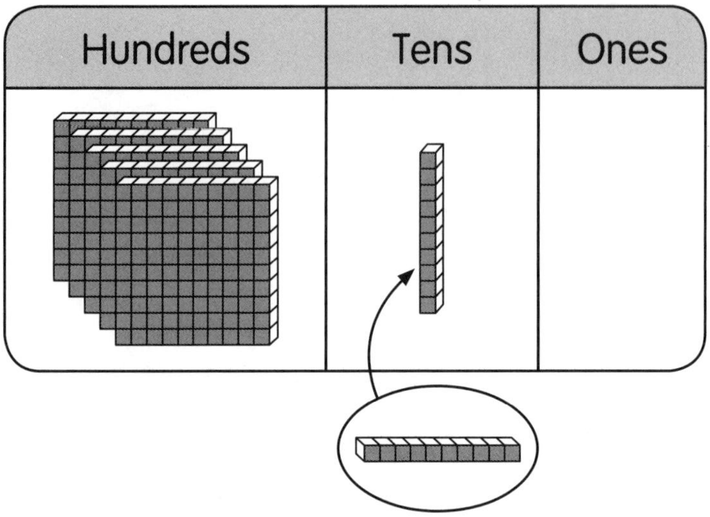

+ 10 + 10

510, 520, 530, 540, 550

12.

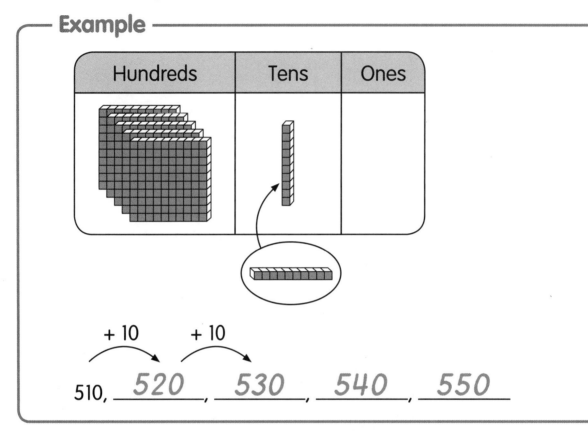

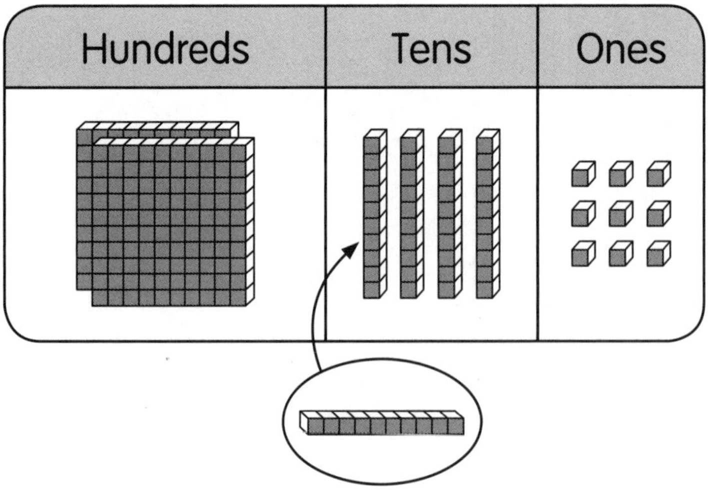

249, ______, ______, ______, ______

13. 716, 726, ______, ______, ______

Name: ______________________ Date: ______________

Count by hundreds.
Find the missing numbers.

Example

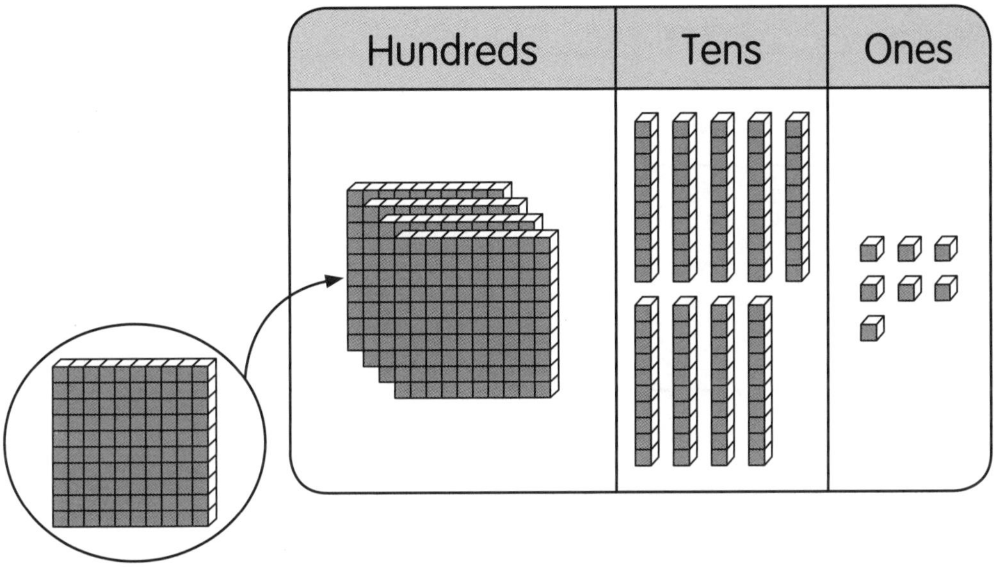

+ 100 + 100

497, 597, 697, 797, 897

14.

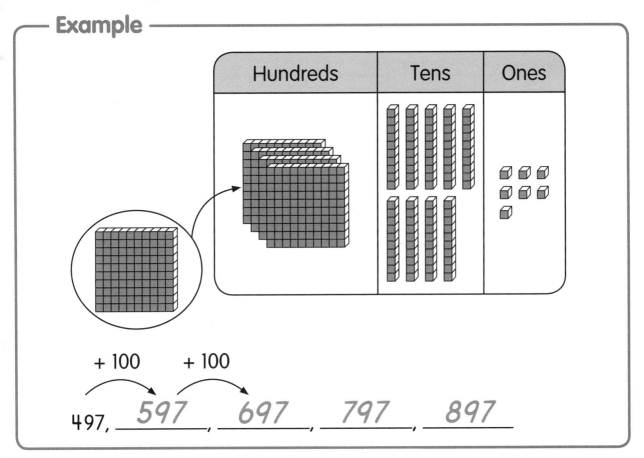

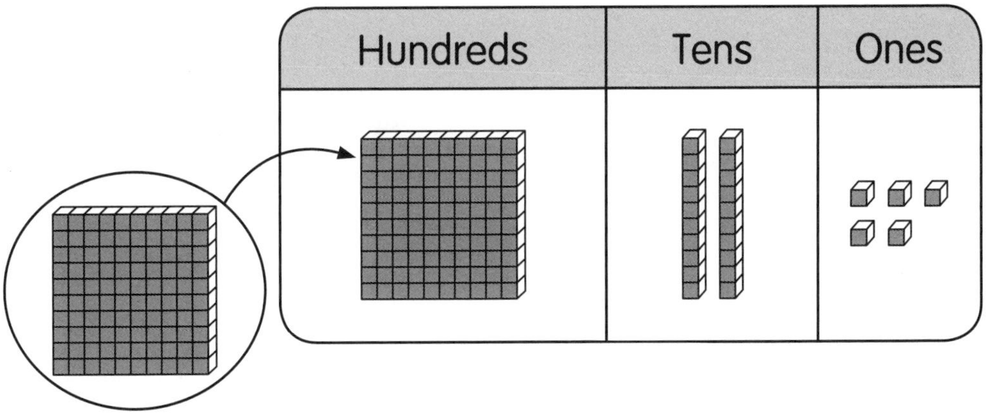

125, ________, ________, ________, ________

15. 356, ________, ________, 656, ________

Name: ______________________ Date: ______________

Find the missing numbers.

16. 459, ________, ________, ________, 463

17. 800, ________, 798, ________, ________

18. 973, 972, ________, ________, ________

19. 120, ________, 140, ________, ________

20. 650, ________, ________, ________, 610

21. 433, ________, 413, ________, ________

22. 100, ________, ________, 400, ________

23. 740, 640, ________, ________, ________

24. 534, ________, 334, ________, ________

Name: ______________________ Date: ______________

Worksheet 2 Place Value

Write the missing numbers.

1.

Tens	Ones
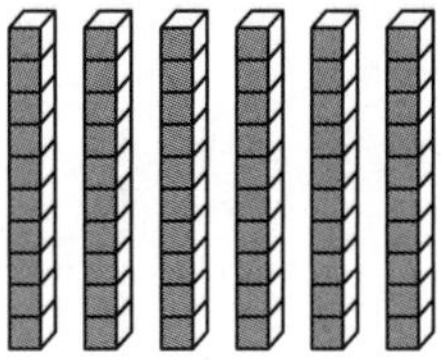	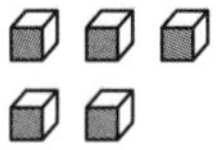

______ and ______ make 65.

______ is 60 and ______.

______ + ______ = 65

Match.

2.

55 ●		● eighty-nine
92 ●		● seventy-one
68 ●		● ninety-two
47 ●		● fifty-five
71 ●		● forty-seven
89 ●		● sixty-eight

Name: ______________________ Date: ______________

Fill in the missing numbers.

Example

Hundreds	Tens	Ones
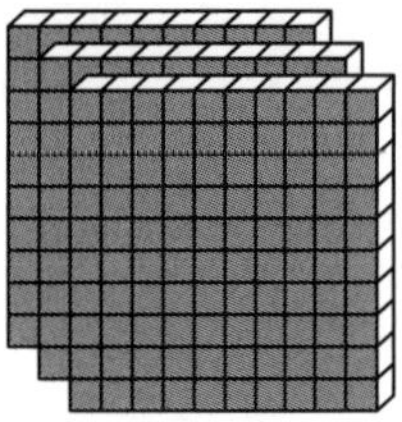	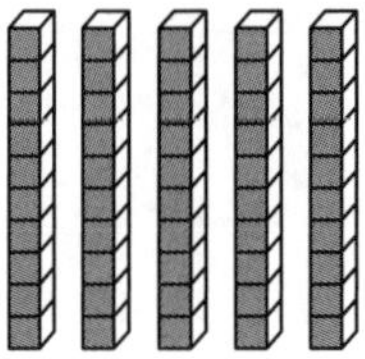	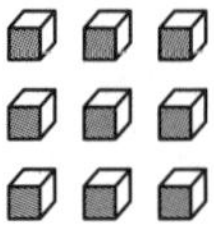
3	5	9

stands for stands for stands for

___3___ hundreds ___5___ tens ___9___ ones

or ___300___ or ___50___ or ___9___

3.

Hundreds	Tens	Ones
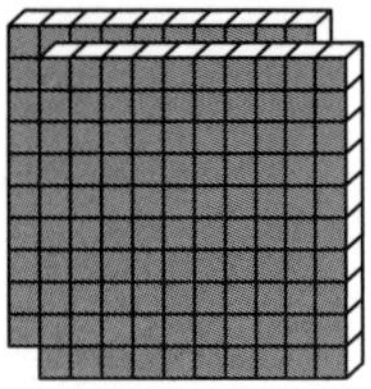	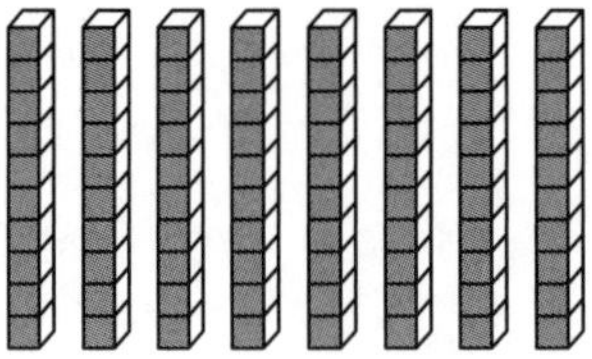	
2	8	1

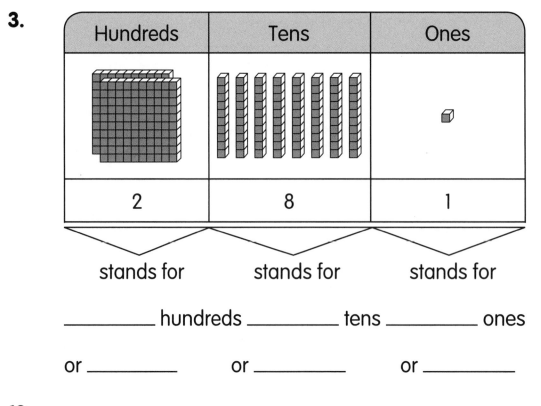

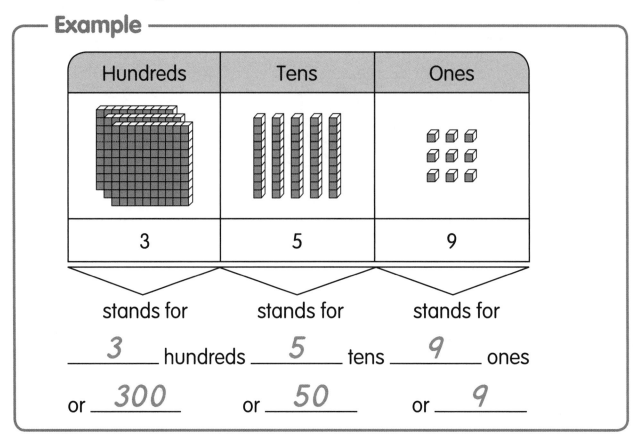

stands for stands for stands for

_______ hundreds _______ tens _______ ones

or _______ or _______ or _______

Name: ______________________ Date: ______________

Fill in the missing numbers.

4.

Hundreds	Tens	Ones
6	2	7

627 = ________ hundreds ________ tens ________ ones

627 = ________ + 20 + ________

5.

Hundreds	Tens	Ones
8	3	5

835 = ________ hundreds ________ tens ________ ones

835 = ________ + ________ + ________

6.

Hundreds	Tens	Ones
9	0	4

904 = ________ hundreds ________ tens ________ ones

904 = ________ + ________ + ________

Name: ______________________ Date: ____________

Fill in the blanks with *hundreds, tens,* or *ones.*

7. In 609,

the digit 6 is in the ______________ place.

the digit 0 is in the ______________ place.

the digit 9 is in the ______________ place.

8. In 852,

the digit 2 is in the ______________ place.

the digit 8 is in the ______________ place.

the digit 5 is in the ______________ place.

Write the number.

9. The digit 5 is in the tens place.
The digit 0 is in the ones place.
The digit 8 is in the hundreds place.

The number is ☐ ☐ ☐.

10. The digit 7 is in the ones place.
The digit 9 is in the hundreds place.
The digit 0 is in the tens place.

The number is ☐ ☐ ☐.

Name: ______________________ Date: ____________

Write the missing numbers and words.

Example

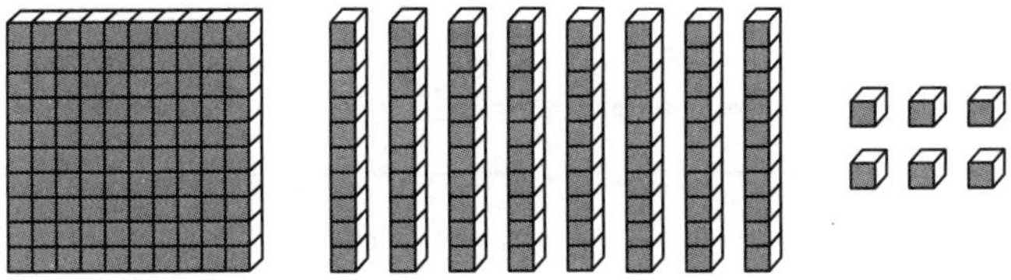

100, 80, and 6 make 186.

186 is the standard form of 186.

one hundred eighty-six is the word form of 186.

100 + 80 + 6 is the expanded form of 186.

11.

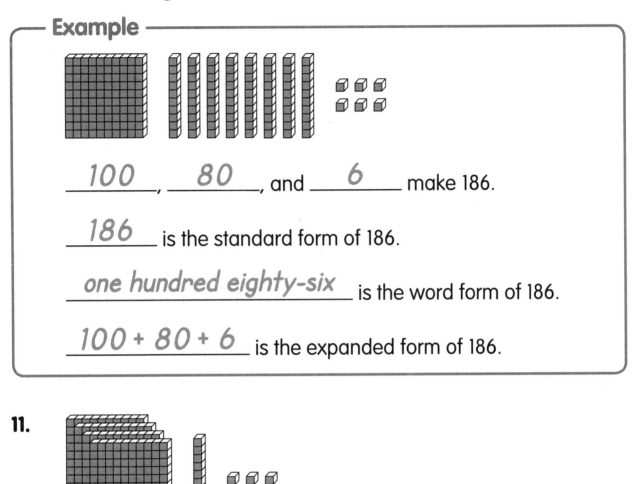

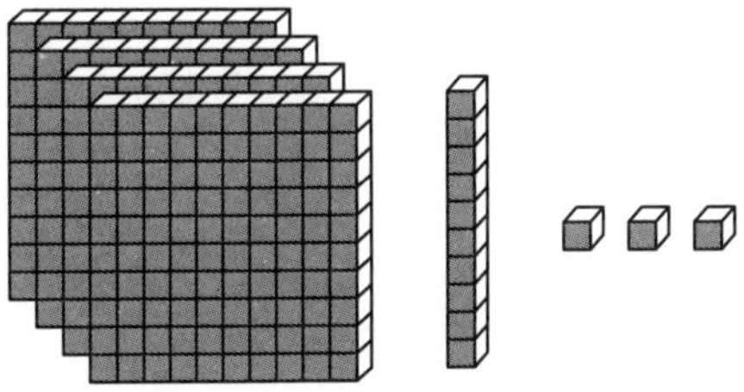

_______, _______, and _______ make 413.

_______ is the standard form of 413.

_______________ is the word form of 413.

_______________ is the expanded form of 413.

Name: ______________________ Date: ______________

Look at the place-value charts.
Then write the numbers in standard form, word form, and expanded form.

Example

Hundreds	Tens	Ones
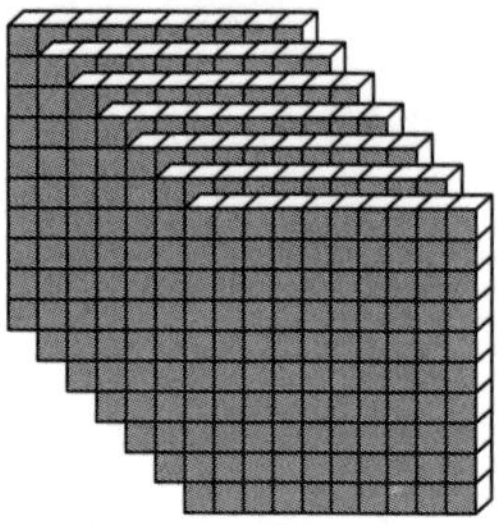	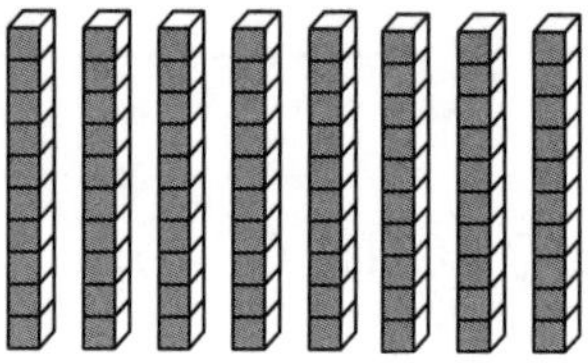	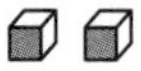
7	8	2
782		
Seven hundred eighty-two		
700 + 80 + 2		

12.

Hundreds	Tens	Ones
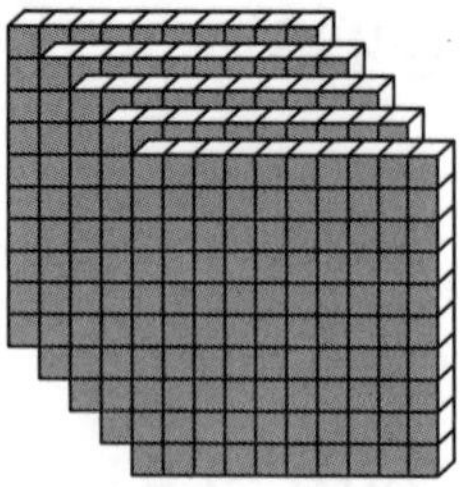		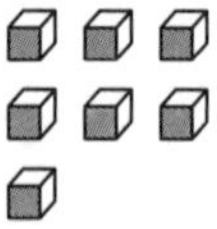

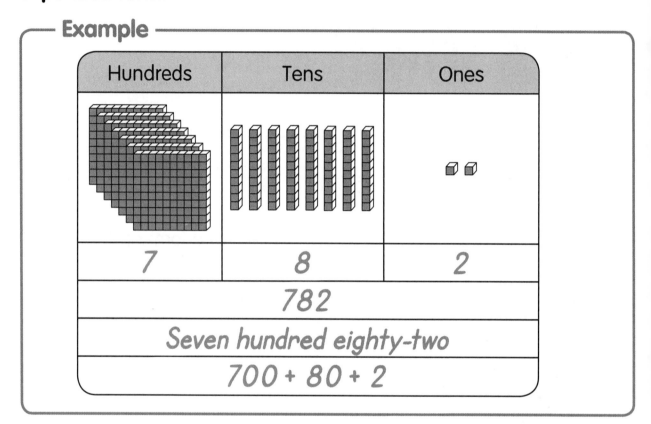

Name: ______________________ Date: ______________

Worksheet 3 Comparing Numbers

Circle the number that is greater.

1. 46 13

2. 55 62

3. 69 94

4. 78 87

Fill in the blanks with *greater than* or *less than*.

5. 72 is ______________ 58.

6. 49 is ______________ 94.

7. 88 is ______________ 77.

8. 60 is ______________ 90.

Name: ______________________ Date: ______________

Use base-ten blocks to compare the numbers.
Fill in the missing numbers.

Example

	Hundreds	Tens	Ones
498	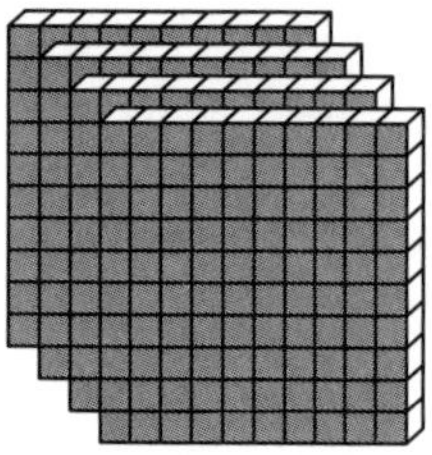	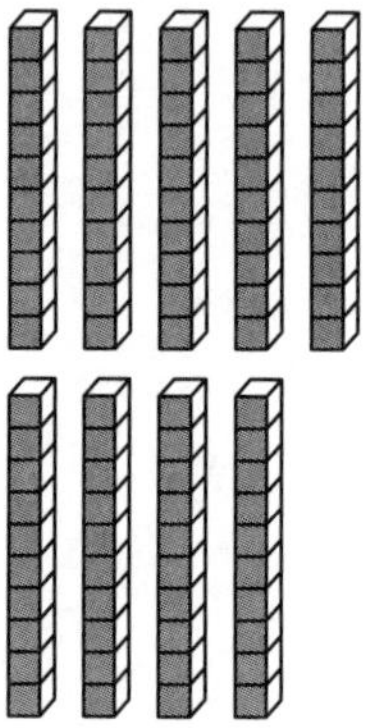	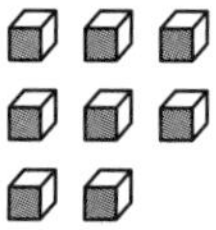
700	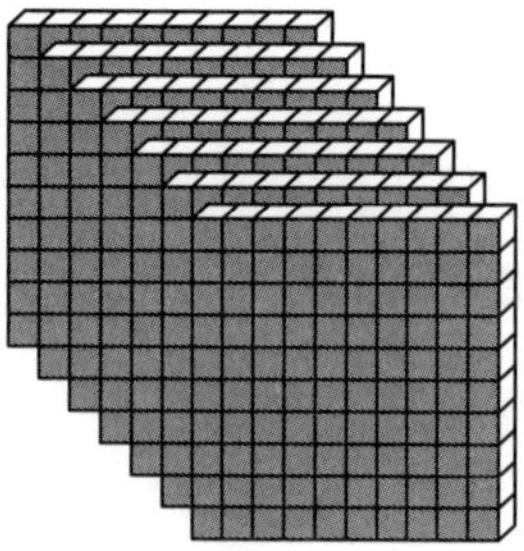		

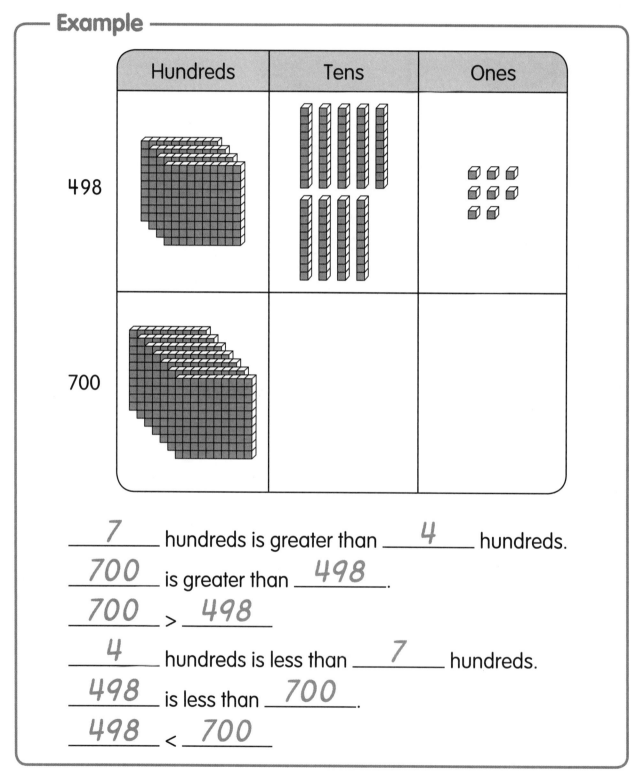

7 hundreds is greater than 4 hundreds.

700 is greater than 498.

700 > 498

4 hundreds is less than 7 hundreds.

498 is less than 700.

498 < 700

Name: ____________________ Date: ____________

Use base-ten blocks to compare the numbers.
Fill in the missing numbers.

9.

	Hundreds	Tens	Ones
825	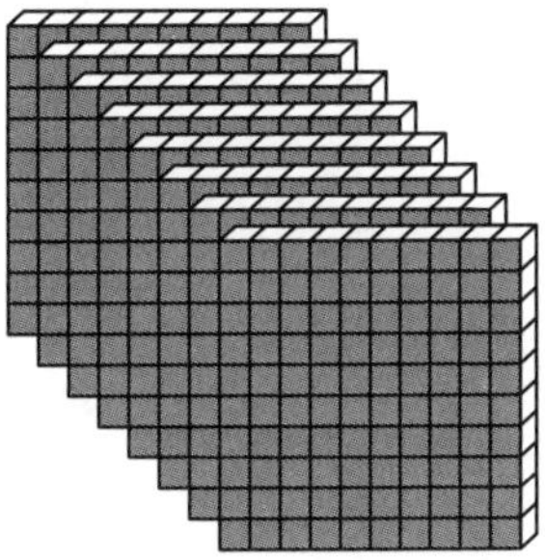	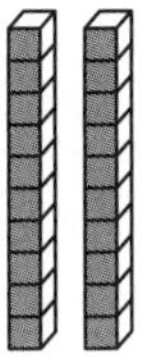	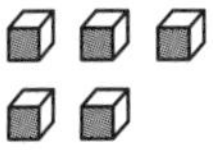
699	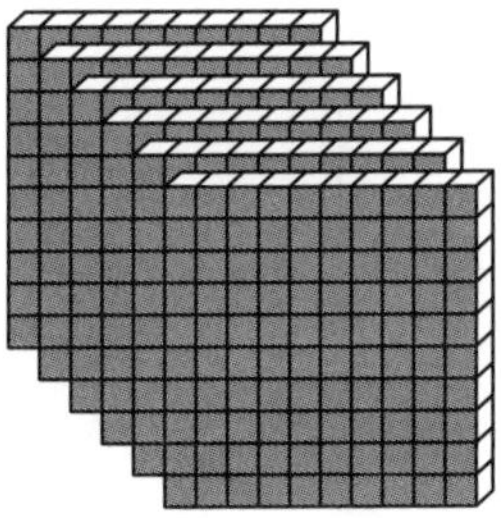	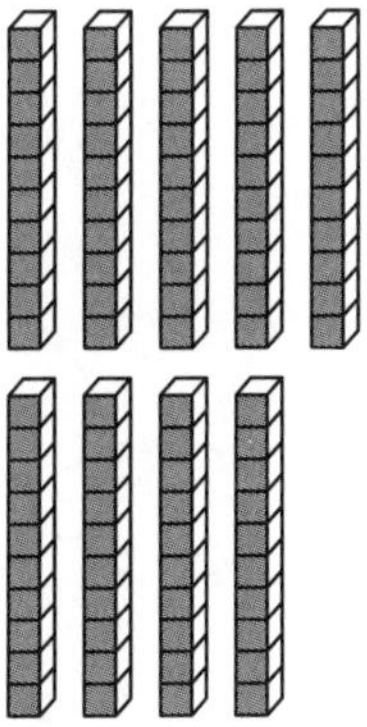	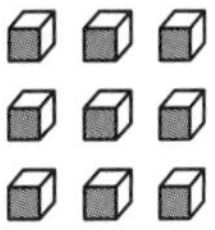

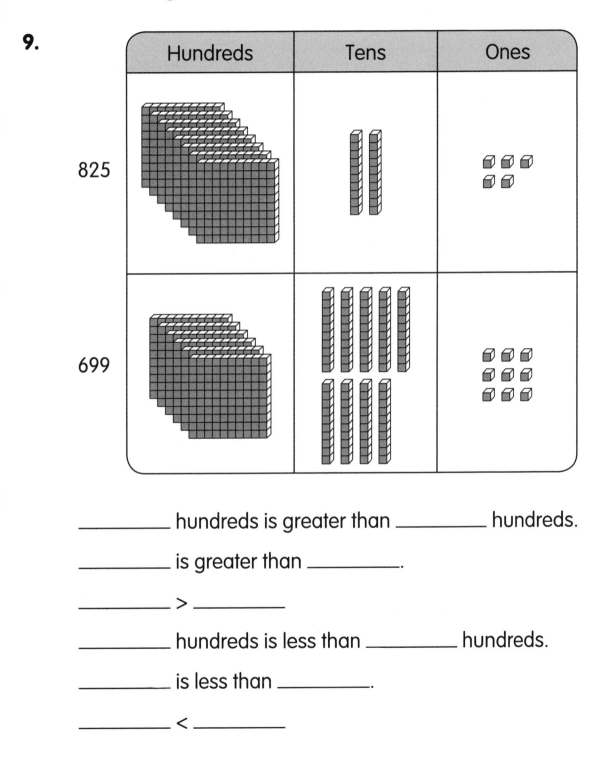

________ hundreds is greater than ________ hundreds.

________ is greater than ________.

________ > ________

________ hundreds is less than ________ hundreds.

________ is less than ________.

________ < ________

Name: ______________________ Date: ______________

Use base-ten blocks to compare the numbers.
Fill in the missing numbers.

Example

	Hundreds	Tens	Ones
305	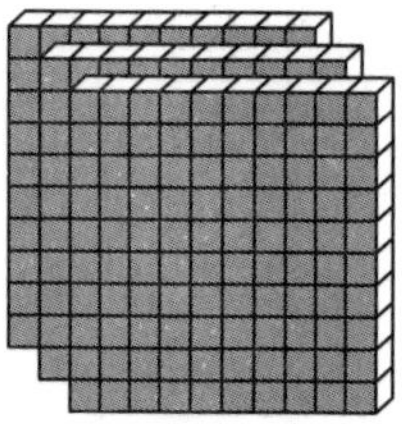		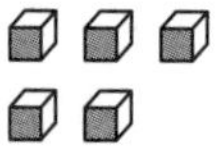
387	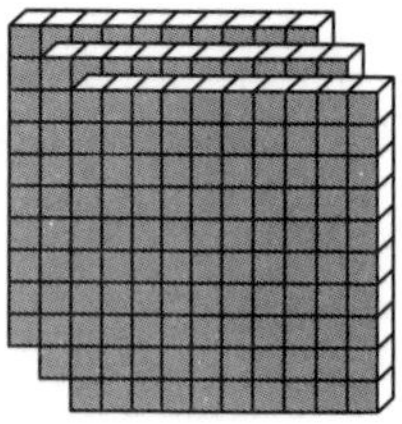	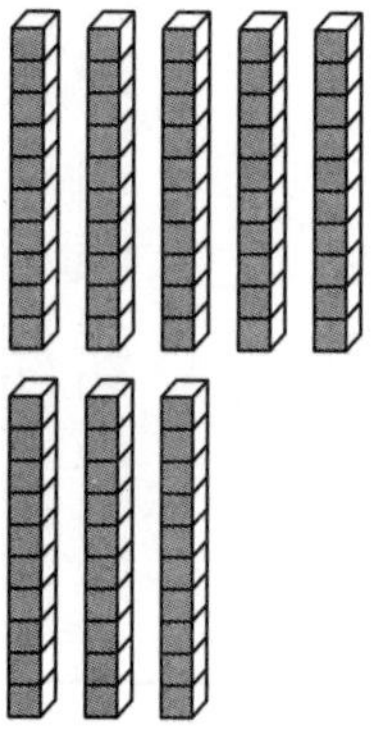	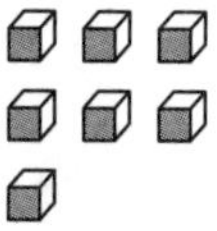

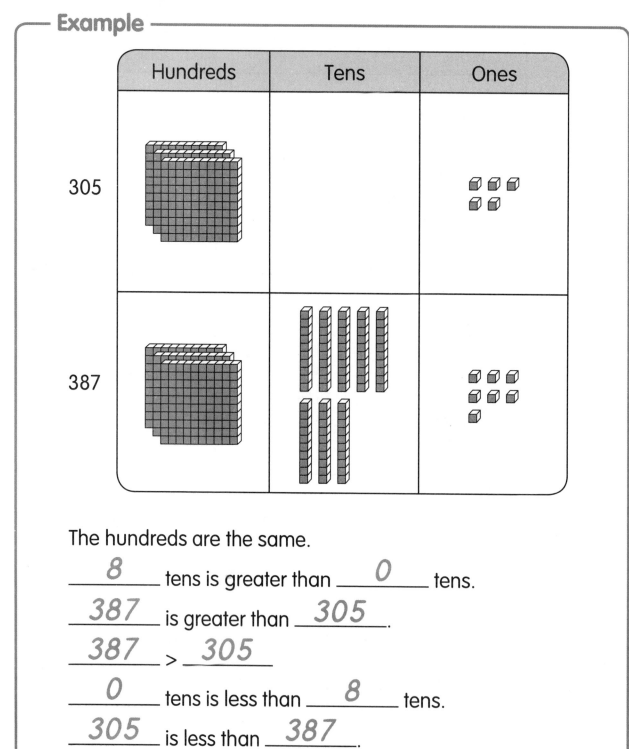

The hundreds are the same.

__8__ tens is greater than __0__ tens.

__387__ is greater than __305__.

__387__ > __305__

__0__ tens is less than __8__ tens.

__305__ is less than __387__.

__305__ < __387__

Name: ____________________ Date: ____________

Use base-ten blocks to compare the numbers.
Fill in the missing numbers.

10.

	Hundreds	Tens	Ones
580	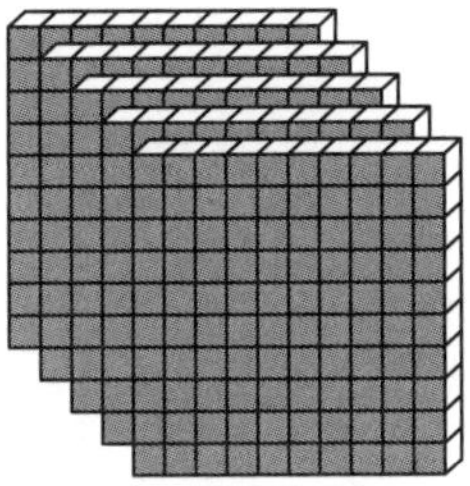	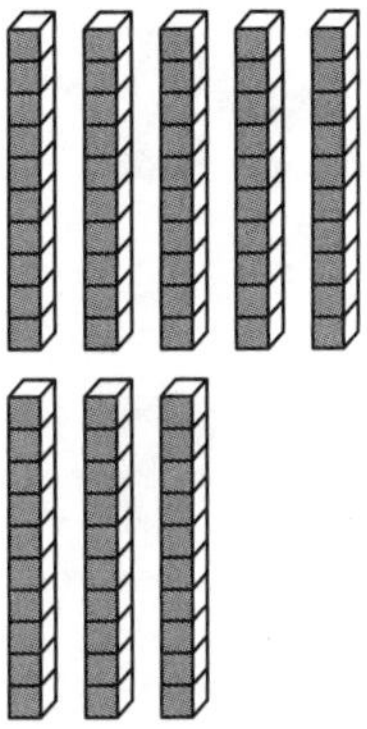	
579	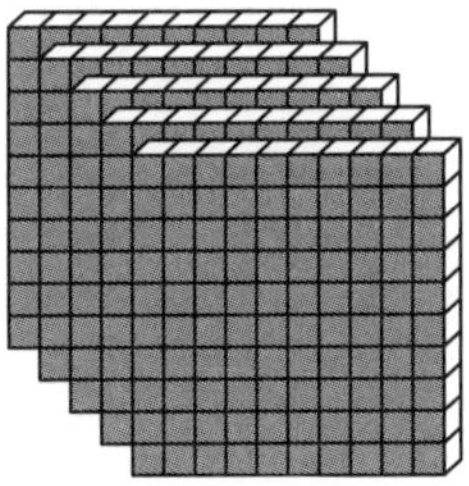	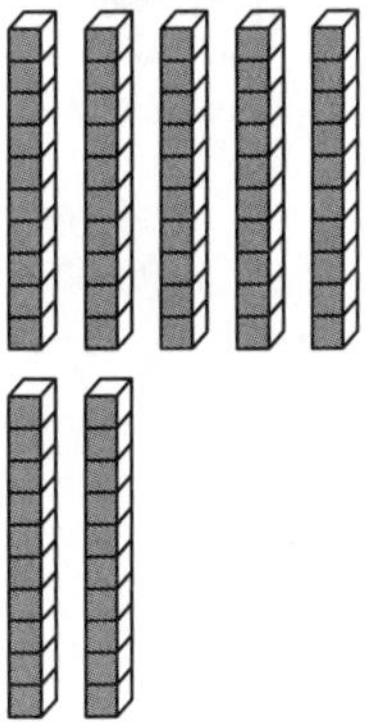	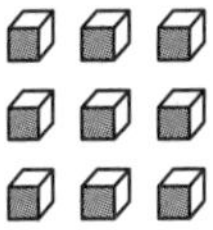

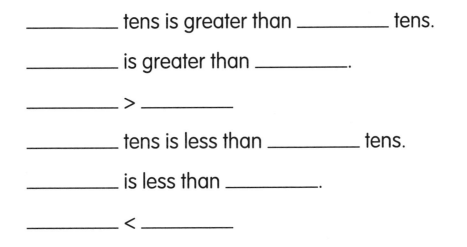

The hundreds are the same.

________ tens is greater than ________ tens.

________ is greater than ________.

________ > ________

________ tens is less than ________ tens.

________ is less than ________.

________ < ________

Name: ________________________ Date: ________________

Circle the number that is less.

11. 628 374

12. 789 798

13. 506 503

14. 475 469

15. 299 198

Write *greater than* or *less than.*

16. 700 is ______________ 709.

17. 877 is ______________ 871.

18. 638 is ______________ 658.

19. 974 is ______________ 947.

20. 638 is ______________ 836.

Name: ______________________________ Date: ______________

Worksheet 4 Order and Pattern

Complete the number patterns.

1. 68, 69, ________, ________, ________, 73

2. 84, ________, ________, 81, 80, ________

Order the numbers from least to greatest.
Use a place-value chart to help you.

Example

	Hundreds	Tens	Ones
457	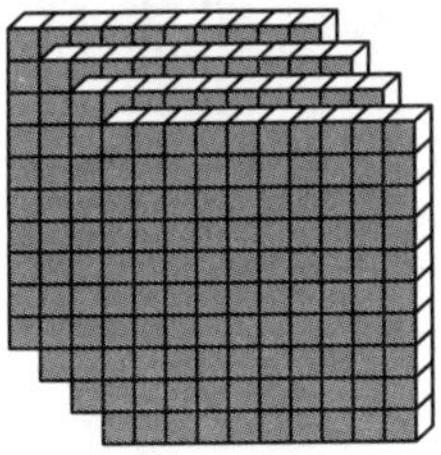	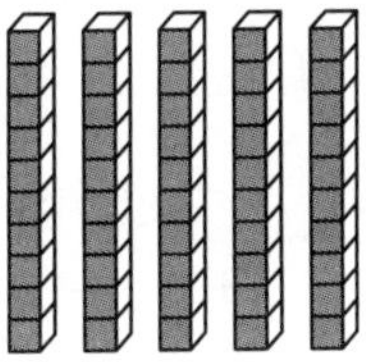	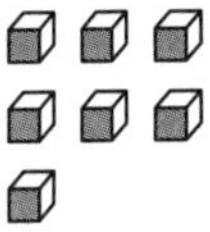
983	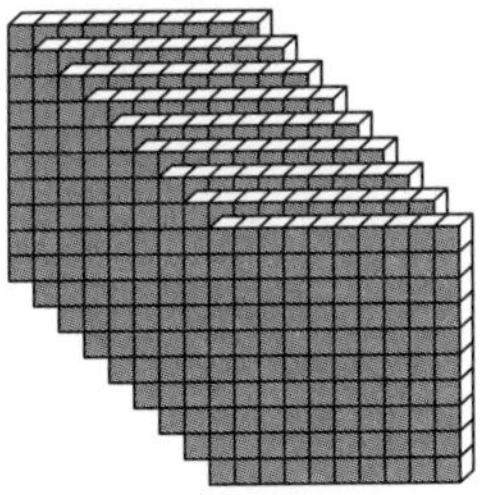	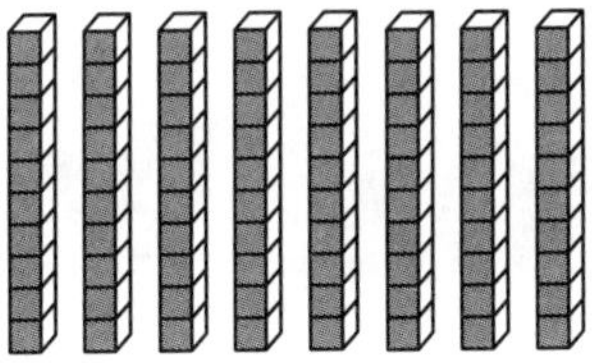	
349	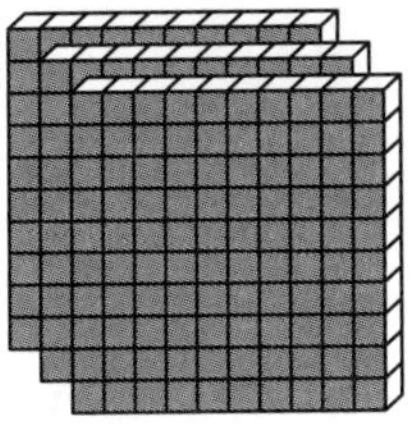	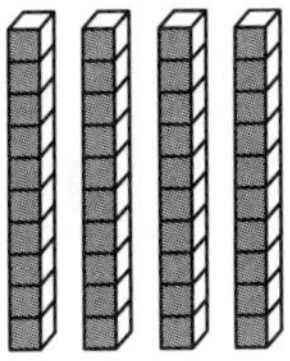	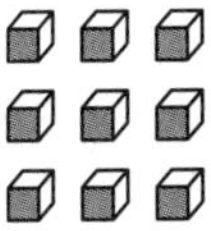

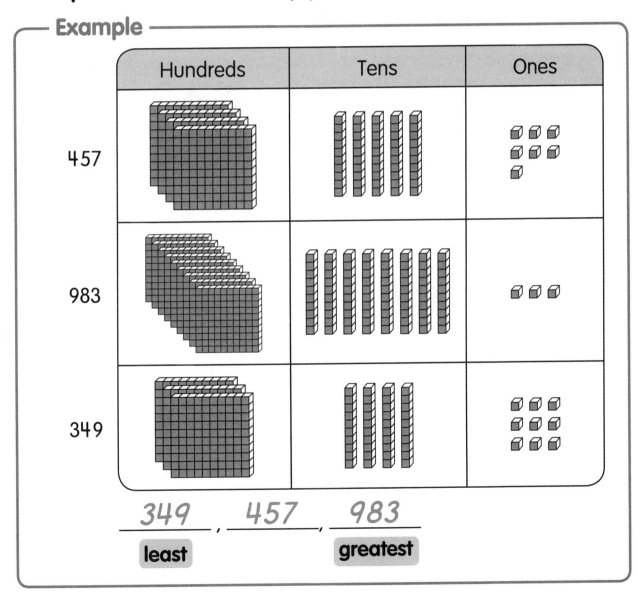

349, 457, 983

least greatest

Name: ______________________ Date: ______________

3.

	Hundreds	Tens	Ones
237	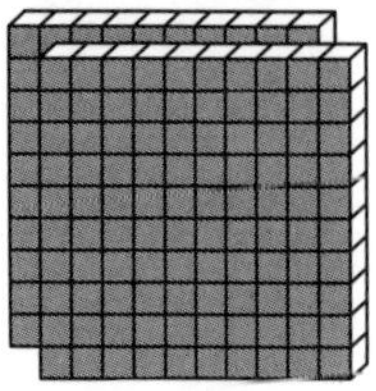	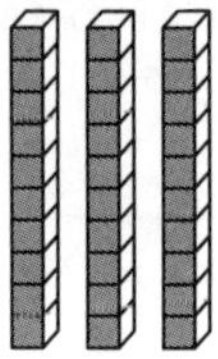	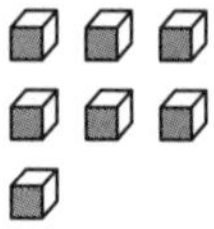
680	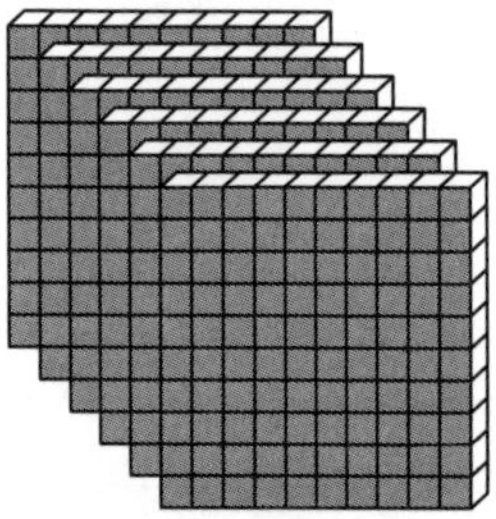	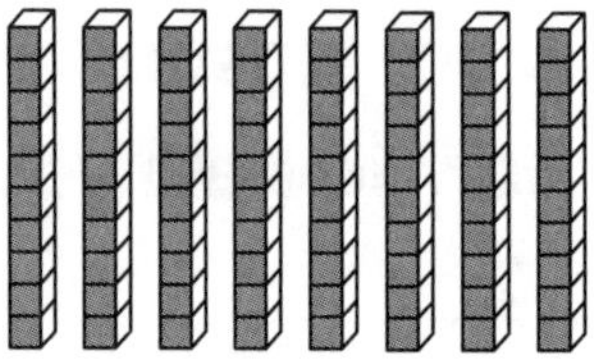	
291	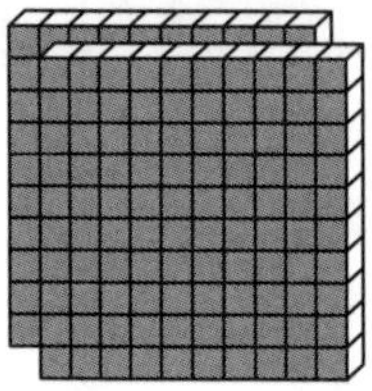	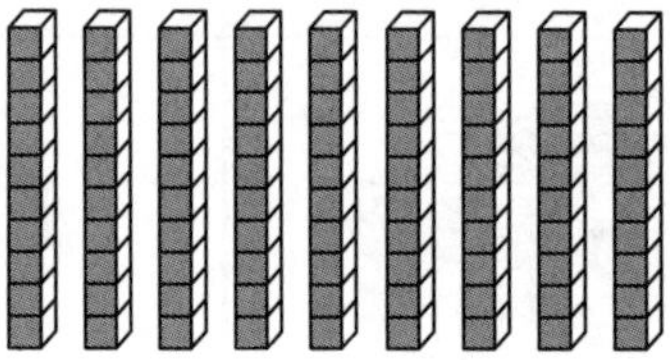	

__________, __________, __________
least

4. **498 403 409**

__________, __________, __________
least

5. **358 458 448**

__________, __________, __________
least

Name: ______________________ **Date:** ____________

Find the missing numbers.
Use a number line to help you.

Example

725 726 ↑ 728 729 730 731 ↑ 733 734

1 **more than** 726 is 727.

1 **less than** 733 is 732.

6.

194 ↑ 214 224 234 244 254 ↑ 274 284

10 more than 194 is ______.

10 less than 274 is ______.

7.

43 ↑ 243 343 443 543 ↑ 743 843 943

100 more than 43 is ______.

100 less than 743 is ______.

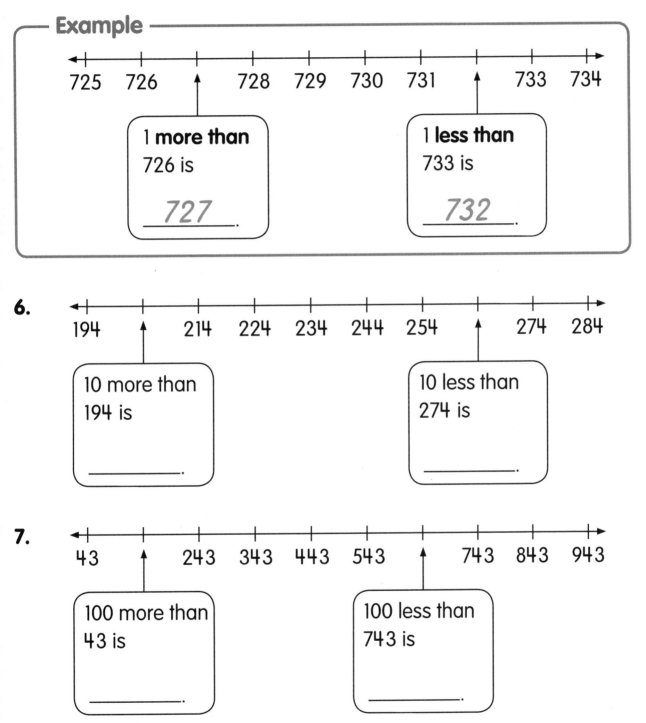

Name: ______________________ Date: ______________

Complete the number patterns.
Use number lines to help you.

8. 404, ______, ______, 407, ______, ______

9. 589, ______, 591, ______, ______, ______

10. 110, 120, ______, ______, ______, 160

11. 290, 300, ______, ______, ______, ______

12. ______, 300, 400, ______, ______, ______

13. ______, ______, 491, ______, 691, ______

Name: ______________________ Date: ____________

CHAPTER 2 Addition up to 1,000

Worksheet 1 Addition and Subtraction Facts Within 20

Find the missing numbers.

1. 2 + ________ = 10

2. ________ + 7 = 10

3. 4 + ________ = 10

4. ________ + 9 = 10

5. 10 = 3 + ________

6. 10 = 5 + ________

Find the missing numbers.

7. 7 + 5 = 7 + ________ + 2 = ________

8. 9 + 6 = 9 + ________ + ________ = ________

Add mentally.

9. 7 + 4 = ________

10. 8 + 5 = ________

11. 9 + 7 = ________

12. 6 + 6 = ________

Name: ______________________________ Date: ______________

Find the missing numbers.

13. $7 + 5 = 2 +$ ________ $+ 5 =$ ________

14. $6 + 6 = 5 +$ ________ $+ 5 +$ ________ $=$ ________

Add mentally.

15. $6 + 8 =$ ________

16. $7 + 4 =$ ________

17. $8 + 7 =$ ________

18. $9 + 6 =$ ________

Complete.

19. $6 = 10 -$ ________

20. $7 = 10 -$ ________

21. $9 = 10 -$ ________

22. $8 = 10 -$ ________

Subtract mentally.

23. $11 - 6 =$ ________

24. $12 - 7 =$ ________

25. $13 - 8 =$ ________

26. $15 - 9 =$ ________

27. $14 - 5 =$ ________

28. $12 - 9 =$ ________

Name: ______________________ Date: ______________

Worksheet 2 Addition Without Regrouping

Add.

1. 53 + 4 = ?

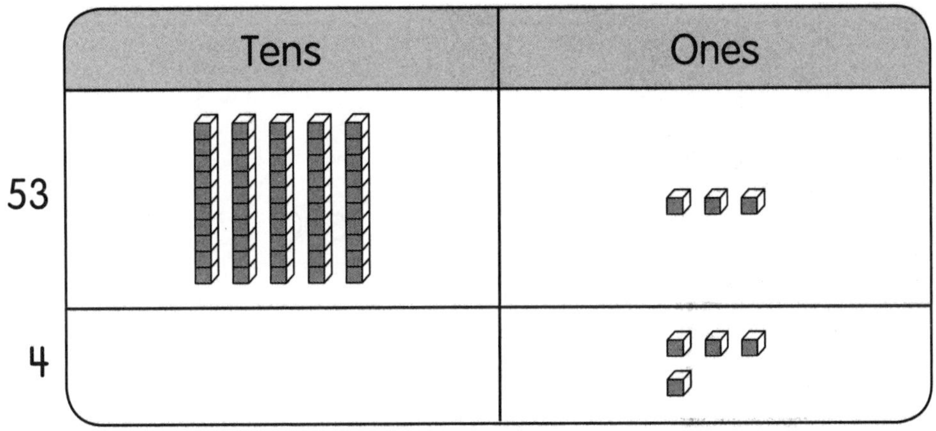

Step 1

Add the ones.

_______ ones + _______ ones = _______ ones

Step 2

Add the tens.

_______ tens + _______ tens = _______ tens

So, 53 + 4 = _______.

Name: ____________________ Date: ____________

Add.

Example

395 + 4 = ?

place-value chart

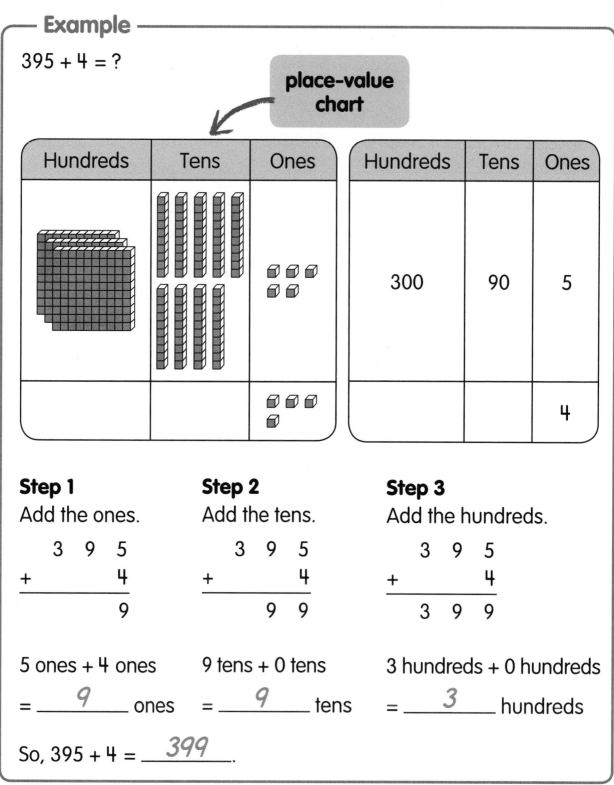

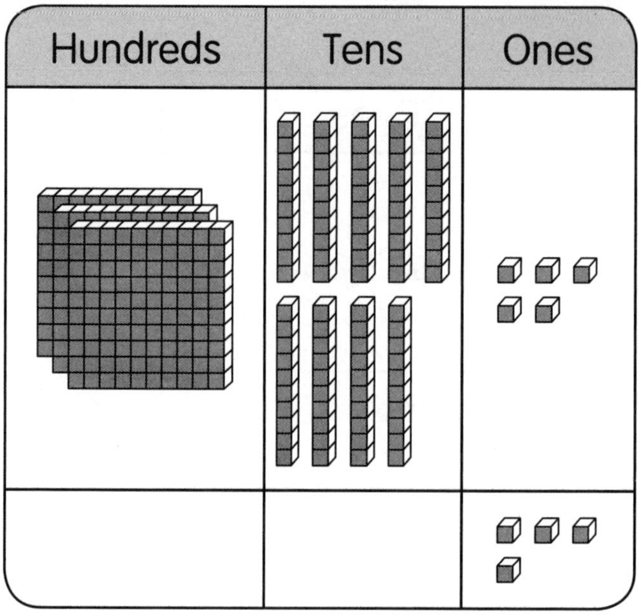

Hundreds	Tens	Ones
300	90	5
		4

Step 1

Add the ones.

```
  3 9 5
+     4
-------
      9
```

5 ones + 4 ones

= 9 ones

Step 2

Add the tens.

```
  3 9 5
+     4
-------
    9 9
```

9 tens + 0 tens

= 9 tens

Step 3

Add the hundreds.

```
  3 9 5
+     4
-------
  3 9 9
```

3 hundreds + 0 hundreds

= 3 hundreds

So, 395 + 4 = 399.

Add.

2. 312 + 7 = ?

Hundreds	Tens	Ones
▨▨▨	▊	▫ ▫
		▫ ▫ ▫ ▫ ▫ ▫ ▫

Hundreds	Tens	Ones
300	10	2
		7

Step 1
Add the ones.

```
  3  1  2
+        7
─────────
         9
```

2 ones + 7 ones

= _____ ones

Step 2
Add the tens.

```
  3  1  2
+        7
─────────
      1  9
```

1 ten + 0 tens

= _____ ten

Step 3
Add the hundreds.

```
  3  1  2
+        7
─────────
  3  1  9
```

3 hundreds + 0 hundreds

= _____ hundreds

So, 312 + 7 = _____.

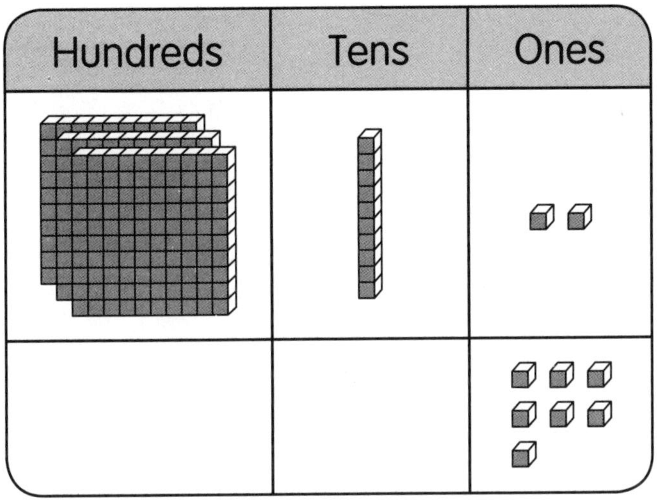

Name: ____________________ Date: ____________

Add.

3. 271 + 3 = ?

Add the ones.

1 one + 3 ones = ________ ones

Add the tens.

7 tens + 0 tens = ________ tens

Add the hundreds.

2 hundreds + 0 hundreds = ________ hundreds

271 + 3 = ________

	2	7	1
+			3

4. 634 + 2 = ________

5. 558 + 1 = ________

6. 456 + 3 = ________

7. 231 + 5 = ________

Name: ______________________________ Date: ______________

Solve.

Example

On Monday, 235 students went to the museum.
On Tuesday, 4 more students went to the museum than on Monday.
How many students went to the museum on Tuesday?

$235 + 4 = 239$

$$\begin{array}{r} 2\,3\,5 \\ +\quad\;\; 4 \\ \hline 2\,3\,9 \end{array}$$

__239__ students went to the museum on Tuesday.

8. Joy buys 140 beads at a craft shop.
Her sister gives her 8 more beads.
How many beads does Joy have now?

Joy has ________ beads now.

Name: ______________________ Date: ______________

Add.

Example

573 + 16 = ?

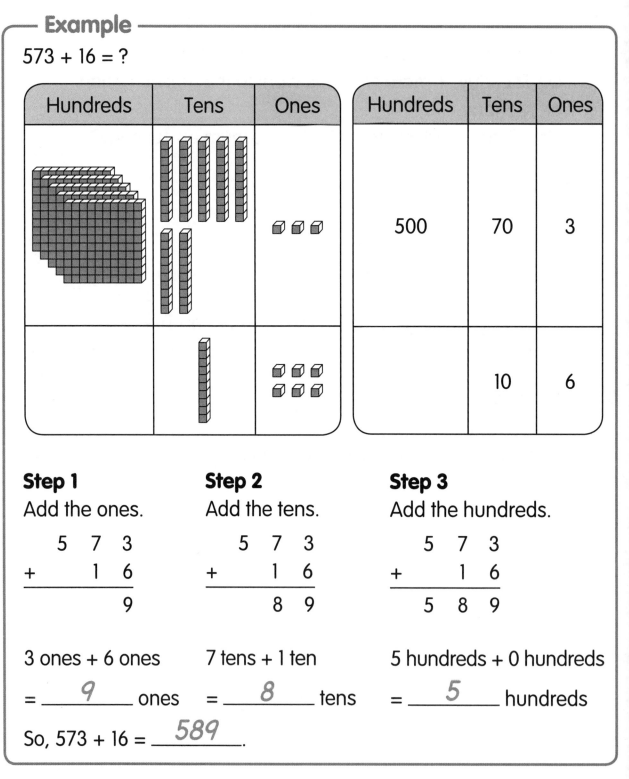

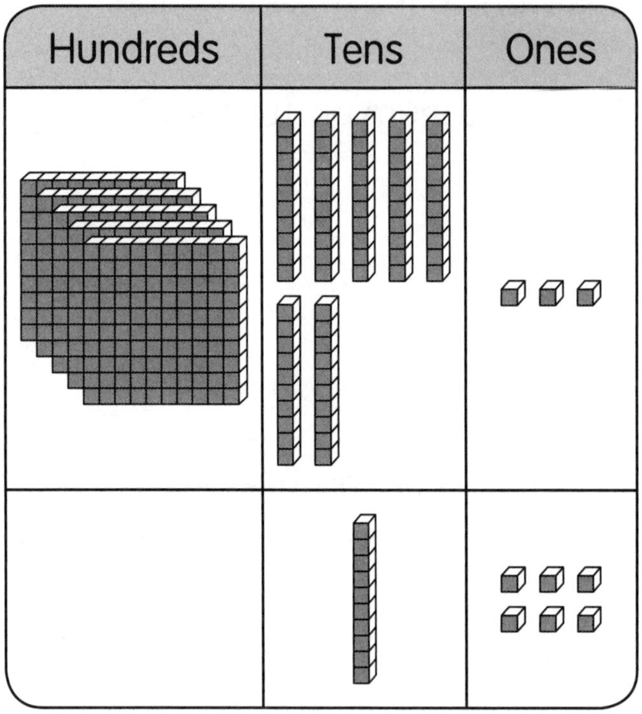

Hundreds	Tens	Ones
500	70	3
	10	6

Step 1

Add the ones.

	5	7	3
+		1	6
			9

3 ones + 6 ones

= 9 ones

Step 2

Add the tens.

	5	7	3
+		1	6
		8	9

7 tens + 1 ten

= 8 tens

Step 3

Add the hundreds.

	5	7	3
+		1	6
	5	8	9

5 hundreds + 0 hundreds

= 5 hundreds

So, 573 + 16 = 589.

Name: ______________________________ Date: ______________

Add.

9. 143 + 22 = ?

Hundreds	Tens	Ones
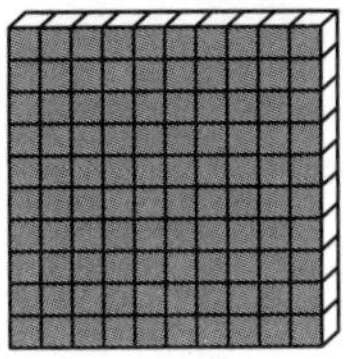	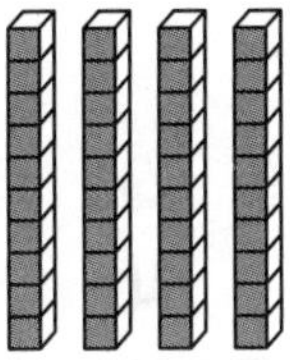	
	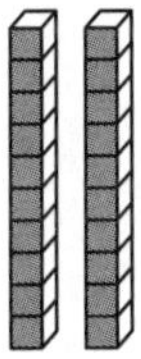	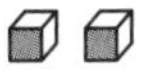

Hundreds	Tens	Ones
100	40	3
	20	2

Step 1

Add the ones.

$$\begin{array}{cccc} & 1 & 4 & 3 \\ + & & 2 & 2 \\ \hline & & & 5 \end{array}$$

3 ones + 2 ones

= __________ ones

Step 2

Add the tens.

$$\begin{array}{cccc} & 1 & 4 & 3 \\ + & & 2 & 2 \\ \hline & & 6 & 5 \end{array}$$

4 tens + 2 tens

= __________ tens

Step 3

Add the hundreds.

$$\begin{array}{cccc} & 1 & 4 & 3 \\ + & & 2 & 2 \\ \hline & 1 & 6 & 5 \end{array}$$

1 hundred + 0 hundreds

= __________ hundred

So, 143 + 22 = __________.

Name: ______________________ Date: ____________

Add.
Use base-ten blocks to help you.

10.
$$\begin{array}{r} 264 \\ +\ \ 23 \\ \hline \end{array}$$

11.
$$\begin{array}{r} 812 \\ +\ \ 57 \\ \hline \end{array}$$

12.
$$\begin{array}{r} 512 \\ +\ \ 71 \\ \hline \end{array}$$

13.
$$\begin{array}{r} 632 \\ +\ \ 47 \\ \hline \end{array}$$

Solve.

Example

Kairu sold 120 cups of lemonade in the morning.
He sold 52 cups of lemonade in the afternoon.
How many cups of lemonade did Kairu sell?

$120 + 52 = 172$

$$\begin{array}{r} 120 \\ +\ \ 52 \\ \hline 172 \end{array}$$

Kairu sold __172__ cups of lemonade.

14. Jorge has 144 magnets.
His aunt buys him 24 magnets.
How many magnets does Jorge have now?

Jorge has ________ magnets now.

Name: ____________________ Date: ____________

Add.

Example

214 + 123 = ?

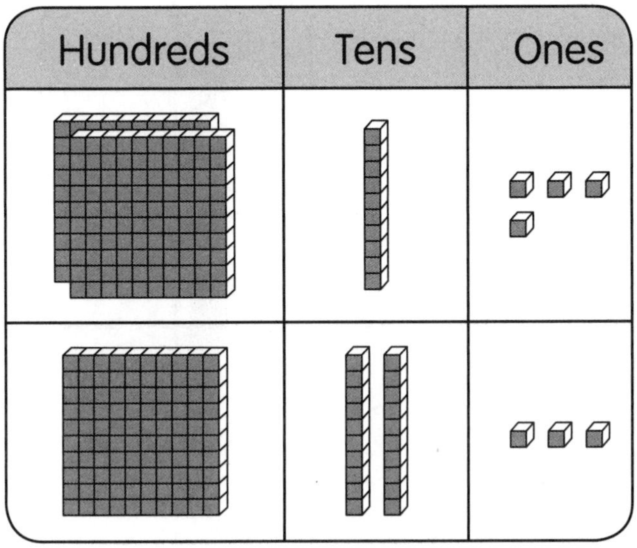

Hundreds	Tens	Ones
200	10	4
100	20	3

Step 1
Add the ones.

```
    2  1  4
+   1  2  3
-----------
          7
```

4 ones + 3 ones
= 7 ones

Step 2
Add the tens.

```
    2  1  4
+   1  2  3
-----------
       3  7
```

1 ten + 2 tens
= 3 tens

Step 3
Add the hundreds.

```
    2  1  4
+   1  2  3
-----------
    3  3  7
```

2 hundreds + 1 hundred
= 3 hundreds

So, 214 + 123 = 337.

Name: ______________________ Date: ______________

Add.

15. 462 + 232 = ?

Hundreds	Tens	Ones
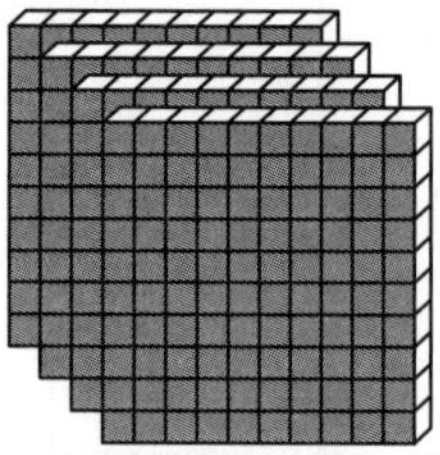	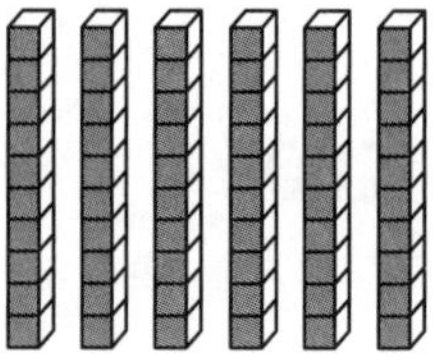	
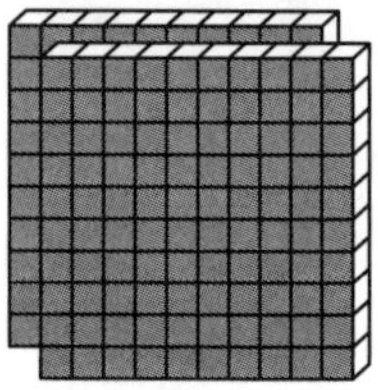	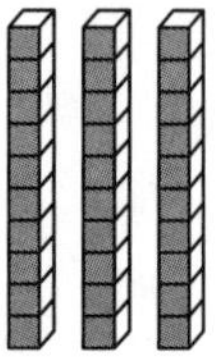	

Hundreds	Tens	Ones
400	60	2
200	30	2

Step 1

Add the ones.

$$\begin{array}{r} 4\ \ 6\ \ 2 \\ +\ \ 2\ \ 3\ \ 2 \\ \hline 4 \end{array}$$

2 ones + 2 ones

= ________ ones

Step 2

Add the tens.

$$\begin{array}{r} 4\ \ 6\ \ 2 \\ +\ \ 2\ \ 3\ \ 2 \\ \hline 9\ \ 4 \end{array}$$

6 tens + 3 tens

= ________ tens

Step 3

Add the hundreds.

$$\begin{array}{r} 4\ \ 6\ \ 2 \\ +\ \ 2\ \ 3\ \ 2 \\ \hline 6\ \ 9\ \ 4 \end{array}$$

6 hundreds + 0 hundreds

= ________ hundreds

So, 462 + 232 = ________.

Name: ______________________ Date: ______________

Add.
Use base-ten blocks to help you.

16.
$$\begin{array}{r} 334 \\ +\ 223 \\ \hline \end{array}$$

17.
$$\begin{array}{r} 722 \\ +\ 213 \\ \hline \end{array}$$

18.
$$\begin{array}{r} 466 \\ +\ 532 \\ \hline \end{array}$$

19.
$$\begin{array}{r} 182 \\ +\ 616 \\ \hline \end{array}$$

Solve.

Example

A farmer drove 122 miles to deliver oranges.
Then he drove back to the farm.
How many miles did the farmer drive in all?

$122 + 122 = 244$

$$\begin{array}{r} 122 \\ +\ 122 \\ \hline 244 \end{array}$$

The farmer drove 244 miles in all.

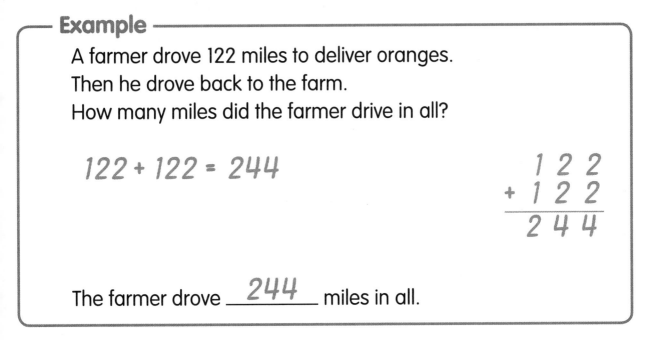

Name: ______________________ Date: ______________

20. A dressmaker has 170 spools of thread.
He buys another 119 spools of thread.
How many spools of thread does the dressmaker have now?

The dressmaker has ________ spools of thread now.

Name: ______________________ Date: ______________

Worksheet 3 Addition with Regrouping in Ones

Add.

1. 15 + 19 = ?

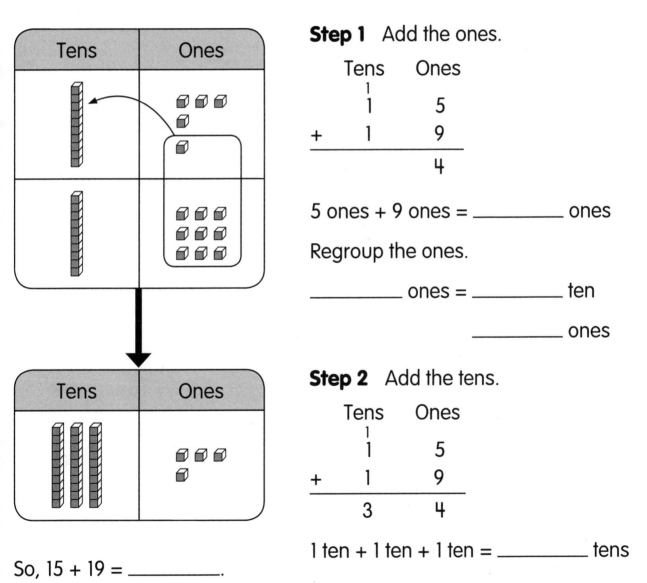

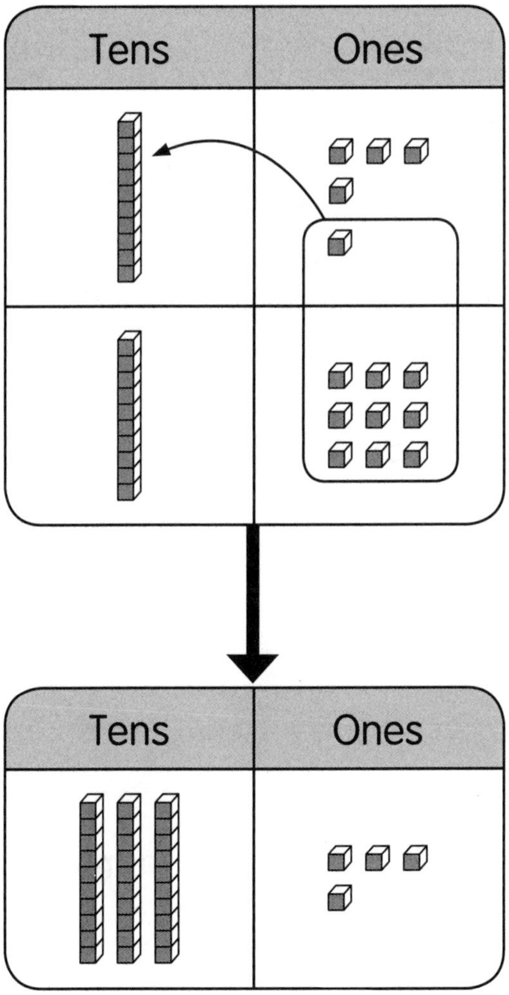

So, 15 + 19 = ________.

Step 1 Add the ones.

	Tens	Ones
	$\overset{1}{1}$	5
+	1	9
		4

5 ones + 9 ones = ________ ones

Regroup the ones.

________ ones = ________ ten

________ ones

Step 2 Add the tens.

	Tens	Ones
	$\overset{1}{1}$	5
+	1	9
	3	4

1 ten + 1 ten + 1 ten = ________ tens

Name: ______________________ Date: ______________

Regroup.
Then add.

Example

278 + 316 = ?

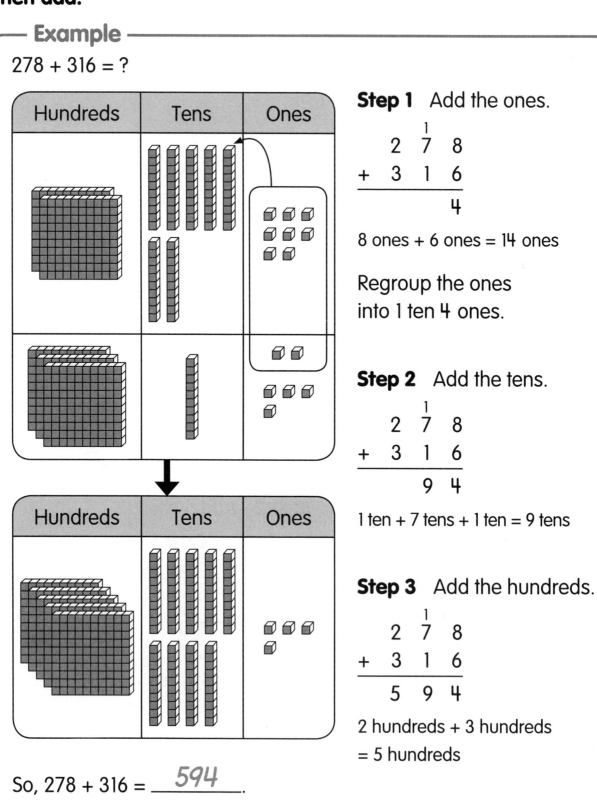

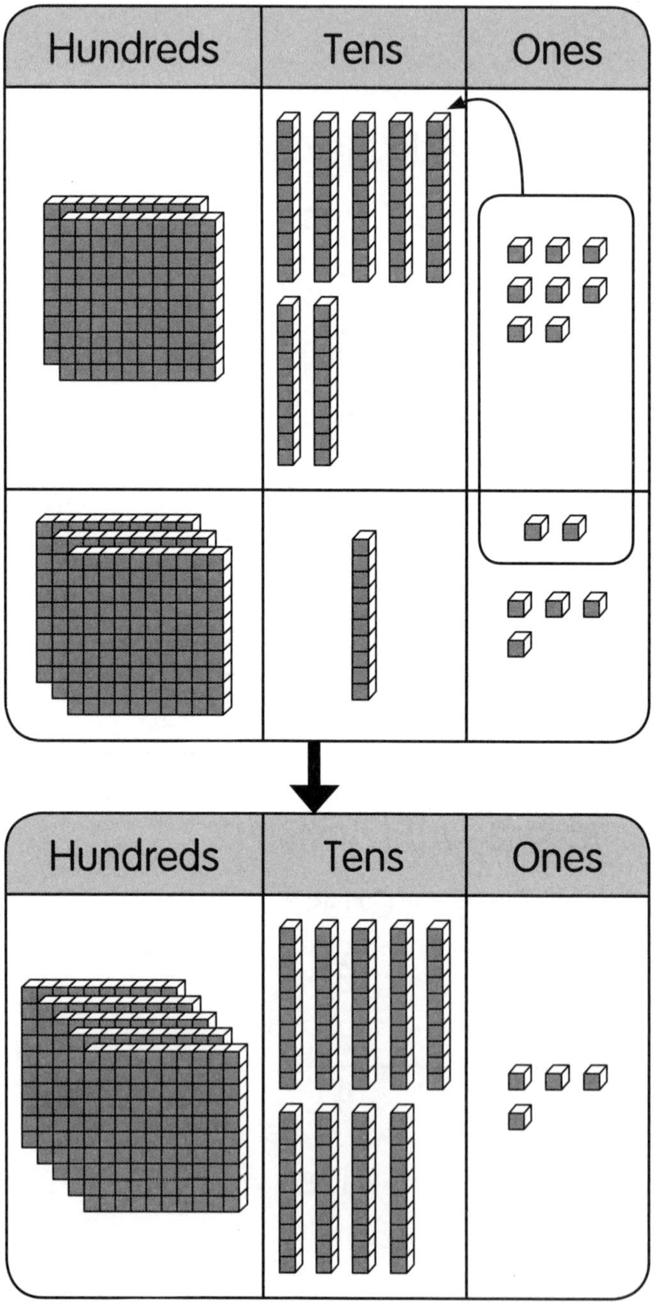

Step 1 Add the ones.

$$\begin{array}{r} \overset{1}{} \\ 2\;7\;8 \\ +\;3\;1\;6 \\ \hline 4 \end{array}$$

8 ones + 6 ones = 14 ones

Regroup the ones
into 1 ten 4 ones.

Step 2 Add the tens.

$$\begin{array}{r} 1 \\ 2\;7\;8 \\ +\;3\;1\;6 \\ \hline 9\;4 \end{array}$$

1 ten + 7 tens + 1 ten = 9 tens

Step 3 Add the hundreds.

$$\begin{array}{r} 1 \\ 2\;7\;8 \\ +\;3\;1\;6 \\ \hline 5\;9\;4 \end{array}$$

2 hundreds + 3 hundreds
= 5 hundreds

So, 278 + 316 = 594.

Name: ____________________ Date: ____________

Regroup.
Then add.

2. 485 + 107 = ?

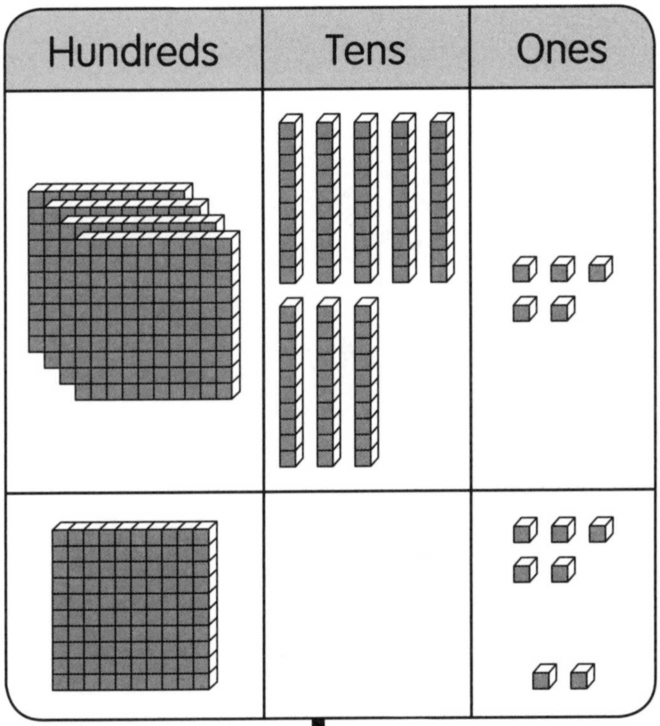

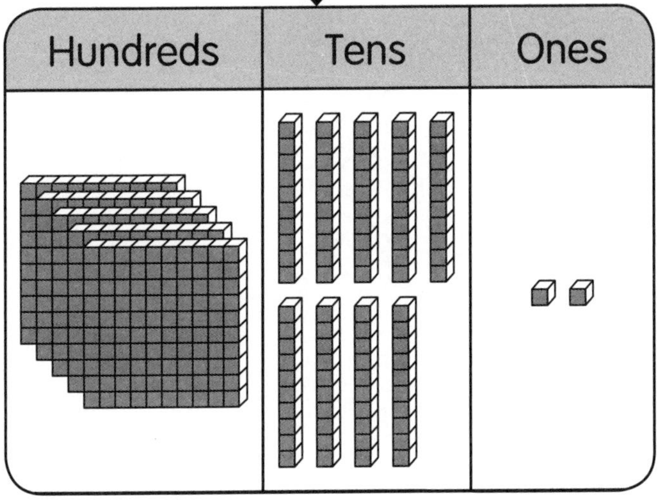

So, 485 + 107 = ________.

Step 1 Add the ones.

$$\begin{array}{cccc} & & {}^{1} & \\ & 4 & 8 & 5 \\ + & 1 & 0 & 7 \\ \hline & & & 2 \end{array}$$

5 ones + 7 ones = 12 ones

Regroup the ones
into 1 ten 2 ones.

Step 2 Add the tens.

$$\begin{array}{cccc} & & {}^{1} & \\ & 4 & 8 & 5 \\ + & 1 & 0 & 7 \\ \hline & & 9 & 2 \end{array}$$

1 ten + 8 tens + 0 tens
= 9 tens

Step 3 Add the hundreds.

$$\begin{array}{cccc} & & {}^{1} & \\ & 4 & 8 & 5 \\ + & 1 & 0 & 7 \\ \hline & 5 & 9 & 2 \end{array}$$

4 hundreds + 1 hundred
= 5 hundreds

Name: ______________________ Date: ______________

3. 713 + 129 = ?

Add and regroup the ones.

3 ones + 9 ones = ________ ones

= ________ ten ________ ones

Add the tens.

1 ten + 1 ten + 2 tens = ________ tens

Add the hundreds.

7 hundreds + 1 hundred = ________ hundreds

713 + 129 = ________

4. 831 + 129 = ________

5. 139 + 556 = ________

6. 468 + 325 = ________

7. 153 + 127 = ________

Name: ______________________________ Date: ______________

Solve.

Example

Gina has 305 orchids.
She needs another 186 orchids to make leis.
How many orchids does Gina need for the leis?

$305 + 186 = 491$

$$\begin{array}{r} \overset{1}{3}\,0\,5 \\ +\ 1\,8\,6 \\ \hline 4\,9\,1 \end{array}$$

Gina needs __491__ orchids for the leis.

8. Thom uses 286 bricks to build a house.
He uses another 104 bricks to build a garden wall.
How many bricks does Thom use?

Thom uses ________ bricks.

Name: ______________________ Date: ______________

Solve.

9. A school has 459 students.
The next year, 105 students join the school.
How many students does the school have now?

The school has ________ students now.

Name: ______________________ Date: ______________

Worksheet 4 Addition with Regrouping in Tens

Regroup.
Then add.

Example

480 + 236 = ?

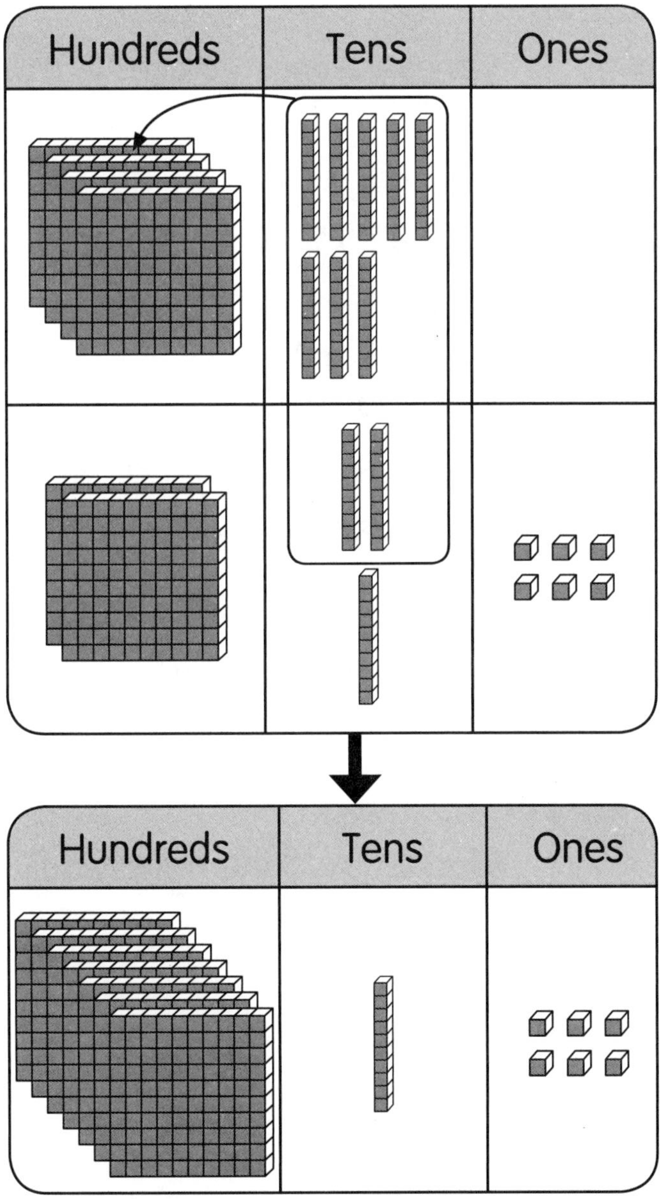

Step 1 Add the ones.

$$\begin{array}{rrrr} & 4 & 8 & 0 \\ + & 2 & 3 & 6 \\ \hline & & & 6 \end{array}$$

0 ones + 6 ones = 6 ones

Step 2 Add the tens.

$$\begin{array}{rrrr} & \overset{1}{4} & 8 & 0 \\ + & 2 & 3 & 6 \\ \hline & & 1 & 6 \end{array}$$

8 tens + 3 tens = 11 tens

Regroup the tens
into 1 hundred 1 ten.

Step 3 Add the hundreds.

$$\begin{array}{rrrr} & \overset{1}{4} & 8 & 0 \\ + & 2 & 3 & 6 \\ \hline & 7 & 1 & 6 \end{array}$$

1 hundred + 4 hundreds
+ 2 hundreds = 7 hundreds

So, 480 + 236 = 716.

Name: ______________________ Date: ______________

Regroup.
Then add.

1. 395 + 150 = ?

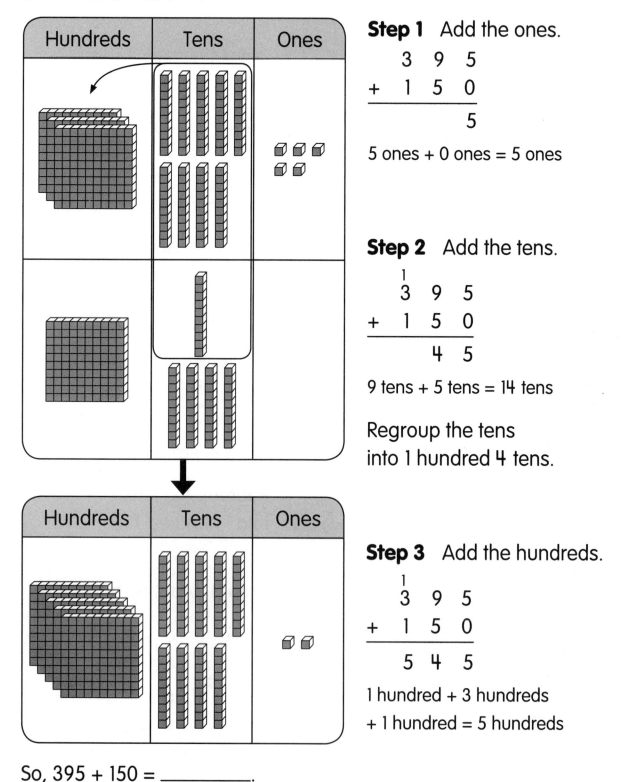

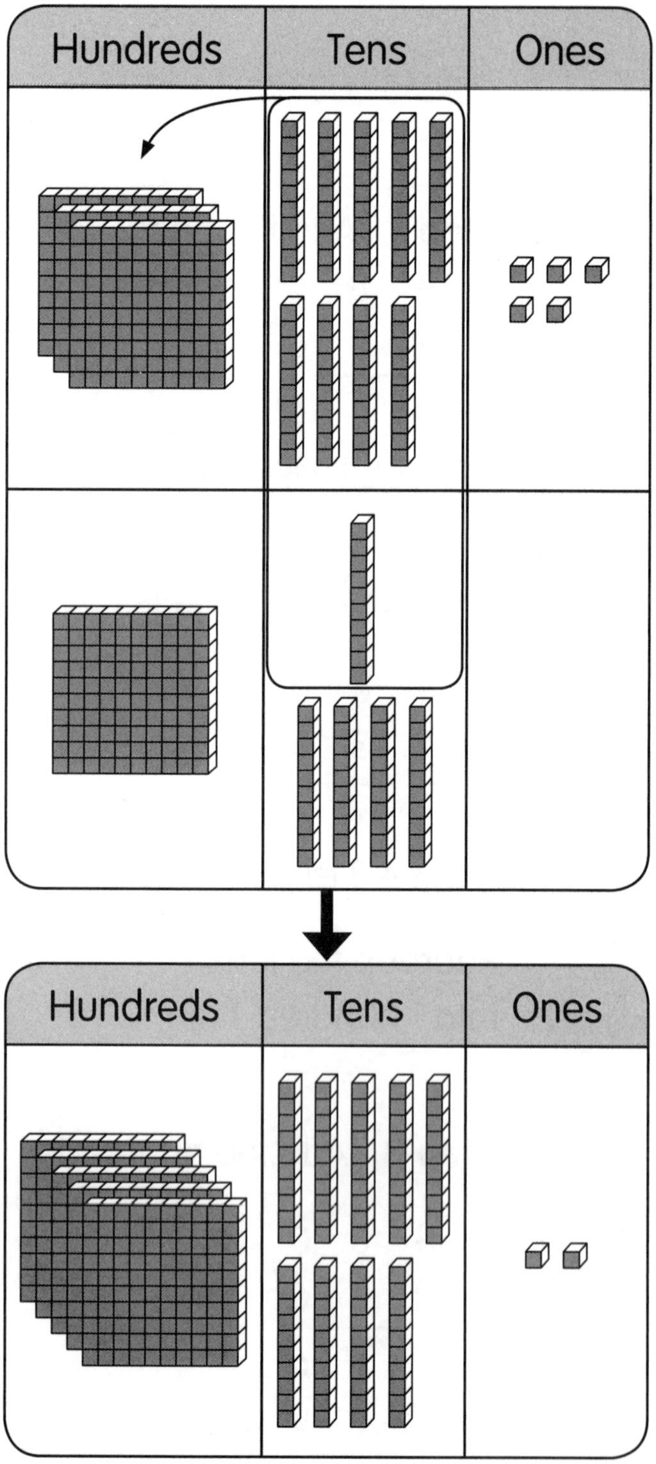

Step 1 Add the ones.

$$\begin{array}{rrrr} & 3 & 9 & 5 \\ + & 1 & 5 & 0 \\ \hline & & & 5 \end{array}$$

5 ones + 0 ones = 5 ones

Step 2 Add the tens.

$$\begin{array}{rrrr} & \overset{1}{3} & 9 & 5 \\ + & 1 & 5 & 0 \\ \hline & & 4 & 5 \end{array}$$

9 tens + 5 tens = 14 tens

Regroup the tens
into 1 hundred 4 tens.

Step 3 Add the hundreds.

$$\begin{array}{rrrr} & \overset{1}{3} & 9 & 5 \\ + & 1 & 5 & 0 \\ \hline & 5 & 4 & 5 \end{array}$$

1 hundred + 3 hundreds
+ 1 hundred = 5 hundreds

So, 395 + 150 = __________.

Name: ______________________ Date: ______________

2. 741 + 168 = ?

Add the ones.

1 one + 8 ones = ________ ones

Add and regroup the tens.

4 tens + 6 tens = ________ tens

= ________ hundred ________ tens

Add the hundreds.

1 hundred + 7 hundreds + 1 hundred = ________ hundreds

741 + 168 = ________

3.
$$\begin{array}{r} 7\ 9\ 3 \\ +\ 1\ 2\ 1 \\ \hline \end{array}$$

4.
$$\begin{array}{r} 1\ 6\ 1 \\ +\ 1\ 5\ 6 \\ \hline \end{array}$$

5.
$$\begin{array}{r} 2\ 6\ 2 \\ +\ 6\ 6\ 4 \\ \hline \end{array}$$

6.
$$\begin{array}{r} 3\ 8\ 3 \\ +\ 2\ 7\ 4 \\ \hline \end{array}$$

7.
$$\begin{array}{r} 3\ 5\ 8 \\ +\ 1\ 8\ 1 \\ \hline \end{array}$$

8.
$$\begin{array}{r} 4\ 8\ 0 \\ +\ 2\ 9\ 6 \\ \hline \end{array}$$

Name: ______________________ Date: ______________

Solve.

Example

Joan collected 170 empty bottles to recycle.
Her grandmother gives her 40 more empty bottles.
How many empty bottles does Joan have now?

$170 + 40 = 210$

$$\begin{array}{r} \overset{1}{1}70 \\ +\ 40 \\ \hline 210 \end{array}$$

Joan has __210__ empty bottles now.

9. There were 460 women at a baseball game.
There were 50 more men than women at the game.
How many men were at the baseball game?

__________ men were at the baseball game.

Name: ______________________ Date: ______________

Worksheet 5 Addition with Regrouping in Ones and Tens

Regroup.
Then add.

Example

369 + 147 = ?

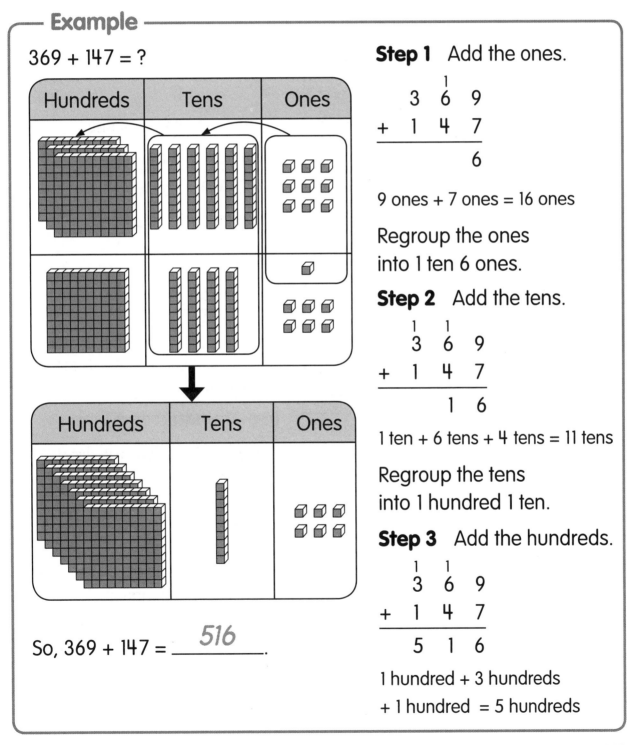

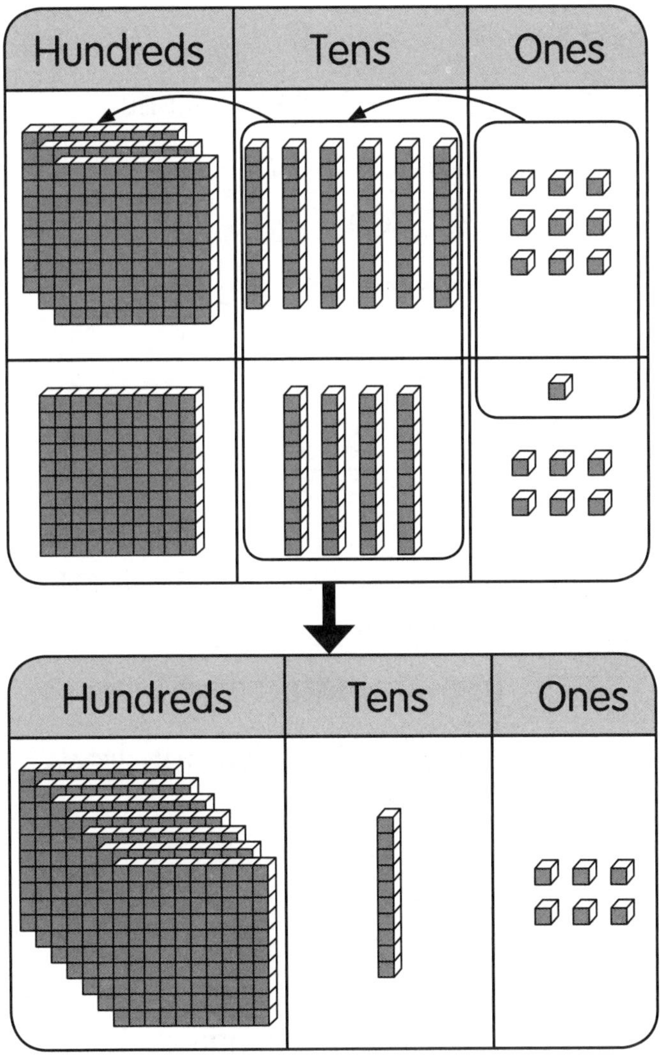

So, 369 + 147 = 516.

Step 1 Add the ones.

$$\begin{array}{r} \scriptstyle 1 \\ 369 \\ +\,147 \\ \hline 6 \end{array}$$

9 ones + 7 ones = 16 ones

Regroup the ones into 1 ten 6 ones.

Step 2 Add the tens.

$$\begin{array}{r} \scriptstyle 1\,1 \\ 369 \\ +\,147 \\ \hline 16 \end{array}$$

1 ten + 6 tens + 4 tens = 11 tens

Regroup the tens into 1 hundred 1 ten.

Step 3 Add the hundreds.

$$\begin{array}{r} \scriptstyle 1\,1 \\ 369 \\ +\,147 \\ \hline 516 \end{array}$$

1 hundred + 3 hundreds + 1 hundred = 5 hundreds

Name: ____________________ Date: ____________

Regroup.
Then add.

1. 587 + 223 = ?

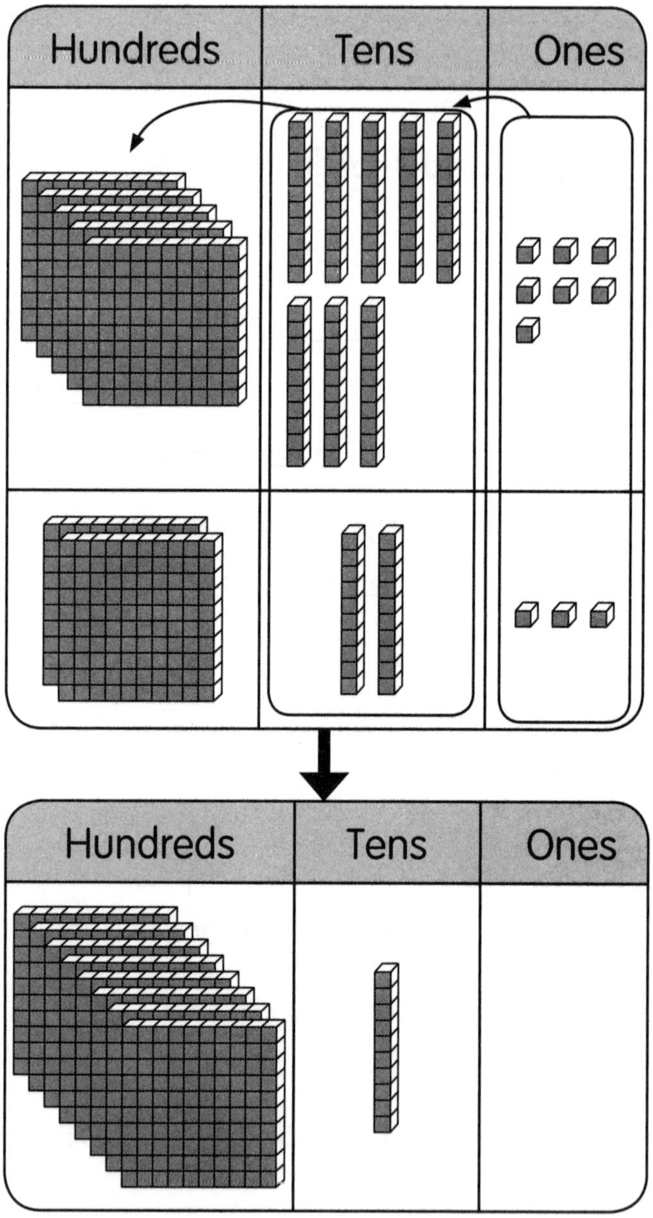

Step 1 Add the ones.

$$\begin{array}{cccc} & & {\scriptstyle 1} & \\ & 5 & 8 & 7 \\ + & 2 & 2 & 3 \\ \hline & & & 0 \end{array}$$

7 ones + 3 ones = 10 ones

Regroup the ones
into 1 ten.

Step 2 Add the tens.

$$\begin{array}{cccc} & {\scriptstyle 1} & {\scriptstyle 1} & \\ & 5 & 8 & 7 \\ + & 2 & 2 & 3 \\ \hline & & 1 & 0 \end{array}$$

1 ten + 8 tens + 2 tens = 11 tens

Regroup the tens
into 1 hundred and 1 ten.

Step 3 Add the hundreds.

$$\begin{array}{cccc} & {\scriptstyle 1} & {\scriptstyle 1} & \\ & 5 & 8 & 7 \\ + & 2 & 2 & 3 \\ \hline & 8 & 1 & 0 \end{array}$$

1 hundred + 5 hundreds
+ 2 hundreds = 8 hundreds

So, 587 + 223 = __________.

Name: ______________________ Date: ______________

2. 157 + 658 = ?

Add and regroup the ones.

7 ones + 8 ones = ________ ones

= ________ ten ________ ones

Add and regroup the tens.

1 ten + 5 tens + 5 tens = ________ tens

= ________ hundred ________ tens

Add the hundreds.

1 hundred + 1 hundred + 6 hundreds = ________ hundreds

157 + 658 = ________

3.
$$\begin{array}{r} 2\ 2\ 2 \\ +\ 2\ 9\ 8 \\ \hline \end{array}$$

4.
$$\begin{array}{r} 1\ 6\ 9 \\ +\ 3\ 6\ 9 \\ \hline \end{array}$$

5.
$$\begin{array}{r} 3\ 5\ 8 \\ +\ 1\ 4\ 2 \\ \hline \end{array}$$

6.
$$\begin{array}{r} 1\ 8\ 4 \\ +\ 4\ 9\ 9 \\ \hline \end{array}$$

7.
$$\begin{array}{r} 7\ 9\ 3 \\ +\ \ \ 2\ 8 \\ \hline \end{array}$$

8.
$$\begin{array}{r} 5\ 2\ 9 \\ +\ 3\ 8\ 4 \\ \hline \end{array}$$

Name: ______________________ Date: ______________

Example

Harry has 185 bookmarks.
His penpal sends him another 25 bookmarks.
How many bookmarks does Harry have now?

$185 + 25 = 210$

$$\begin{array}{r} {}^{1}\,{}^{1} \\ 185 \\ +\ \ 25 \\ \hline 210 \end{array}$$

Harry has __210__ bookmarks now.

9. A fish pond has 217 fish.
Mr. Reynolds adds another 95 fish.
How many fish are there in the pond now?

________ fish are in the pond now.

Name: ______________________________ Date: ______________

CHAPTER 3 Subtraction up to 1,000

Worksheet 1 Subtraction Without Regrouping

Subtract.

1. 34 − 13 = ?

34

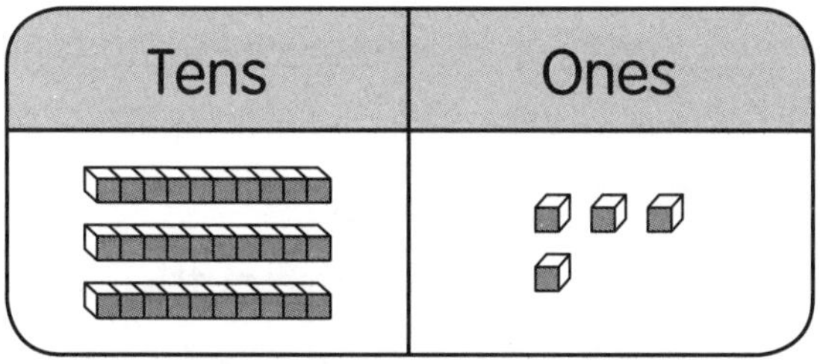

13

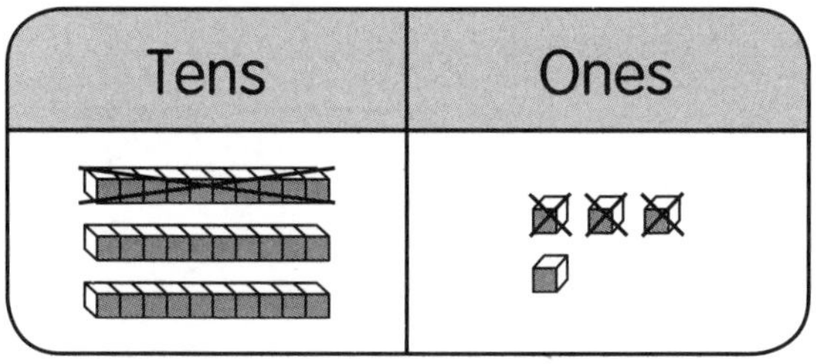

Step 1

Subtract the ones.

__________ ones − __________ ones = __________ one

Step 2

Subtract the tens.

__________ tens − __________ ten = __________ tens

So, 34 − 13 = __________.

Name: ______________________ Date: ______________

Subtract.

Example

365 – 2 = ?

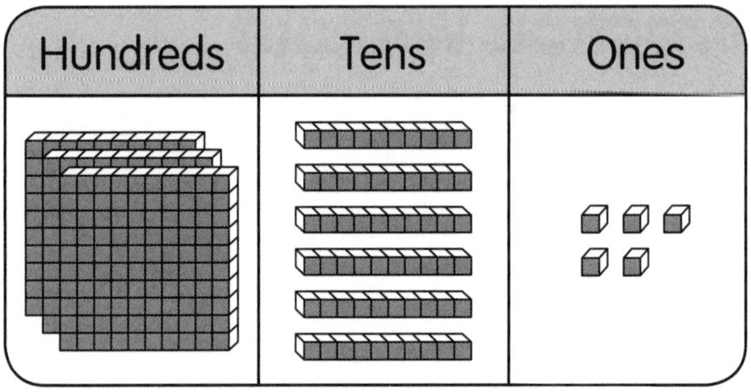

Step 1
Subtract the ones.

$$\begin{array}{r} 3\;6\;5 \\ -\quad\;\; 2 \\ \hline 3 \end{array}$$

5 ones – 2 ones
= __3__ ones

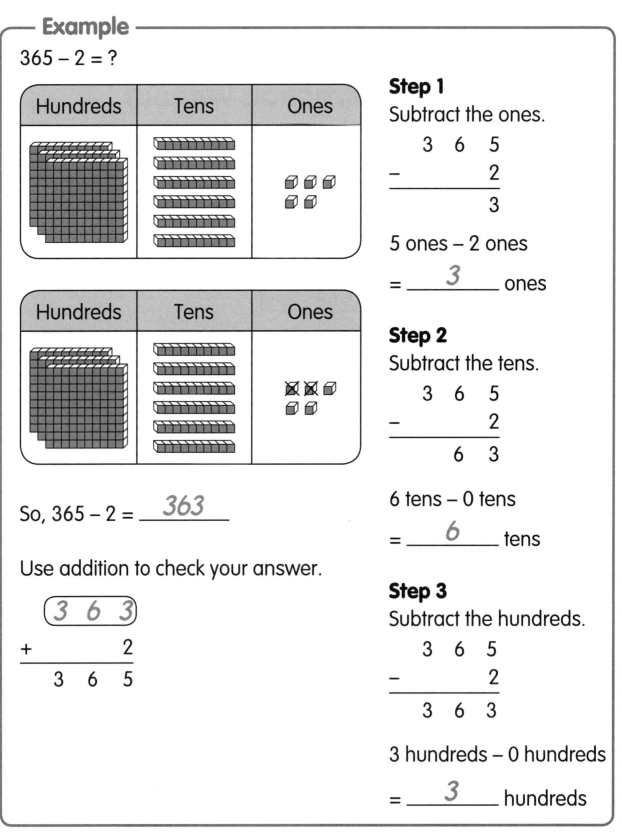

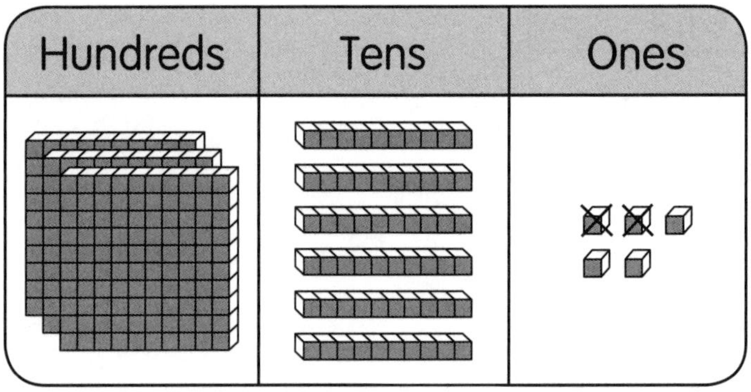

Step 2
Subtract the tens.

$$\begin{array}{r} 3\;6\;5 \\ -\quad\;\; 2 \\ \hline 6\;3 \end{array}$$

6 tens – 0 tens
= __6__ tens

So, 365 – 2 = __363__

Use addition to check your answer.

$$\begin{array}{r} \boxed{3\;6\;3} \\ +\quad\;\; 2 \\ \hline 3\;6\;5 \end{array}$$

Step 3
Subtract the hundreds.

$$\begin{array}{r} 3\;6\;5 \\ -\quad\;\; 2 \\ \hline 3\;6\;3 \end{array}$$

3 hundreds – 0 hundreds
= __3__ hundreds

Name: ______________________ Date: ______________

Subtract.

2. 849 – 6 = ?

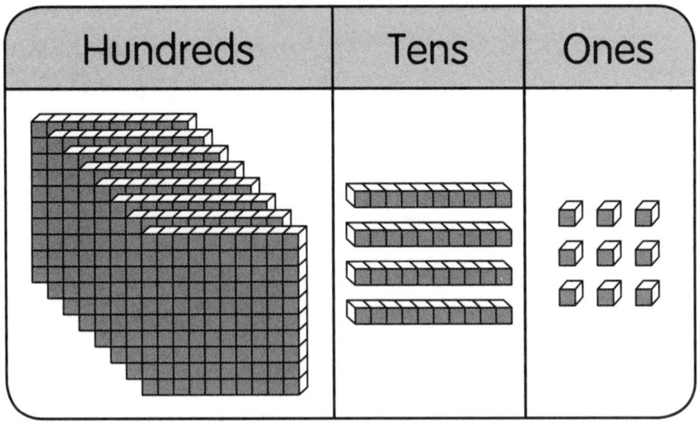

Step 1

Subtract the ones.

$$\begin{array}{r} 8\ 4\ 9 \\ -\quad\ \ 6 \\ \hline 3 \end{array}$$

9 ones – 6 ones

= ________ ones

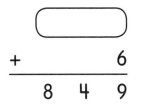

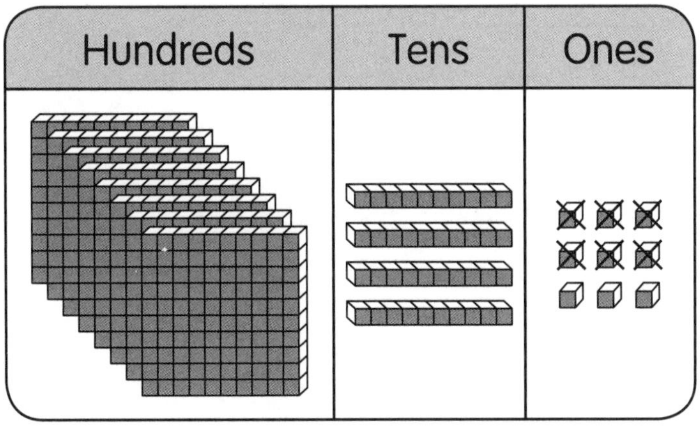

Step 2

Subtract the tens.

$$\begin{array}{r} 8\ 4\ 9 \\ -\quad\ \ 6 \\ \hline 4\ 3 \end{array}$$

4 tens – 0 tens

= ________ tens

Step 3

Subtract the hundreds.

$$\begin{array}{r} 8\ 4\ 9 \\ -\quad\ \ 6 \\ \hline 8\ 4\ 3 \end{array}$$

8 hundreds – 0 hundreds

= ________ hundreds

So, 849 – 6 = ________.

Use addition to check your answer.

$$\begin{array}{r} \boxed{} \\ +\quad\ \ 6 \\ \hline 8\ 4\ 9 \end{array}$$

Name: ____________________ Date: ____________

Subtract.
Add to check your answer.

3. 486 – 5 = ?

Subtract the ones.

6 ones – 5 ones = ________ one

	4	8	6
–			5

Subtract the tens.

8 tens – 0 tens = ________ tens

Subtract the hundreds.

4 hundreds – 0 hundreds = ________ hundreds

486 – 5 = ________

4. 837 – 2 = ________

5. 557 – 4 = ________

6. 854 – 4 = ________

7. 298 – 7 = ________

Name: ______________________ Date: ____________

Solve.
Show how to check your answer.

Example

A gardener had 459 seedlings.
She gave 5 seedlings to Tanya.
How many seedlings does the gardener have now?

$459 - 5 = 454$

$$\begin{array}{r} 459 \\ -\quad 5 \\ \hline 454 \end{array} \qquad \begin{array}{r} 454 \\ +\quad 5 \\ \hline 459 \end{array}$$

The gardener has ___454___ seedlings now.

8. Jody has 146 eggs.
4 of the eggs hatch into chicks.
How many eggs does Jody have now?

Jody has __________ eggs now.

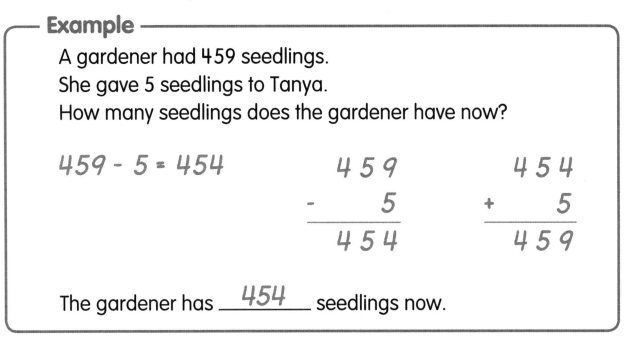

Name: ______________________ Date: ______________

Subtract.

Example

485 – 74 = ?

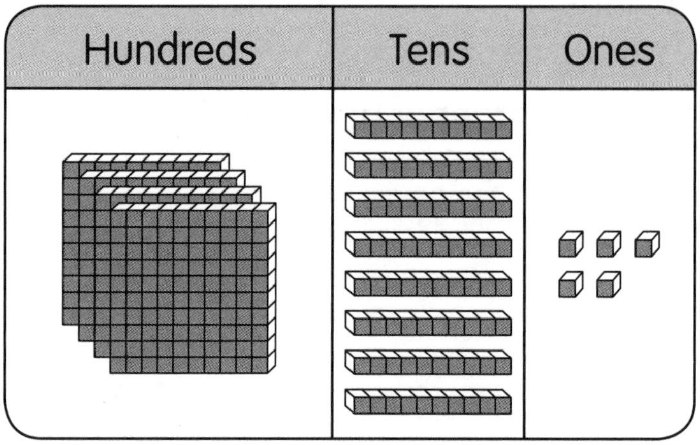

Step 1

Subtract the ones.

$$\begin{array}{rrr} 4 & 8 & 5 \\ - & 7 & 4 \\ \hline & & 1 \end{array}$$

5 ones – 4 ones

= __1__ one

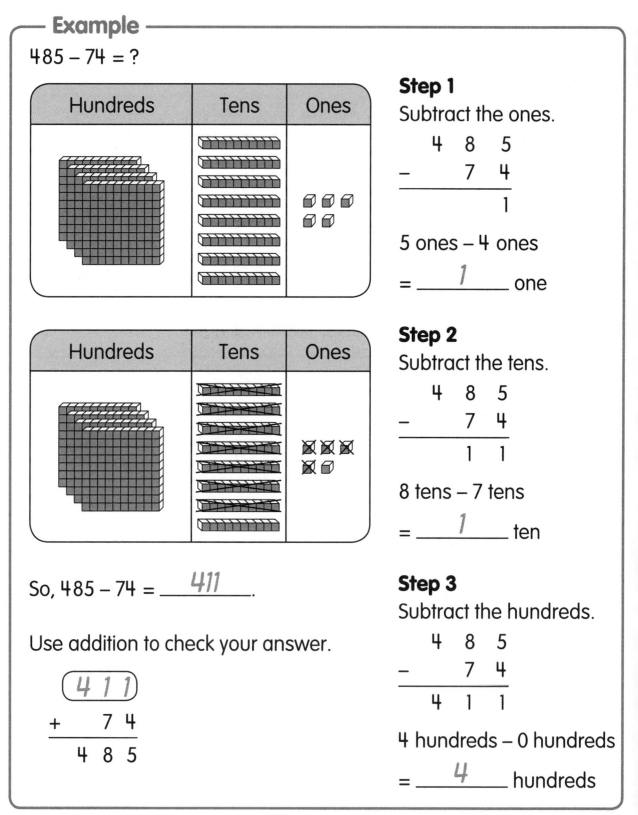

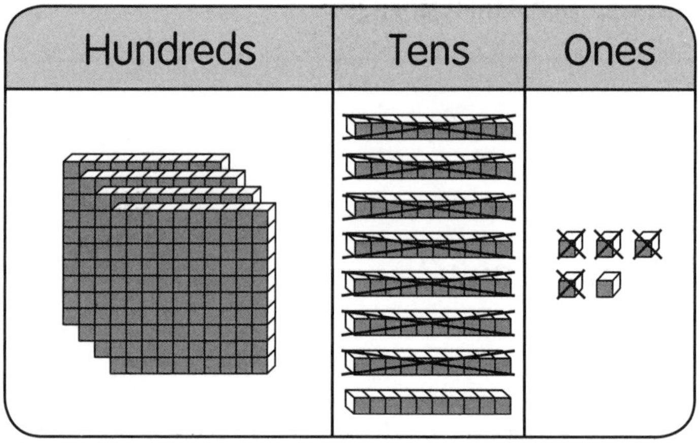

Step 2

Subtract the tens.

$$\begin{array}{rrr} 4 & 8 & 5 \\ - & 7 & 4 \\ \hline & 1 & 1 \end{array}$$

8 tens – 7 tens

= __1__ ten

So, 485 – 74 = __411__.

Step 3

Subtract the hundreds.

$$\begin{array}{rrr} 4 & 8 & 5 \\ - & 7 & 4 \\ \hline 4 & 1 & 1 \end{array}$$

4 hundreds – 0 hundreds

= __4__ hundreds

Use addition to check your answer.

$$\begin{array}{rrrr} & 4 & 1 & 1 \\ + & & 7 & 4 \\ \hline & 4 & 8 & 5 \end{array}$$

Name: ____________________ Date: ____________

Subtract.

9. 586 – 10 = ?

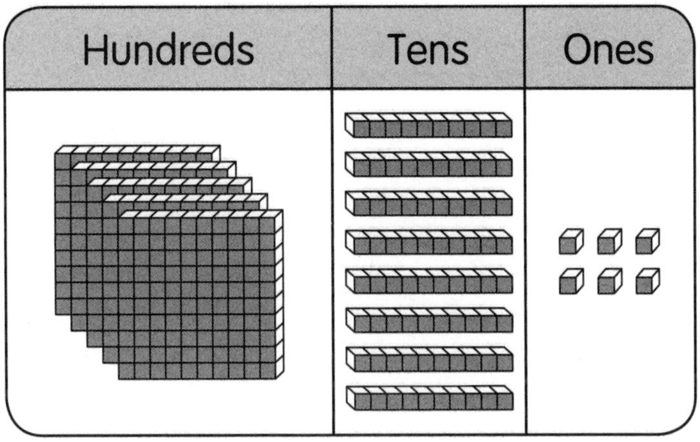

Step 1
Subtract the ones.

$$\begin{array}{rrrr} & 5 & 8 & 6 \\ - & & 1 & 0 \\ \hline & & & 6 \end{array}$$

6 ones – 0 ones

= ________ ones

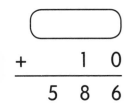

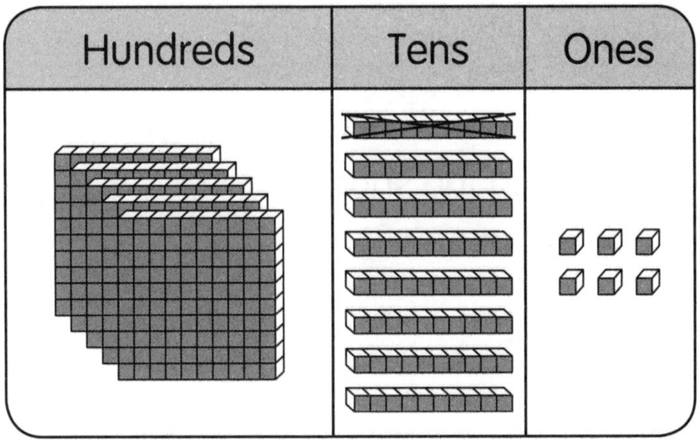

Step 2
Subtract the tens.

$$\begin{array}{rrrr} & 5 & 8 & 6 \\ - & & 1 & 0 \\ \hline & & 7 & 6 \end{array}$$

8 tens – 1 ten

= ________ tens

Step 3
Subtract the hundreds.

$$\begin{array}{rrrr} & 5 & 8 & 6 \\ - & & 1 & 0 \\ \hline & 5 & 7 & 6 \end{array}$$

5 hundreds – 0 hundreds

= ________ hundreds

So, 586 – 10 = ________.

Use addition to check your answer.

$$\begin{array}{rrrr} & \boxed{} & & \\ + & & 1 & 0 \\ \hline & 5 & 8 & 6 \end{array}$$

Name: ______________________ Date: ______________

Subtract.
Add to check your answer.

10.
$$\begin{array}{r} 359 \\ -\ \ 45 \\ \hline \end{array}$$

11.
$$\begin{array}{r} 128 \\ -\ \ 25 \\ \hline \end{array}$$

12.
$$\begin{array}{r} 975 \\ -\ \ 71 \\ \hline \end{array}$$

13.
$$\begin{array}{r} 255 \\ -\ \ 12 \\ \hline \end{array}$$

Solve.
Show how to check your answer.

Example

A baker bought 125 eggs.
He broke 12 eggs on the way back to the shop.
How many eggs does the baker have now?

$125 - 12 = 113$

$$\begin{array}{r} 125 \\ -\ \ 12 \\ \hline 113 \end{array} \qquad \begin{array}{r} 113 \\ +\ \ 12 \\ \hline 125 \end{array}$$

The baker has __113__ eggs now.

14. Xavier makes 243 bookmarks for a charity sale.
He sells 33 bookmarks at the sale.
How many bookmarks does Xavier have left?

Xavier has ________ bookmarks left.

Name: ______________________ Date: ______________

Subtract.

Example

597 – 453 = ?

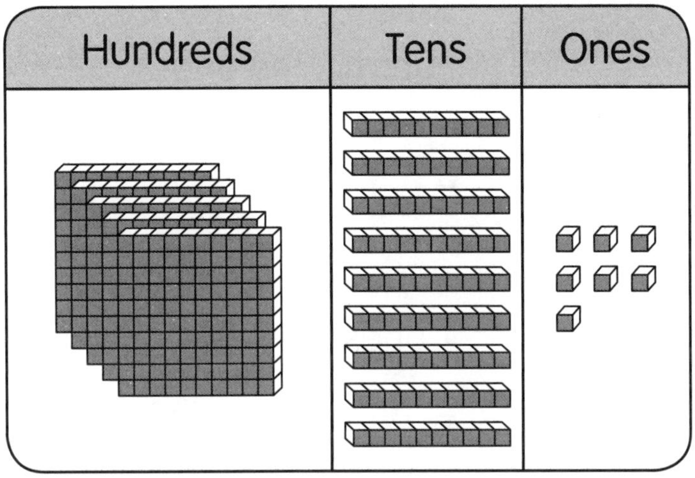

Step 1

Subtract the ones.

```
   5  9  7
–  4  5  3
----------
         4
```

7 ones – 3 ones

= ___4___ ones

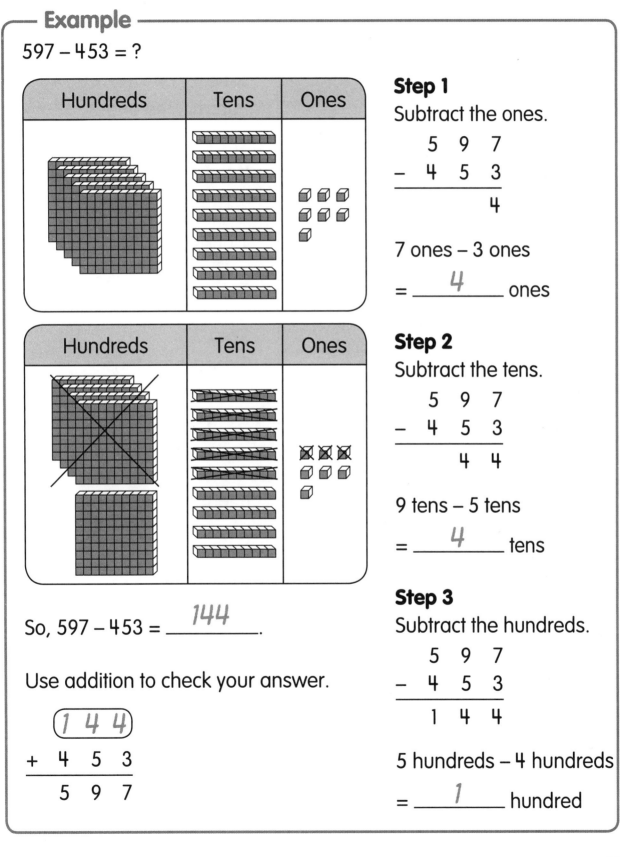

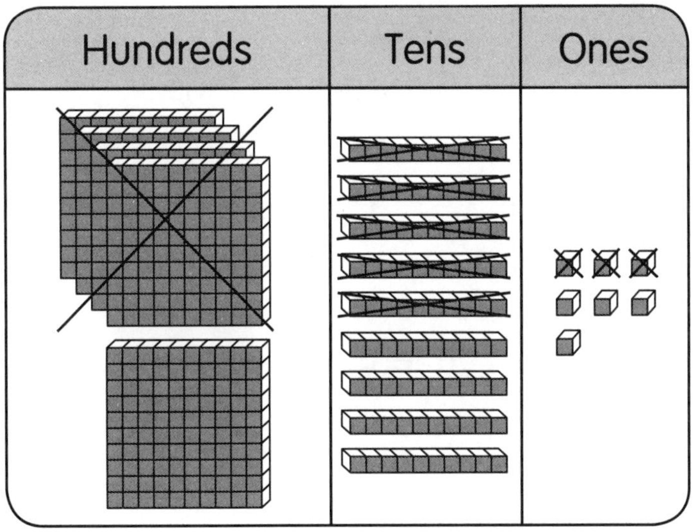

Step 2

Subtract the tens.

```
   5  9  7
–  4  5  3
----------
      4  4
```

9 tens – 5 tens

= ___4___ tens

Step 3

Subtract the hundreds.

```
   5  9  7
–  4  5  3
----------
   1  4  4
```

5 hundreds – 4 hundreds

= ___1___ hundred

So, 597 – 453 = ___144___.

Use addition to check your answer.

```
   1  4  4
+  4  5  3
----------
   5  9  7
```

Name: ______________________ Date: ______________

Subtract.

15. 687 – 153 = ?

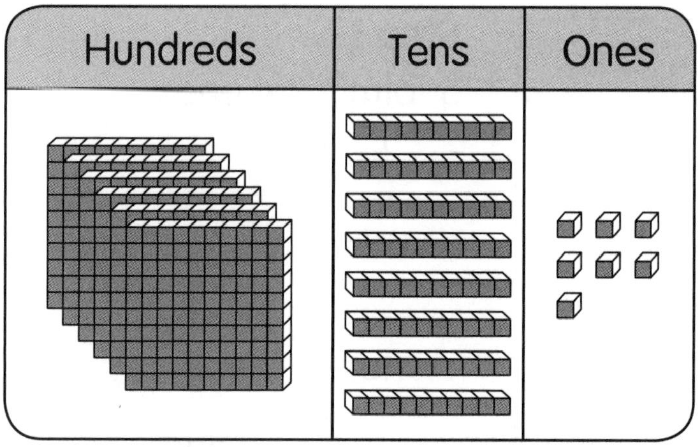

Step 1
Subtract the ones.

```
   6  8  7
–  1  5  3
----------
         4
```

7 ones – 3 ones

= ________ ones

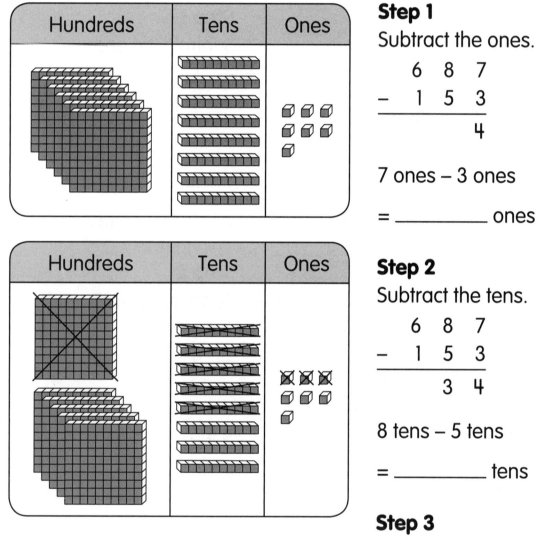

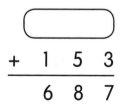

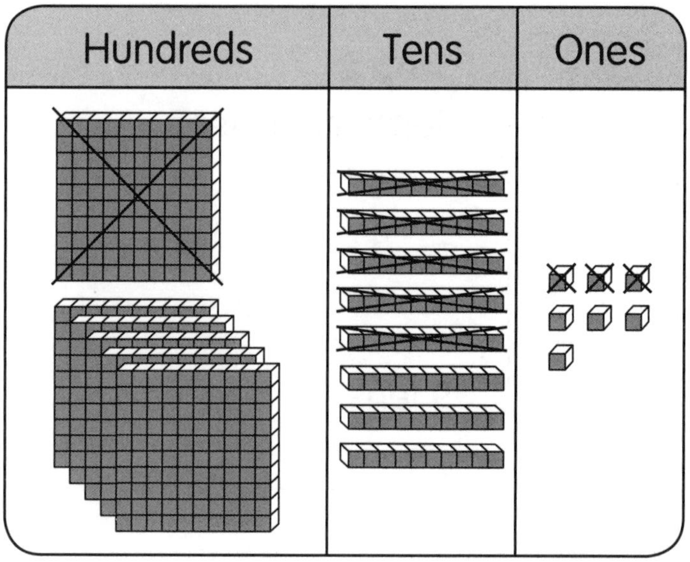

Step 2
Subtract the tens.

```
   6  8  7
–  1  5  3
----------
      3  4
```

8 tens – 5 tens

= ________ tens

Step 3
Subtract the hundreds.

```
   6  8  7
–  1  5  3
----------
   5  3  4
```

6 hundreds – 1 hundred

= ________ hundreds

So, 687 – 153 = ________.

Use addition to check your answer.

```
   [      ]
+  1  5  3
----------
   6  8  7
```

Name: ______________________ Date: ______________

Subtract.
Use addition to check your answer.

16.
$$\begin{array}{r} 835 \\ -\ 314 \\ \hline \end{array}$$

17.
$$\begin{array}{r} 467 \\ -\ 156 \\ \hline \end{array}$$

18.
$$\begin{array}{r} 999 \\ -\ 471 \\ \hline \end{array}$$

19.
$$\begin{array}{r} 574 \\ -\ 161 \\ \hline \end{array}$$

Solve.
Show how to check your answer.

Example

Mrs. Grey buys a suitcase for $258.
Mrs. Hudson buys the same suitcase for $216.
How much more did Mrs. Grey pay?

$258 - $216 = $42

$$\begin{array}{r} \$258 \\ -\ \$216 \\ \hline \$42 \end{array} \qquad \begin{array}{r} \$216 \\ +\ 42 \\ \hline \$258 \end{array}$$

Mrs. Grey paid __$42__ more.

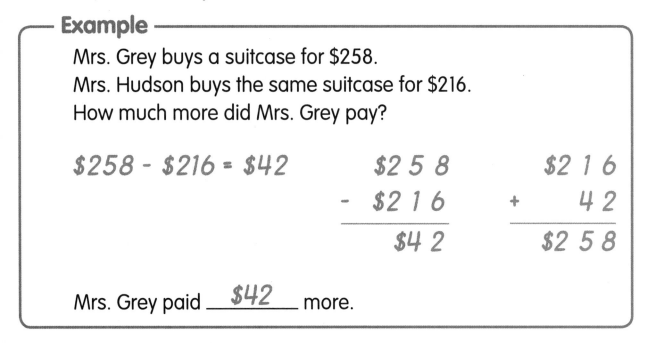

Name: ____________________ **Date:** ____________

20. A cook needs 175 cloves of garlic.
She has 155 cloves of garlic.
How many more cloves of garlic does she need?

She needs ________ more cloves of garlic.

Name: ______________________ Date: ______________

Worksheet 2 Subtraction with Regrouping in Tens and Ones

Subtract.

1. 33 – 8 = ?

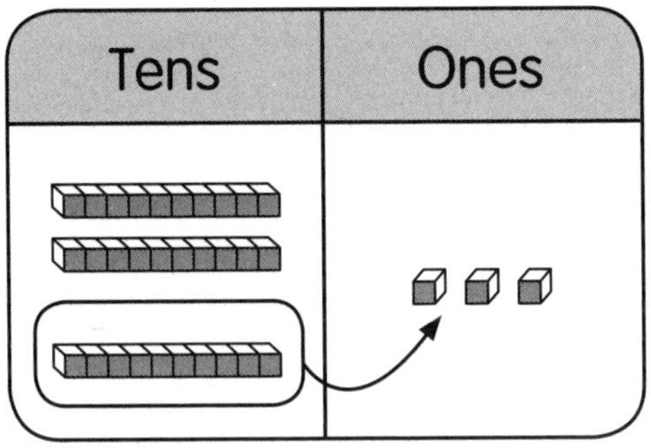

Step 1

Regroup the tens and ones

3 tens 3 ones = ________ tens

________ ones

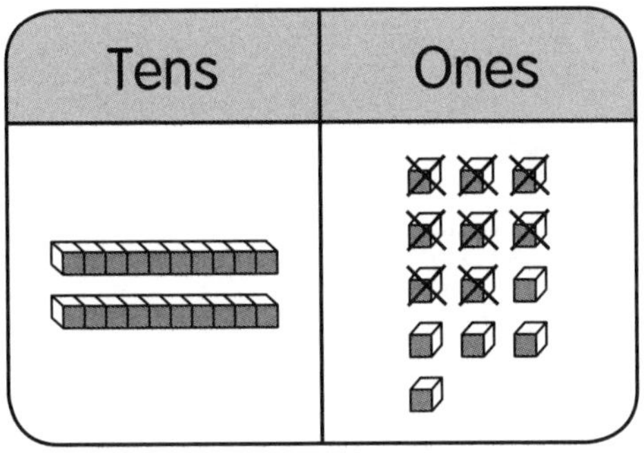

Subtract the ones.

Tens	Ones
~~3~~ (2)	(1)3
–	8
	5

So, 33 – 8 = ________.

13 ones – 8 ones = ________ ones

Step 2

Subtract the tens.

Tens	Ones
~~3~~ (2)	(1)3
–	8
2	5

2 tens – 0 tens = ________ tens

Name: ______________________ Date: ______________

Regroup the tens and ones.
Then subtract.

Example

542 – 329 = ?

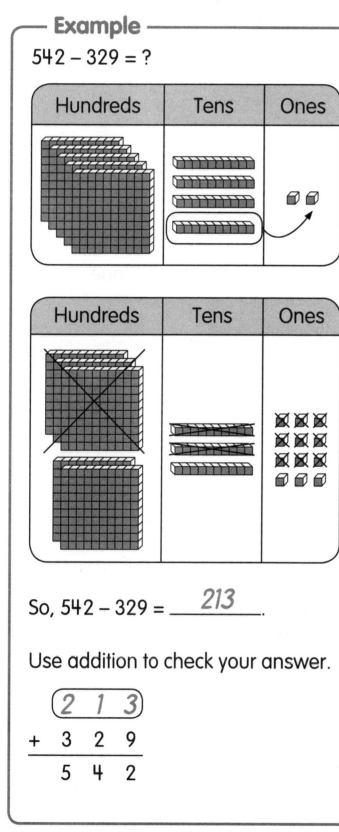

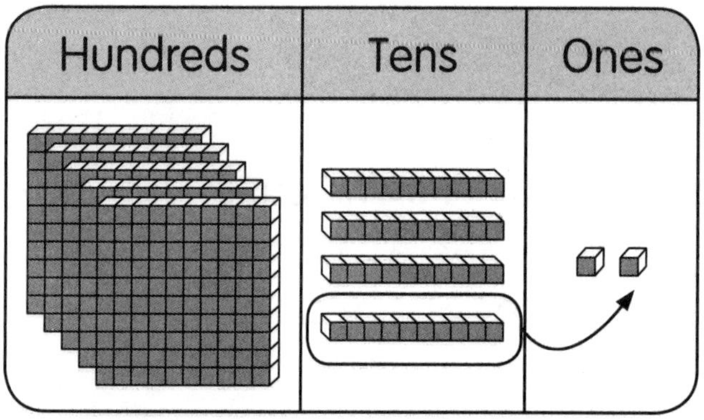

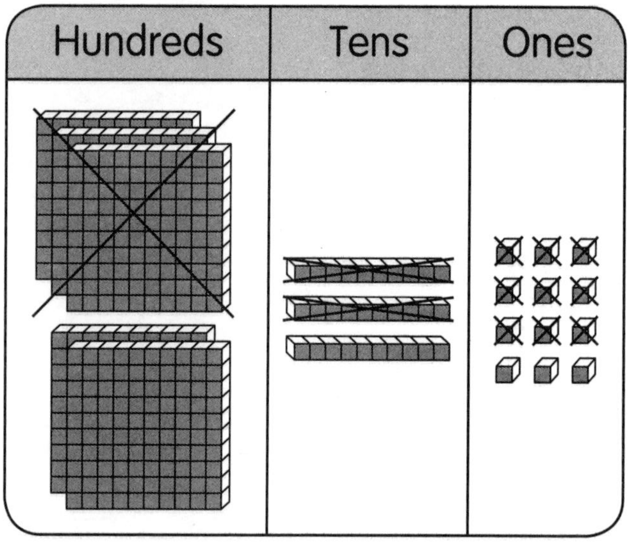

So, 542 – 329 = 213.

Use addition to check your answer.

	2	1	3
+	3	2	9
	5	4	2

Step 1

Regroup the tens and ones.

4 tens 2 ones = 3 tens 12 ones

Subtract the ones.

	5	~~4~~ 3	[1]2
–	3	2	9
			3

12 ones – 9 ones = 3 ones

Step 2

Subtract the tens.

	5	~~4~~ 3	[1]2
–	3	2	9
		1	3

3 tens – 2 tens = 1 ten

Step 3

Subtract the hundreds.

	5	~~4~~ 3	[1]2
–	3	2	9
	2	1	3

5 hundreds – 3 hundreds = 2 hundreds

Name: ______________________ Date: ______________

Regroup the tens and ones.
Then subtract.

2. 425 – 116 = ?

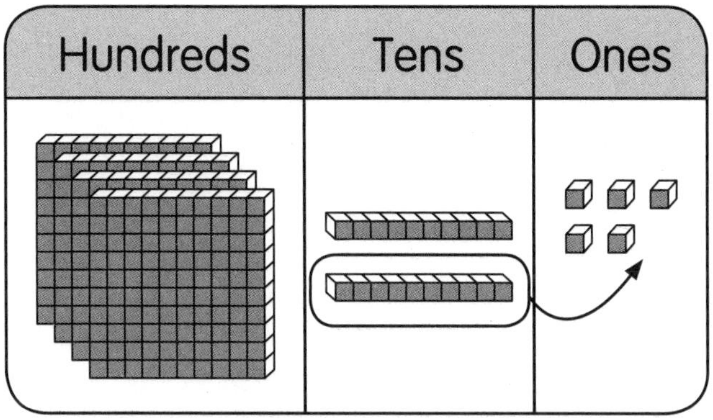

Step 1
Regroup the tens and ones.
2 tens 5 ones = 1 ten
15 ones
Subtract the ones.

$$\begin{array}{r} 4\ \overset{1}{\not{2}}\ {}^{1}5 \\ -\ 1\ \ 1\ \ 6 \\ \hline 9 \end{array}$$

15 ones – 6 ones = ____ ones

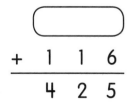

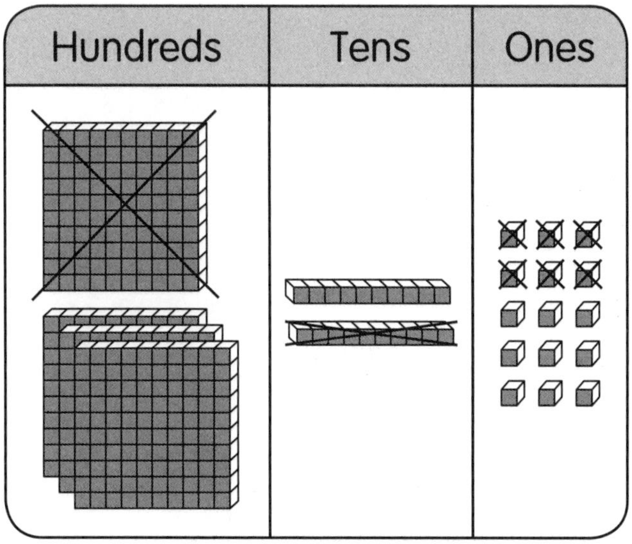

Step 2
Subtract the tens.

$$\begin{array}{r} 4\ \overset{1}{\not{2}}\ {}^{1}5 \\ -\ 1\ \ 1\ \ 6 \\ \hline 0\ \ 9 \end{array}$$

1 ten – 1 ten = ____ tens

Step 3
Subtract the hundreds.

$$\begin{array}{r} 4\ \overset{1}{\not{2}}\ {}^{1}5 \\ -\ 1\ \ 1\ \ 6 \\ \hline 3\ \ 0\ \ 9 \end{array}$$

4 hundreds – 1 hundred
= ____ hundreds

So, 425 – 116 = ____________.

Use addition to check your answer.

$$\begin{array}{r} \boxed{} \\ +\ 1\ \ 1\ \ 6 \\ \hline 4\ \ 2\ \ 5 \end{array}$$

Name: ______________________ Date: ______________

Subtract.
Add to check your answer.

3. 792 – 426 = ?

Regroup the tens and ones.

9 tens 2 ones = ________ tens ________ ones

Subtract the ones.

12 ones – 6 ones = ________ ones

Subtract the tens.

8 tens – 2 tens = ________ tens

Subtract the hundreds.

7 hundreds – 4 hundreds = ________ hundreds

792 – 426 = ________

4. 543 – 224 = ________

5. 992 – 784 = ________

Name: ______________________________ Date: ______________

Solve.
Show how to check your answer.

Example

Mrs. Kim bakes 564 muffins to sell.
She sells 238 muffins.
How many muffins does Mrs. Kim have left?

$564 - 238 = 326$

$$\begin{array}{r} \overset{5}{\cancel{6}}\overset{1}{} \\ 5\,\cancel{6}\,4 \\ -\ 2\,3\,8 \\ \hline 3\,2\,6 \end{array} \qquad \begin{array}{r} 3\,2\,6 \\ +\ 2\,3\,8 \\ \hline 5\,6\,4 \end{array}$$

Mrs. Kim has ___326___ muffins left.

6. Stella buys 460 straws.
She uses 115 straws for a craft project.
How many straws does Stella have left?

Stella has __________ straws left.

Name: ______________________ Date: ______________

Solve.
Show how to check your answer.

7. Pauline has 355 coins.
She gives 109 coins to her cousin.
How many coins does Pauline have left?

Pauline has ________ coins left.

Name: ______________________ Date: ______________

Worksheet 3 Subtraction with Regrouping in Hundreds and Tens

Regroup the hundreds and tens. Then subtract.

Example

618 – 291 = ?

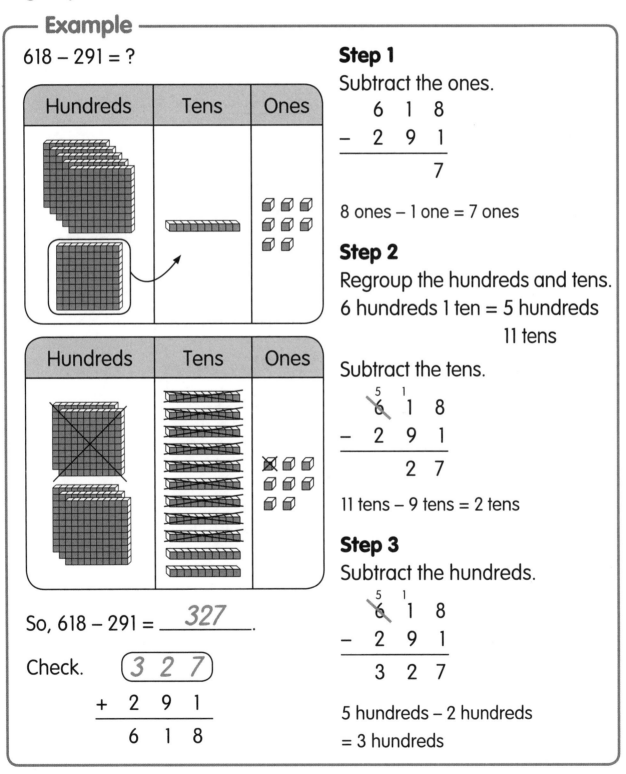

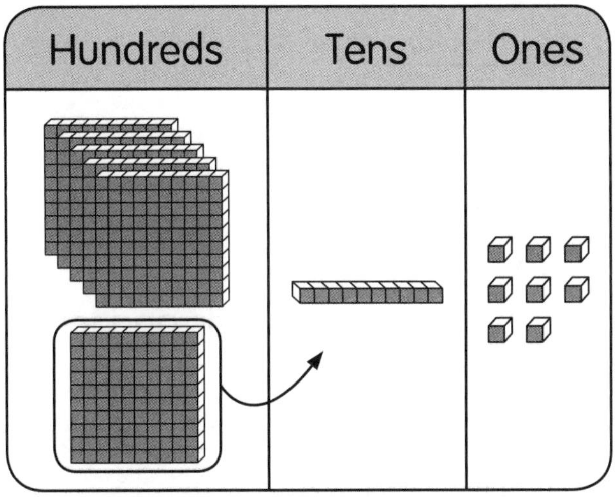

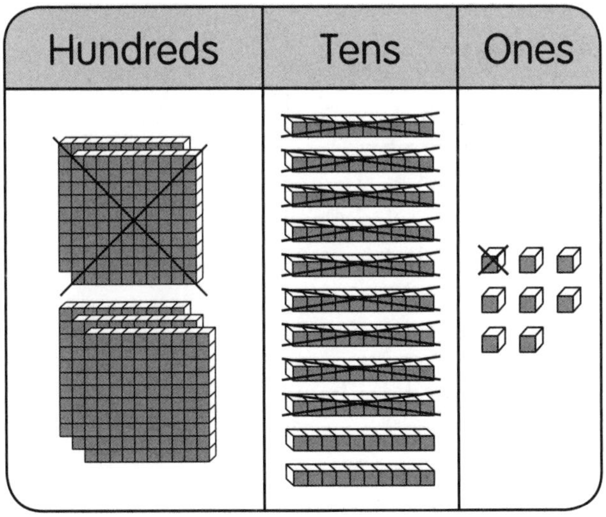

So, 618 – 291 = 327.

Check.

$$\begin{array}{r} 3\ 2\ 7 \\ +\ 2\ 9\ 1 \\ \hline 6\ 1\ 8 \end{array}$$

Step 1

Subtract the ones.

$$\begin{array}{r} 6\ 1\ 8 \\ -\ 2\ 9\ 1 \\ \hline 7 \end{array}$$

8 ones – 1 one = 7 ones

Step 2

Regroup the hundreds and tens.

6 hundreds 1 ten = 5 hundreds 11 tens

Subtract the tens.

$$\begin{array}{r} \overset{5}{\cancel{6}}\ \overset{1}{1}\ 8 \\ -\ 2\ 9\ 1 \\ \hline 2\ 7 \end{array}$$

11 tens – 9 tens = 2 tens

Step 3

Subtract the hundreds.

$$\begin{array}{r} \overset{5}{\cancel{6}}\ \overset{1}{1}\ 8 \\ -\ 2\ 9\ 1 \\ \hline 3\ 2\ 7 \end{array}$$

5 hundreds – 2 hundreds = 3 hundreds

Name: ______________________ Date: ____________

Regroup the hundreds and tens.
Then subtract.

1. 823 – 142 = ?

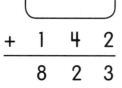

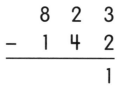

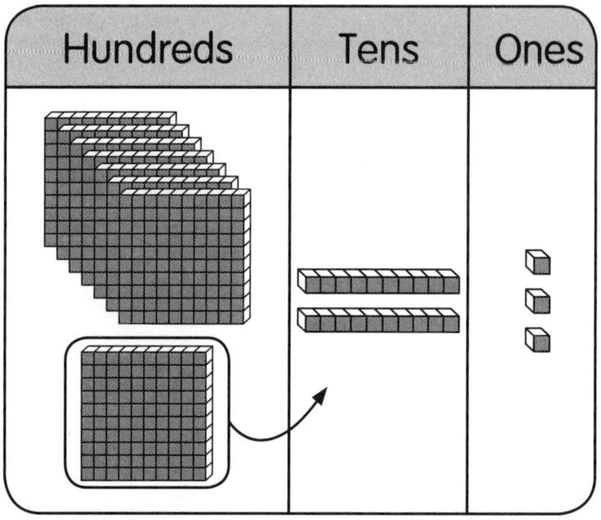

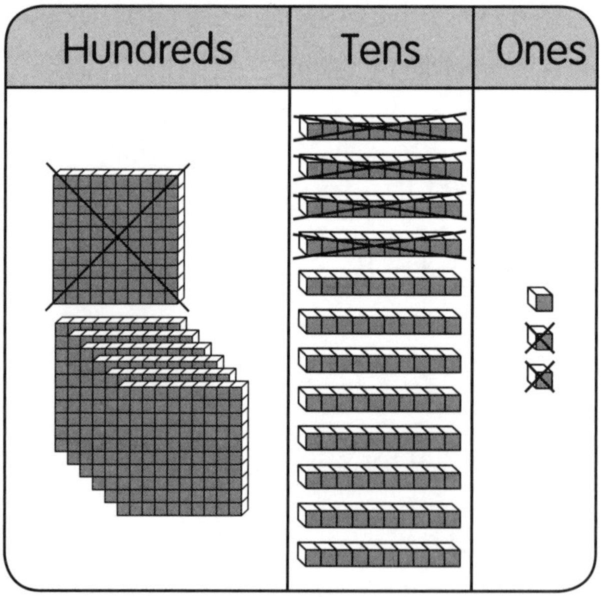

So, 823 – 142 = ________.

Check.

$$\begin{array}{r} \boxed{} \\ +\ 1\ 4\ 2 \\ \hline 8\ 2\ 3 \end{array}$$

Step 1

Subtract the ones.

$$\begin{array}{r} 8\ 2\ 3 \\ -\ 1\ 4\ 2 \\ \hline 1 \end{array}$$

3 ones – 2 ones = ____ one

Step 2

Regroup the hundreds and tens.

8 hundreds 2 tens = ____ hundreds ____ tens

Subtract the tens.

$$\begin{array}{r} \overset{7}{\cancel{8}}\ \overset{1}{}2\ 3 \\ -\ 1\ 4\ 2 \\ \hline 8\ 1 \end{array}$$

12 tens – 4 tens = ____ tens

Step 3

Subtract the hundreds.

$$\begin{array}{r} \overset{7}{\cancel{8}}\ \overset{1}{}2\ 3 \\ -\ 1\ 4\ 2 \\ \hline 6\ 8\ 1 \end{array}$$

7 hundreds – 1 hundred = ____ hundreds

Name: ____________________ Date: ____________

Subtract.
Add to check your answer.

2. 419 – 132 = ?

Subtract the ones.

9 ones – 2 ones = ________ ones

Regroup the hundreds and tens.

4 hundreds 1 ten = ________ hundreds ________ tens

Subtract the tens.

11 tens – 3 tens = ________ tens

Subtract the hundreds.

3 hundreds – 1 hundred = ________ hundreds

419 – 132 = ________

3.
$$\begin{array}{r} 573 \\ -\ 381 \\ \hline \end{array}$$

4.
$$\begin{array}{r} 736 \\ -\ 285 \\ \hline \end{array}$$

5.
$$\begin{array}{r} 613 \\ -\ 481 \\ \hline \end{array}$$

6.
$$\begin{array}{r} 187 \\ -\ 94 \\ \hline \end{array}$$

7.
$$\begin{array}{r} 427 \\ -\ 385 \\ \hline \end{array}$$

8.
$$\begin{array}{r} 909 \\ -\ 353 \\ \hline \end{array}$$

Name: ______________________ Date: ______________

Solve.
Show how to check your answer.

Example

There were 435 people at a concert.
During a break, 295 people left.
How many people were still left at the concert?

$435 - 295 = 140$

$$\begin{array}{r} \overset{3}{\cancel{4}}\overset{1}{3}5 \\ -\ 295 \\ \hline 140 \end{array} \qquad \begin{array}{r} 140 \\ +\ 295 \\ \hline 435 \end{array}$$

<u>140</u> people were still left at the concert.

9. Mr. Johnson drives 450 miles to a ski resort.
Mr. Rivers drives 190 miles less than Mr. Johnson.
How many miles does Mr. Rivers drive?

Mr. Rivers drives ________ miles.

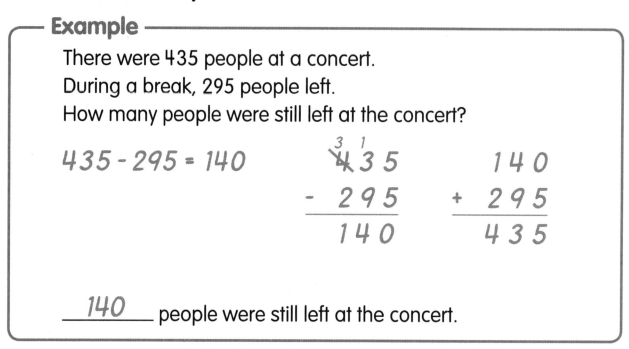

Name: ______________________ Date: ______________

Worksheet 4 Subtraction with Regrouping in Hundreds, Tens, and Ones

Regroup the hundreds, tens, and ones. Then subtract.

Example

532 – 298 = ?

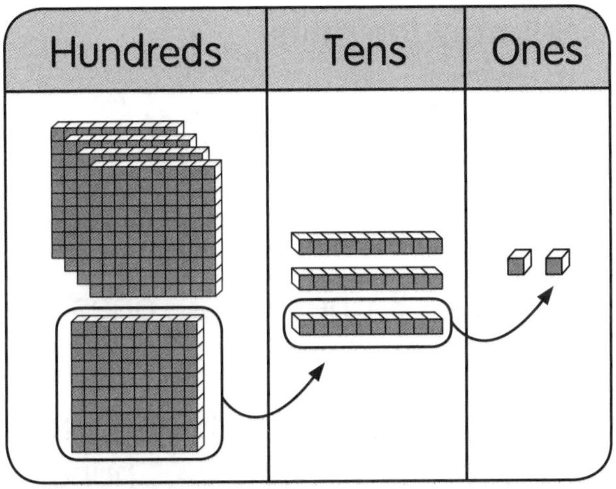

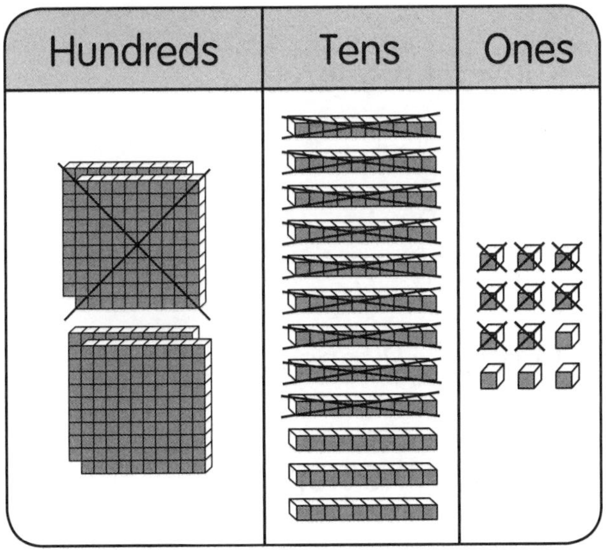

So, 532 – 298 = 234.

Check.

$$\begin{array}{r} 234 \\ +\ 298 \\ \hline 532 \end{array}$$

Step 1

Regroup the tens and ones.

3 tens 2 ones = 2 tens 12 ones

Subtract the ones.

$$\begin{array}{r} 5\ \overset{2}{\not 3}\ \overset{1}{2} \\ -\ 2\ 9\ 8 \\ \hline 4 \end{array}$$

12 ones – 8 ones = 4 ones

Step 2

Regroup the hundreds and tens.

5 hundreds 2 tens = 4 hundreds 12 tens

Subtract the tens.

$$\begin{array}{r} \overset{4}{\not 5}\ \overset{12}{\not 3}\ \overset{1}{2} \\ -\ 2\ 9\ 8 \\ \hline 3\ 4 \end{array}$$

12 tens – 9 tens = 3 tens

Step 3

Subtract the hundreds.

$$\begin{array}{r} \overset{4}{\not 5}\ \overset{12}{\not 3}\ \overset{1}{2} \\ -\ 2\ 9\ 8 \\ \hline 2\ 3\ 4 \end{array}$$

4 hundreds – 2 hundreds = 2 hundreds

Name: ______________________ Date: ______________

Regroup.
Then subtract.

1. 751 – 594 = ?

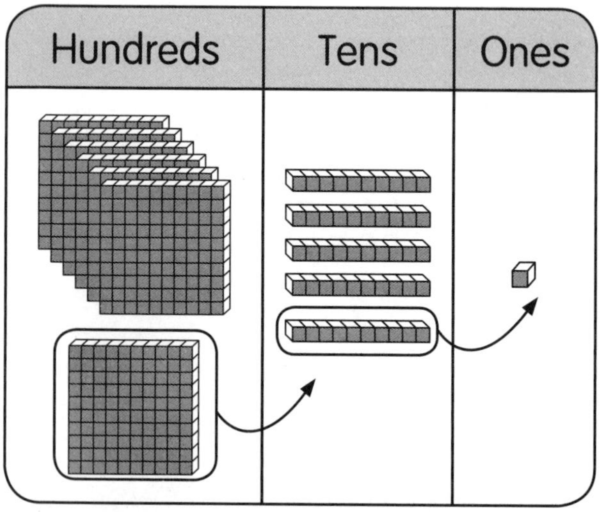

Step 1
Regroup the tens and ones.
5 tens 1 one = ____ tens ____ ones
Subtract the ones.

$$\begin{array}{r} 7\ \overset{4}{\not{5}}\ \overset{1}{1} \\ -\ 5\ 9\ 4 \\ \hline 7 \end{array}$$

11 ones – 4 ones = ____ ones

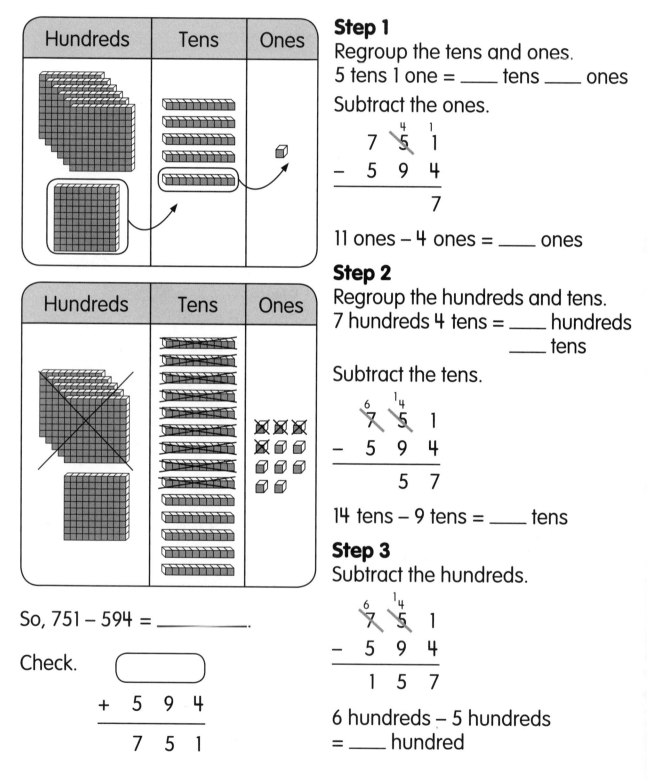

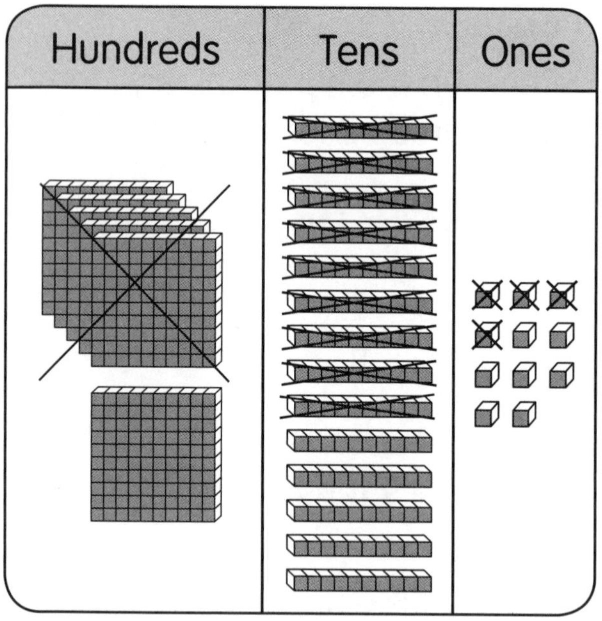

Step 2
Regroup the hundreds and tens.
7 hundreds 4 tens = ____ hundreds ____ tens
Subtract the tens.

$$\begin{array}{r} \overset{6}{\not{7}}\ \overset{14}{\not{5}}\ 1 \\ -\ 5\ 9\ 4 \\ \hline 5\ 7 \end{array}$$

14 tens – 9 tens = ____ tens

Step 3
Subtract the hundreds.

$$\begin{array}{r} \overset{6}{\not{7}}\ \overset{14}{\not{5}}\ 1 \\ -\ 5\ 9\ 4 \\ \hline 1\ 5\ 7 \end{array}$$

6 hundreds – 5 hundreds
= ____ hundred

So, 751 – 594 = ________.

Check.

$$\begin{array}{r} \boxed{} \\ +\ 5\ 9\ 4 \\ \hline 7\ 5\ 1 \end{array}$$

Name: ______________________ Date: ______________

Subtract.
Add to check your answer.

2. 785 – 297 = ?

Regroup the tens and ones.

8 tens 5 ones = ________ tens ________ ones

Subtract the ones.

15 ones – 7 ones = ________ ones

Regroup the hundreds and tens.

7 hundreds 7 tens = ________ hundreds ________ tens

Subtract the tens.

17 tens – 9 tens = ________ tens

Subtract the hundreds.

6 hundreds – 2 hundreds = ________ hundreds

785 – 297 = ________

3.
$$\begin{array}{r} 8\ 2\ 2 \\ -\ 3\ 7\ 7 \\ \hline \end{array}$$

4.
$$\begin{array}{r} 4\ 3\ 8 \\ -\ 3\ 6\ 4 \\ \hline \end{array}$$

5.
$$\begin{array}{r} 3\ 2\ 1 \\ -\ 2\ 6\ 4 \\ \hline \end{array}$$

6.
$$\begin{array}{r} 9\ 3\ 3 \\ -\ 4\ 9\ 4 \\ \hline \end{array}$$

7.
$$\begin{array}{r} 6\ 5\ 4 \\ -\ \ \ 9\ 7 \\ \hline \end{array}$$

8.
$$\begin{array}{r} 5\ 1\ 6 \\ -\ 1\ 5\ 7 \\ \hline \end{array}$$

Name: ______________________ Date: ______________

Solve.
Show how to check your answer.

Example

Penny skips 250 times.
Bianca skips 95 times less than Penny.
How many times does Bianca skip?

$250 - 95 = 155$

$$\begin{array}{r} \overset{1}{\cancel{2}}\,\overset{14}{\cancel{5}}\,\overset{1}{0} \\ -\ \ 9\,5 \\ \hline 1\,5\,5 \end{array} \qquad \begin{array}{r} 1\,5\,5 \\ +\ \ 9\,5 \\ \hline 2\,5\,0 \end{array}$$

Bianca skips ___155___ times.

9. Susan picked 120 apples.
35 of the apples are rotten.
How many apples are not rotten?

__________ apples are not rotten.

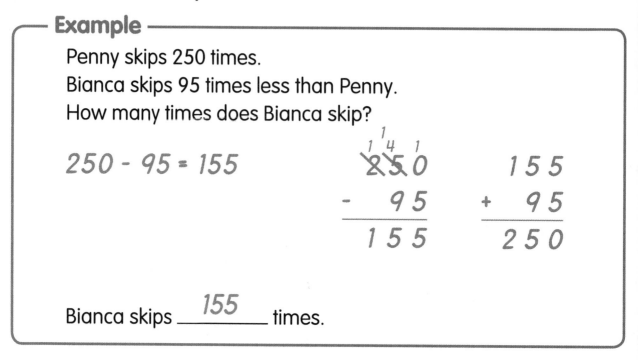

Name: ______________________ Date: ______________

Worksheet 5 Subtraction Across Zeros

Regroup. Then subtract.

Example

200 – 158 = ?

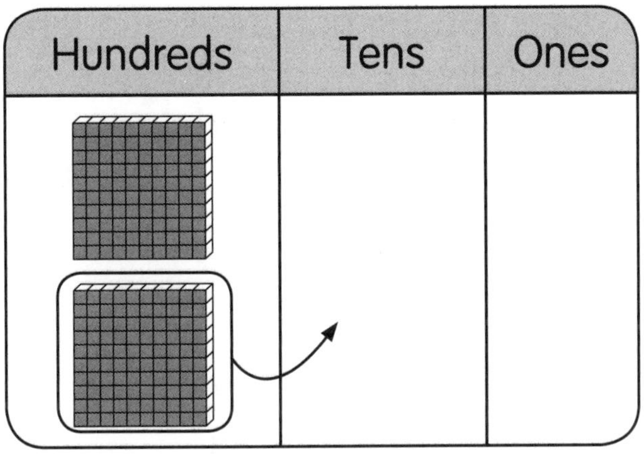

Step 1
Regroup the hundreds and tens.
2 hundreds = 1 hundred 10 tens
Regroup the tens and ones.
10 tens = 9 tens 10 ones

Subtract the ones.

$$\begin{array}{rccc} & \overset{1}{\cancel{2}} & \overset{1\,9}{\cancel{0}} & \overset{1}{0} \\ - & 1 & 5 & 8 \\ \hline & & & 2 \end{array}$$

10 ones – 8 ones = 2 ones

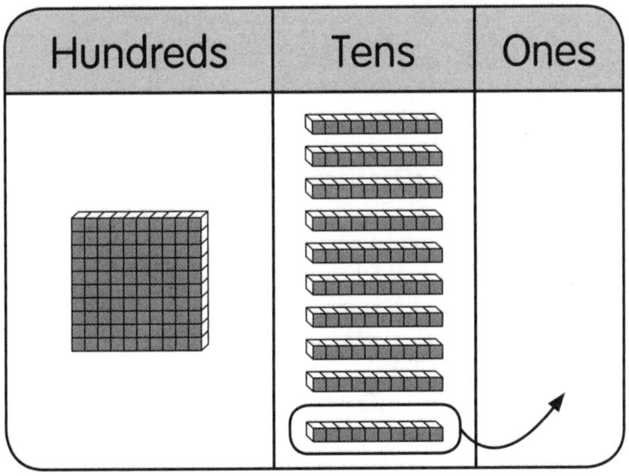

Step 2
Subtract the tens.

$$\begin{array}{rccc} & \overset{1}{\cancel{2}} & \overset{1\,9}{\cancel{0}} & \overset{1}{0} \\ - & 1 & 5 & 8 \\ \hline & & 4 & 2 \end{array}$$

9 tens – 5 tens = 4 tens

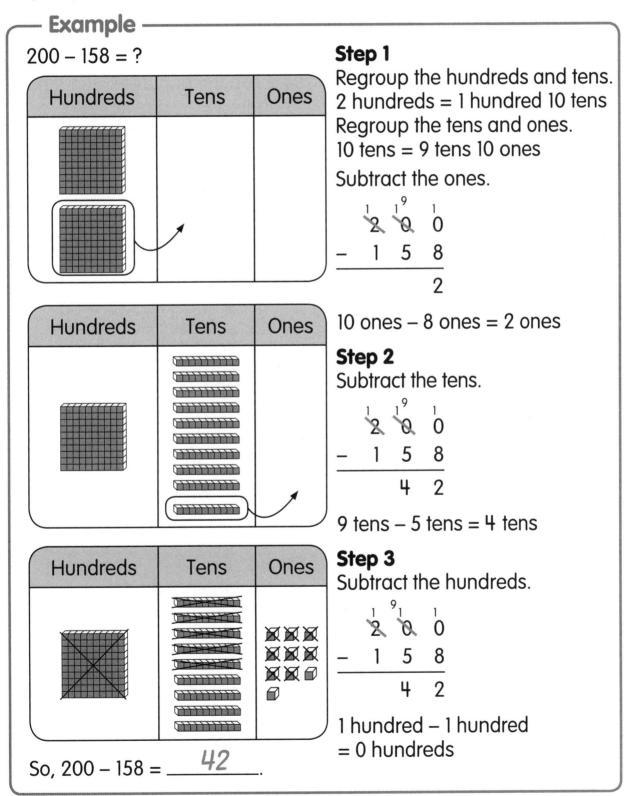

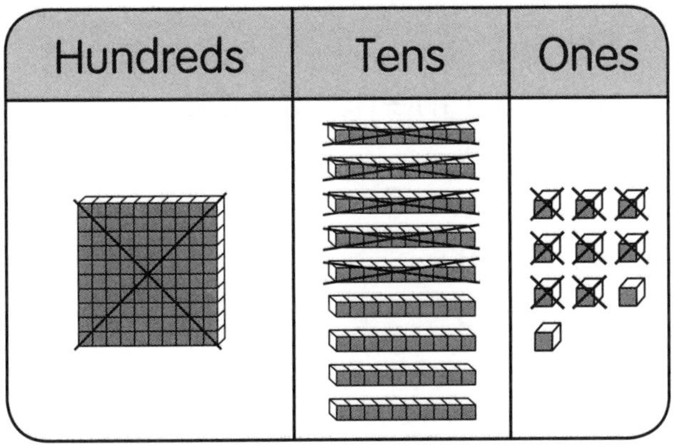

Step 3
Subtract the hundreds.

$$\begin{array}{rccc} & \overset{1}{\cancel{2}} & \overset{9\,1}{\cancel{0}} & \overset{1}{0} \\ - & 1 & 5 & 8 \\ \hline & & 4 & 2 \end{array}$$

1 hundred – 1 hundred
= 0 hundreds

So, 200 – 158 = 42.

Name: ______________________________ Date: ______________

Regroup.
Then subtract.

1. 100 – 45 = ?

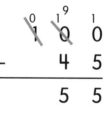

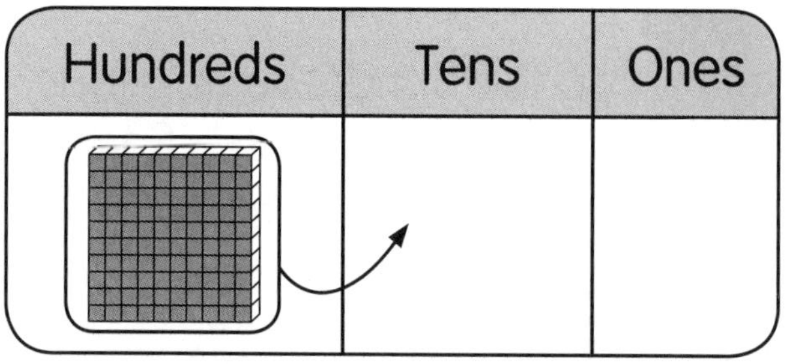

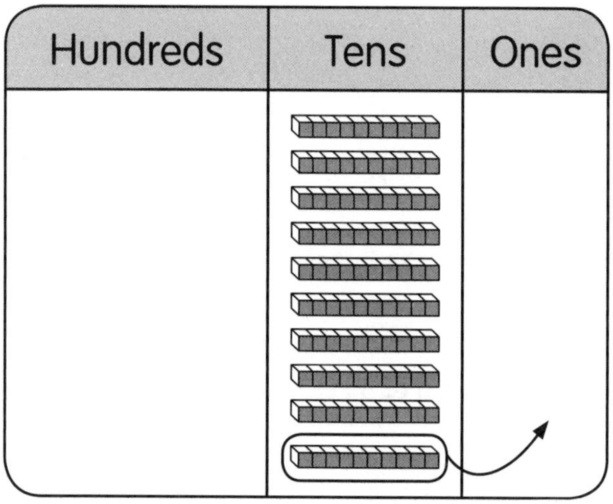

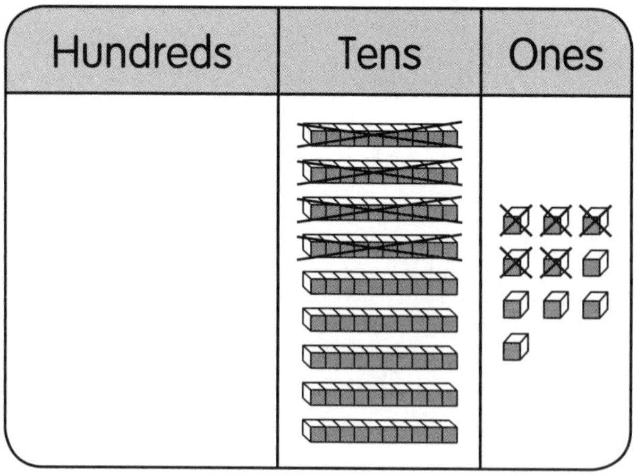

So, 100 – 45 = __________.

Step 1
Regroup the hundreds and tens.
1 hundred = ____ tens
Regroup the tens and ones.
10 tens = ____ tens ____ ones
Subtract the ones.

$$\begin{array}{rrrr} & \overset{0}{\cancel{1}} & \overset{1\,9}{\cancel{0}} & \overset{1}{0} \\ - & & 4 & 5 \\ \hline & & & 5 \end{array}$$

10 ones – 5 ones = ____ ones

Step 2
Subtract the tens.

$$\begin{array}{rrrr} & \overset{0}{\cancel{1}} & \overset{1\,9}{\cancel{0}} & \overset{1}{0} \\ - & & 4 & 5 \\ \hline & & 5 & 5 \end{array}$$

9 tens – 4 tens = ____ tens

Step 3
Subtract the hundreds.

$$\begin{array}{rrrr} & \overset{0}{\cancel{1}} & \overset{1\,9}{\cancel{0}} & \overset{1}{0} \\ - & & 4 & 5 \\ \hline & & 5 & 5 \end{array}$$

0 hundreds – 0 hundreds
= ____ hundreds

Name: ______________________ Date: ______________

Solve.
Add to check your answer.

2. 900 – 461 = ?

Regroup the hundreds and tens.

9 hundreds = ________ hundreds ________ tens

Regroup the tens and ones.

10 tens = ________ tens ________ ones

Subtract the ones.

10 ones – 1 one = ________ ones

Subtract the tens.

9 tens – 6 tens = ________ tens

Subtract the hundreds.

8 hundreds – 4 hundreds = ________ hundreds

900 – 461 = ________

3.
```
  8 0 0
– 2 6 4
-------
```

4.
```
  2 0 0
– 1 2 8
-------
```

5.
```
  5 0 0
– 3 8 1
-------
```

6.
```
  7 0 0
– 5 4 2
-------
```

7.
```
  6 0 0
– 2 5 8
-------
```

8.
```
  3 0 0
–   6 9
-------
```

Name: ______________________ Date: ____________

Solve.

Show how to check your answer.

Example

Bradley has $300.
He buys a pair of running shoes for $125.
How much does Bradley have left?

$\$300 - \$125 = \$175$

$$\begin{array}{r} \overset{2}{\cancel{3}}\overset{\overset{9}{1}}{\cancel{0}}\overset{1}{0} \\ -\ 125 \\ \hline 175 \end{array} \qquad \begin{array}{r} 175 \\ +\ 125 \\ \hline 300 \end{array}$$

Bradley has $175 left.

9. Rowan has 200 stamps.
147 stamps are U.S. stamps.
How many stamps are not U.S. stamps?

_______ stamps are not U.S. stamps.

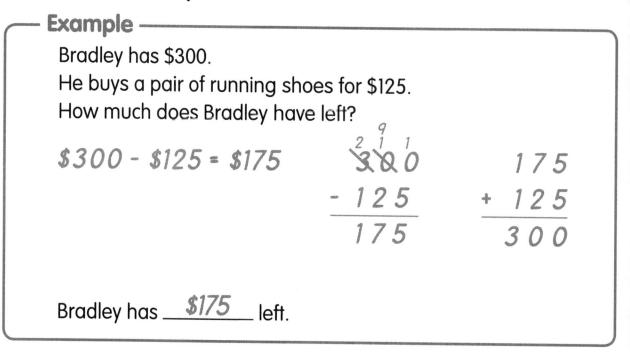

Name: ______________________ Date: ______________

CHAPTER 4 Using Bar Models: Addition and Subtraction

Worksheet 1 Using Part-Part-Whole in Addition and Subtraction

Solve.
Check your answer.

1. Lydia has 3 □.
Kai has 4 more □ than Lydia.
How many □ does Kai have?

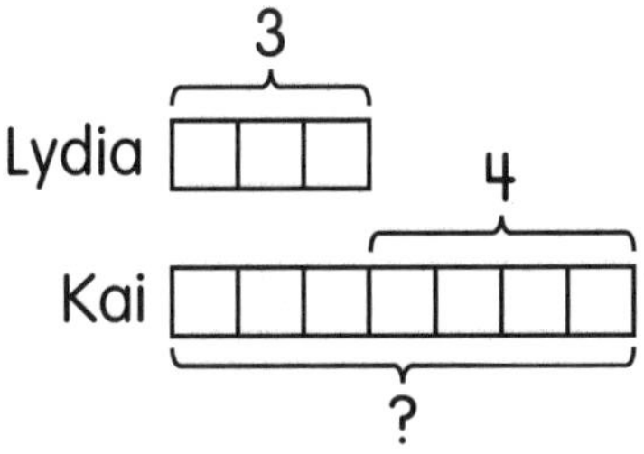

________ + ________ = ________

Kai has ________ □.

2. Prudence has 5 pens.
Tonya has 9 pens.
How many more pens does Tonya have?

Use □ to show the number of pens.

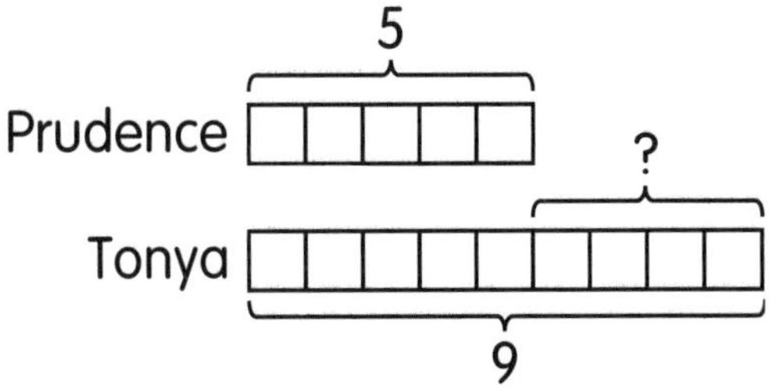

________ − ________ = ________

Tonya has ________ more pens.

Name: ____________________ Date: ____________

Find the missing numbers.
Use the bar models to help you.
Subtract to check your answer.

Example

Emma has 10 red bracelets.
Anna has 5 blue bracelets.
How many bracelets do they have in all?

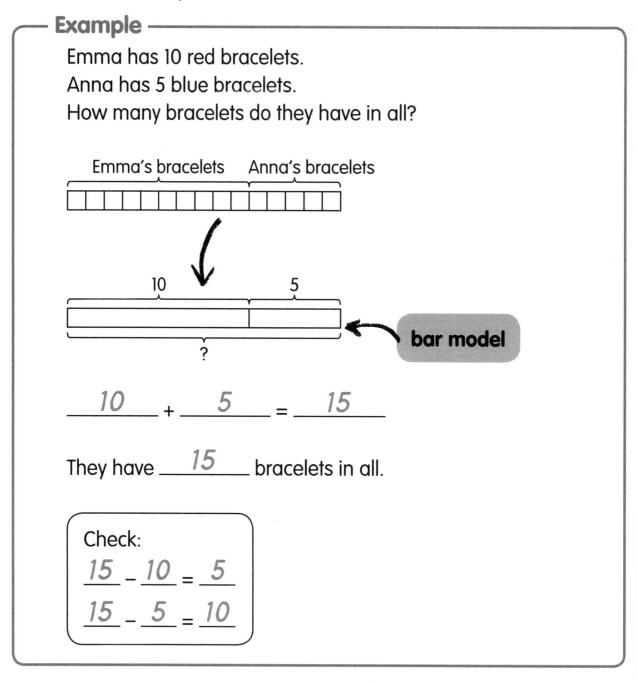

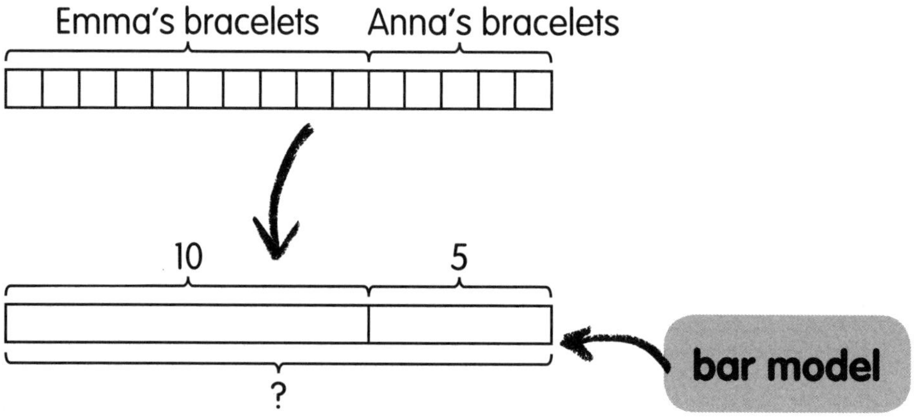

10 + 5 = 15

They have 15 bracelets in all.

Check:
15 – 10 = 5
15 – 5 = 10

Name: ____________________ Date: ____________

3. Ling has 15 coins.
Norah has 2 coins.
How many coins do they have in all?

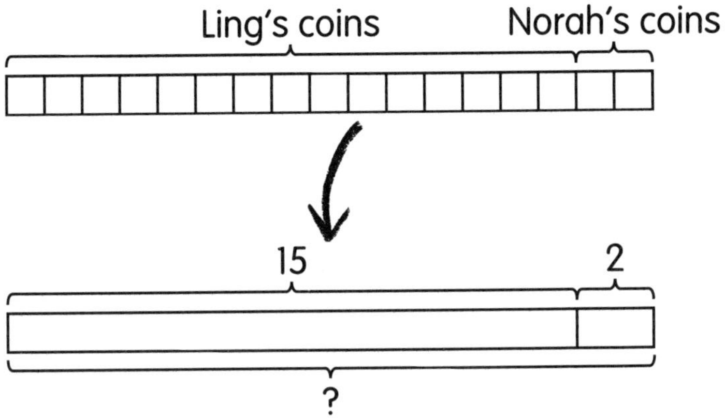

_____ + _____ = _____

They have _____ coins in all.

Check:

___ − ___ = ___

___ − ___ = ___

4. Dora has 40 cherries.
Ava has 60 cherries.
How many cherries do they have in all?

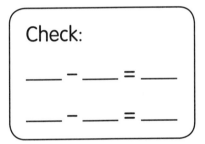

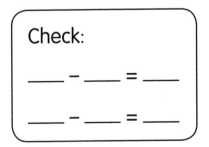

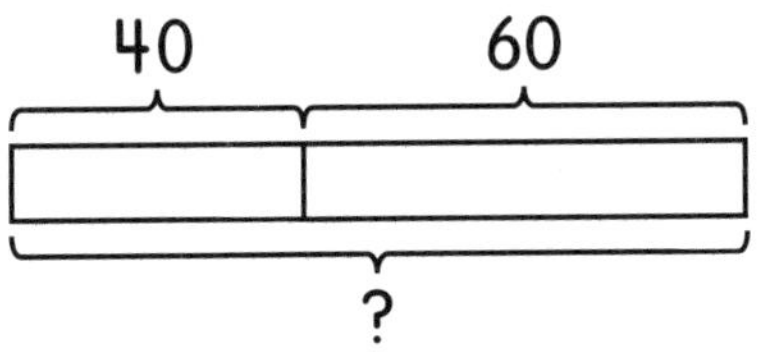

_____ + _____ = _____

They have _____ cherries in all.

Check:

___ − ___ = ___

___ − ___ = ___

Name: ______________________ Date: ______________

Find the missing numbers.
Use the bar models to help you.
Add to check your answer.

Example

Justin has 9 tomatoes.
He eats 2 tomatoes.
How many tomatoes are left?

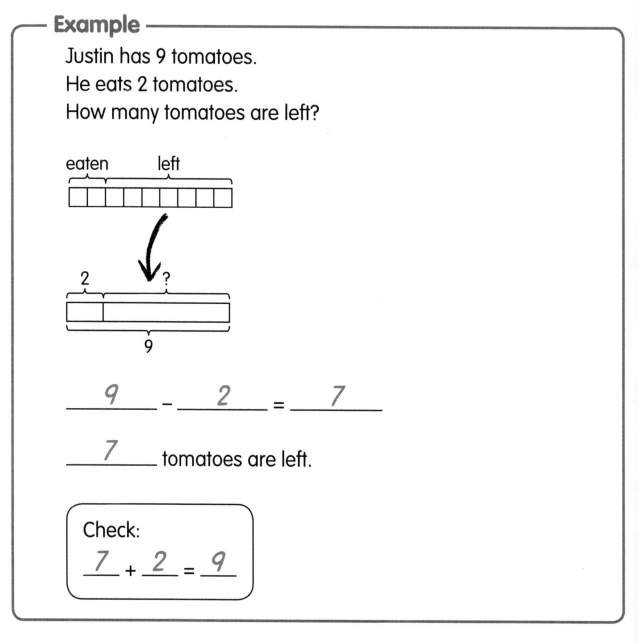

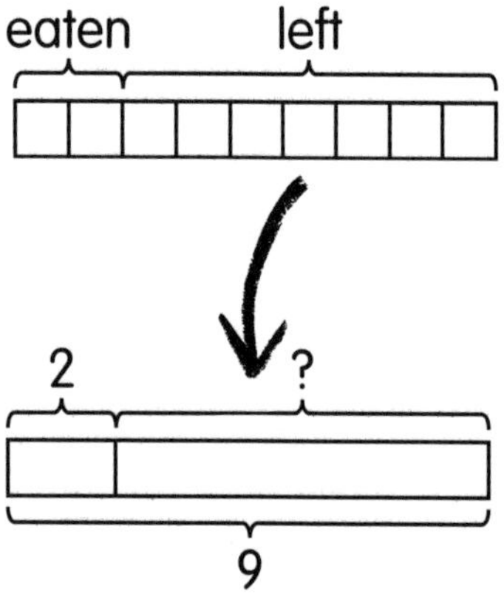

9 – 2 = 7

7 tomatoes are left.

Check:
7 + 2 = 9

Name: ______________________ Date: ______________

5. There are 10 birds on a branch.
3 birds fly away.
How many birds are left?

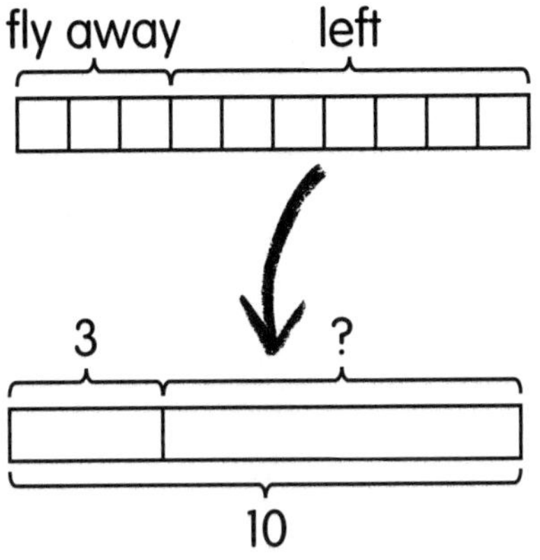

Check:

___ + ___ = ___

_______ − _______ = _______

_______ birds are left.

6. A library has 450 books.
315 of the books are English books.
The rest of the books are Spanish books.
How many Spanish books are in the library?

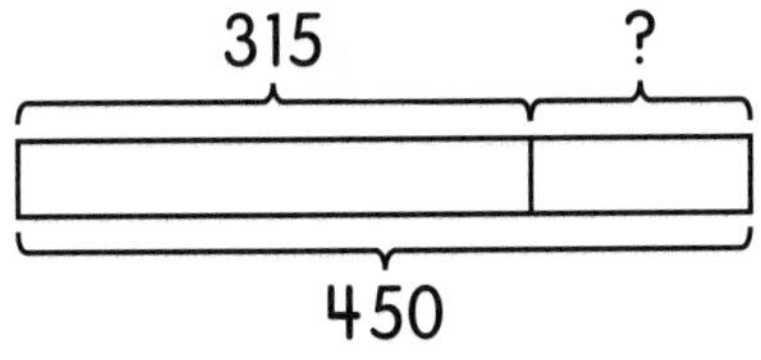

Check:

___ + ___ = ___

_______ − _______ = _______

_______ Spanish books are in the library.

Name: ______________________________ Date: ______________

Solve.
Draw bar models to help you.
Show how to check your answer.

7. Jasper folds 107 paper cranes.
His sister folds 44 paper cranes.
How many paper cranes do they fold in all?

They fold ________ paper cranes in all.

8. Aiden has 145 trading cards.
He buys another 35 trading cards.
How many trading cards does Aiden have now?

Aiden has ________ trading cards now.

Name: ______________________ Date: ______________

Worksheet 2 Adding On and Taking Away Sets

Solve.
Use the bar models to help you.

Example

Corinne has 12 apples.
She buys another 3 apples.
How many apples does Corinne have now?

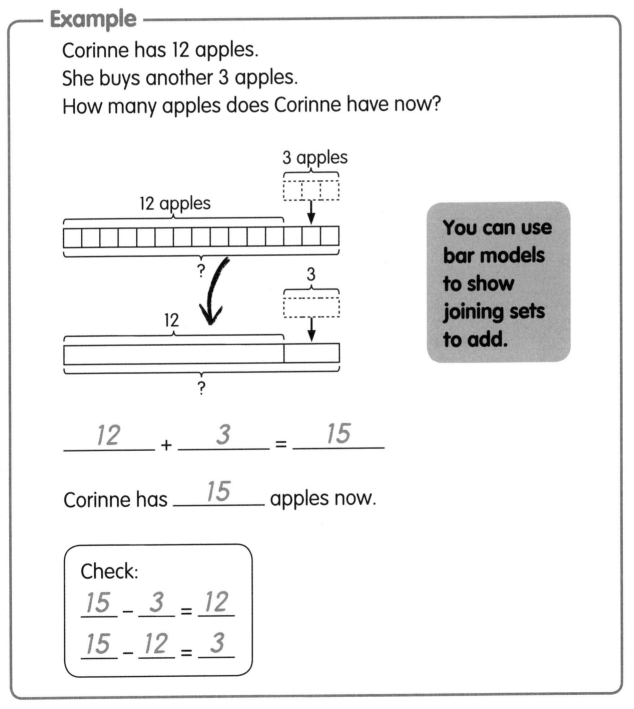

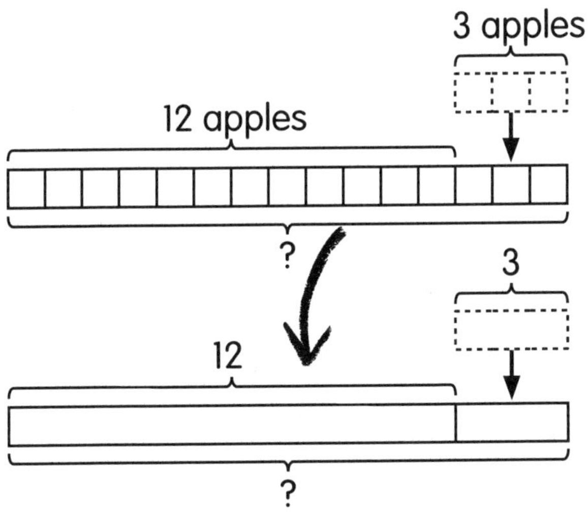

You can use bar models to show joining sets to add.

12 + 3 = 15

Corinne has 15 apples now.

Check:
15 − 3 = 12
15 − 12 = 3

Name: ______________________ Date: ______________

1. There are 5 books on the bookshelf.
Mrs. Swift puts another 6 books on the bookshelf.
How many books are on the bookshelf now?

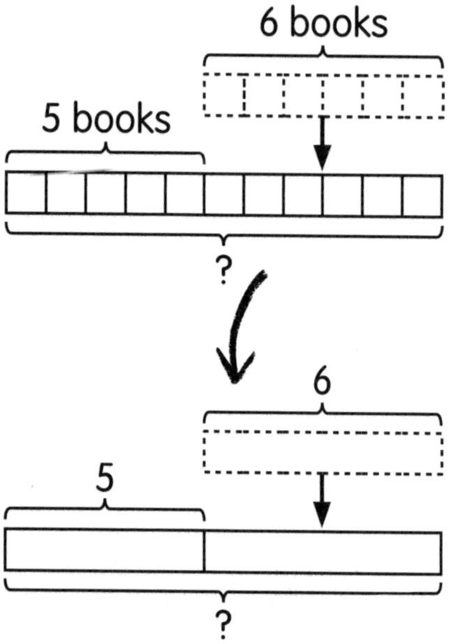

______ + ______ = ______

Check:

____ − ____ = ____

____ − ____ = ____

______ books are on the bookshelf now.

2. A florist has 180 red roses.
He buys another 60 red roses.
How many red roses does he have now?

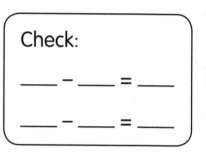

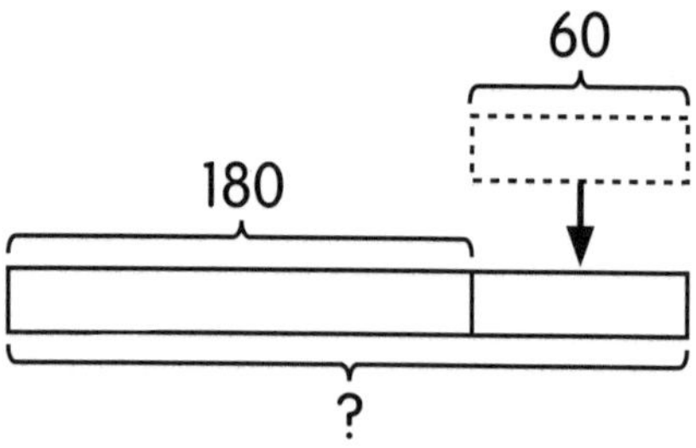

______ + ______ = ______

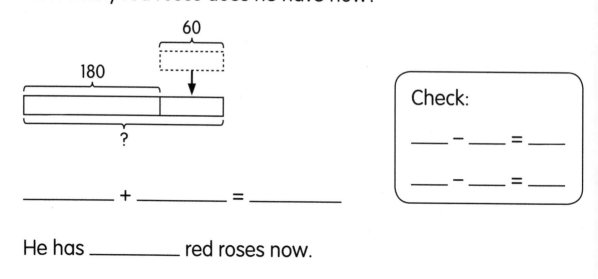

Check:

____ − ____ = ____

____ − ____ = ____

He has ______ red roses now.

Name: ______________________ Date: ______________

Solve.
Use the bar models to help you.

Example

A clown has 15 balloons.
He gives away 5 balloons.
How many balloons does he have now?

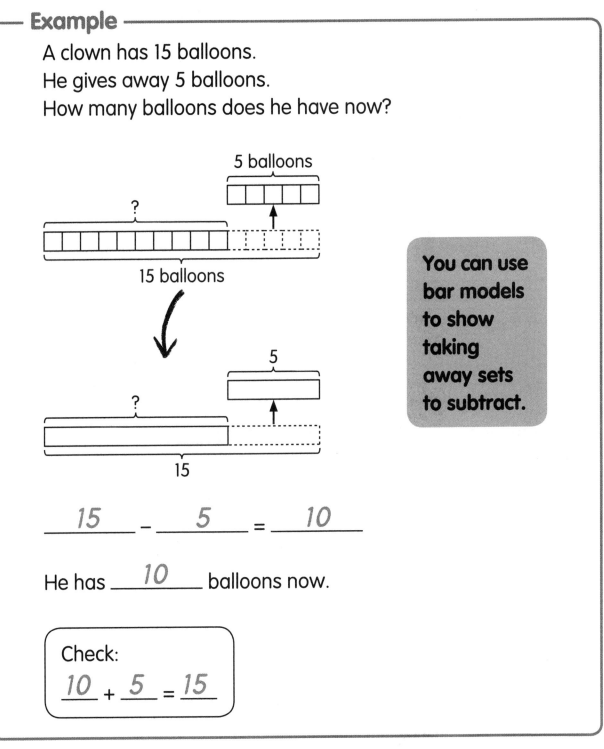

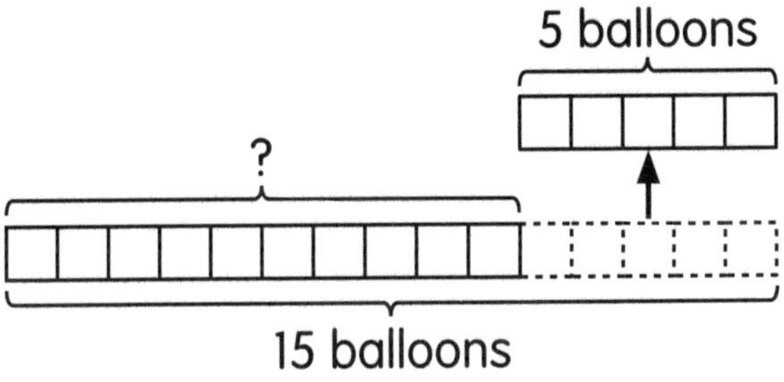

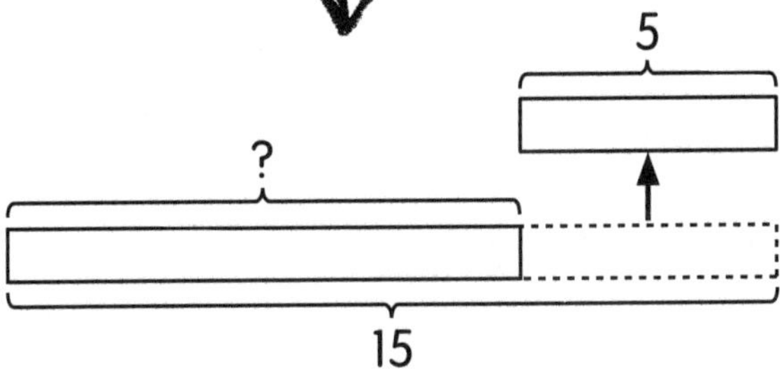

You can use bar models to show taking away sets to subtract.

15 – 5 = 10

He has 10 balloons now.

Check:
10 + 5 = 15

Name: ______________________ Date: ______________

3. Peter has 13 baseball cards.
He gives 4 baseball cards to Jamal.
How many baseball cards does Peter have now?

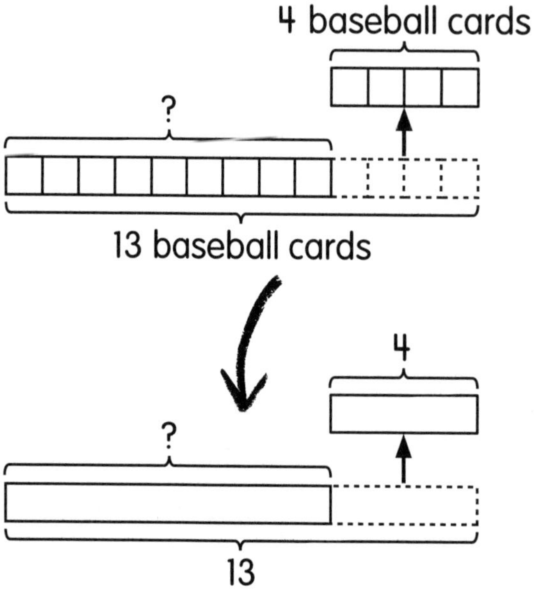

Check:

____ + ____ = ____

________ − ________ = ________

Peter has ________ baseball cards now.

4. A school supply closet has 125 markers.
The teacher takes out 45 markers.
How many markers are left in the supply closet?

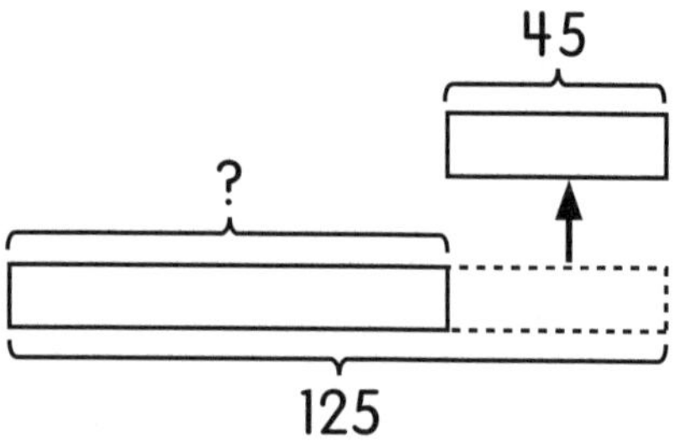

Check:

____ + ____ = ____

________ − ________ = ________

________ markers are left in the supply closet.

Name: ______________________ Date: ______________

Worksheet 3 Comparing Two Sets

Solve.
Use the bar models to help you.
Subtract to check your answer.

Example

Lily has 5 stickers in her notebook.
Kenley has 7 more stickers than Lily.
How many stickers does Kenley have in her notebook?

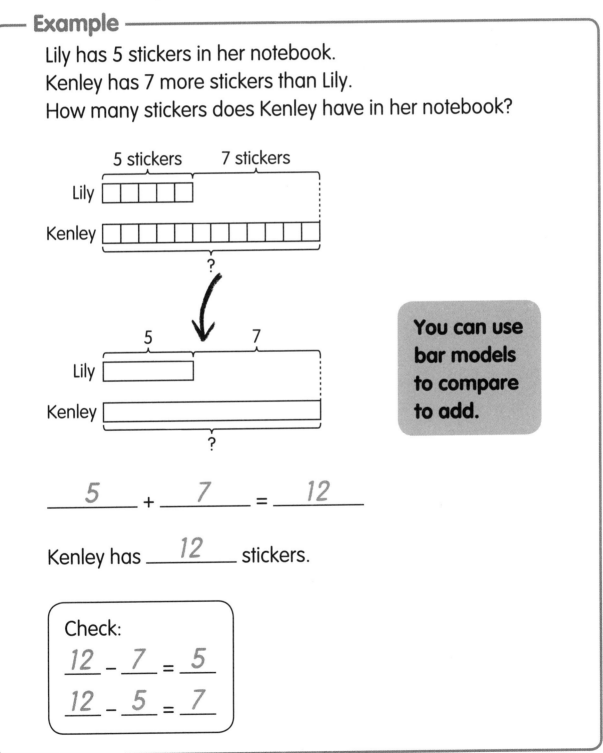

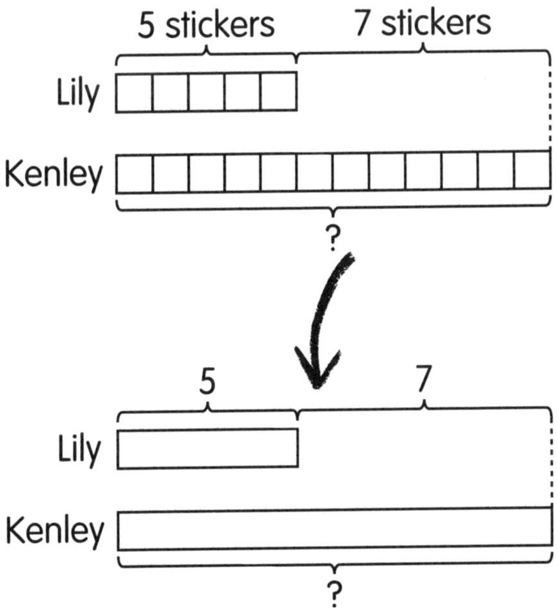

You can use bar models to compare to add.

__5__ + __7__ = __12__

Kenley has __12__ stickers.

Check:
__12__ – __7__ = __5__
__12__ – __5__ = __7__

Name: ______________________ Date: ______________

1. Bill has \$6.
Jerome has \$6 more than Bill.
How much money does Jerome have?

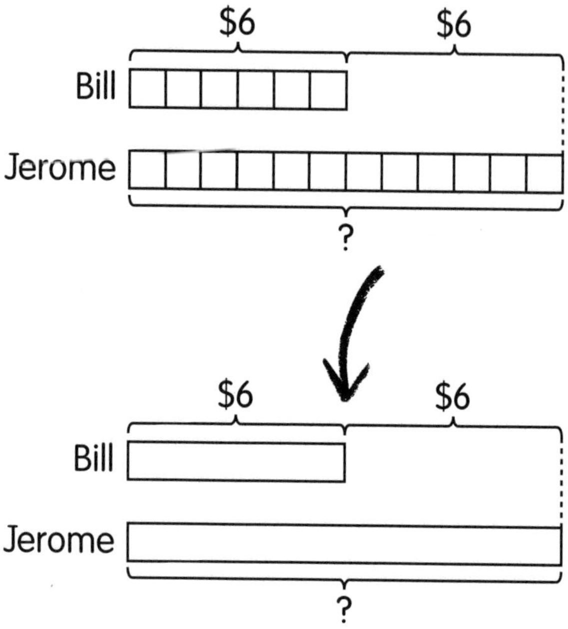

\$______ + \$______ = \$______

Check:

____ − ____ = ____

____ − ____ = ____

Jerome has \$______.

2. Samuel has 372 cows on his farm.
He has 148 more sheep than cows on his farm.
How many sheep does Samuel have?

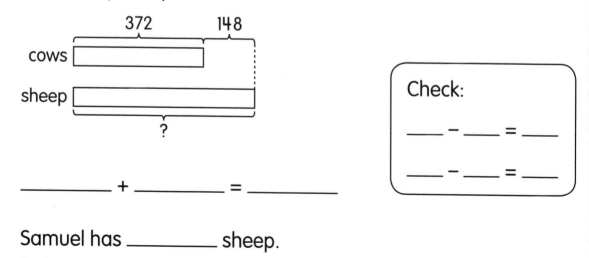

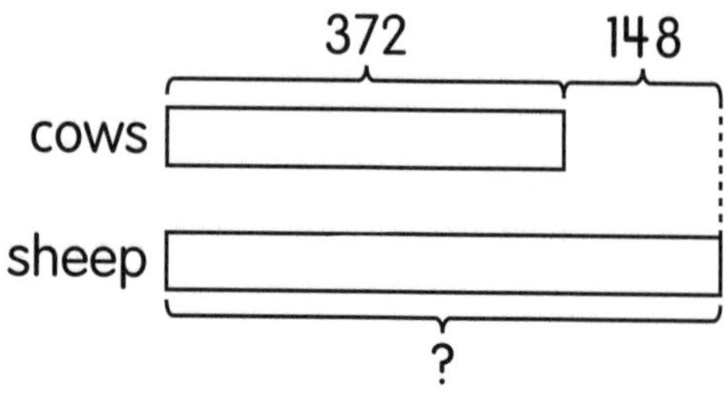

______ + ______ = ______

Check:

____ − ____ = ____

____ − ____ = ____

Samuel has ______ sheep.

Name: ______________________ Date: ______________

Solve.
Use the bar models to help you.
Add to check your answer.

Example

15 girls are in the swimming pool.
10 fewer boys are in the swimming pool.
How many boys are in the swimming pool?

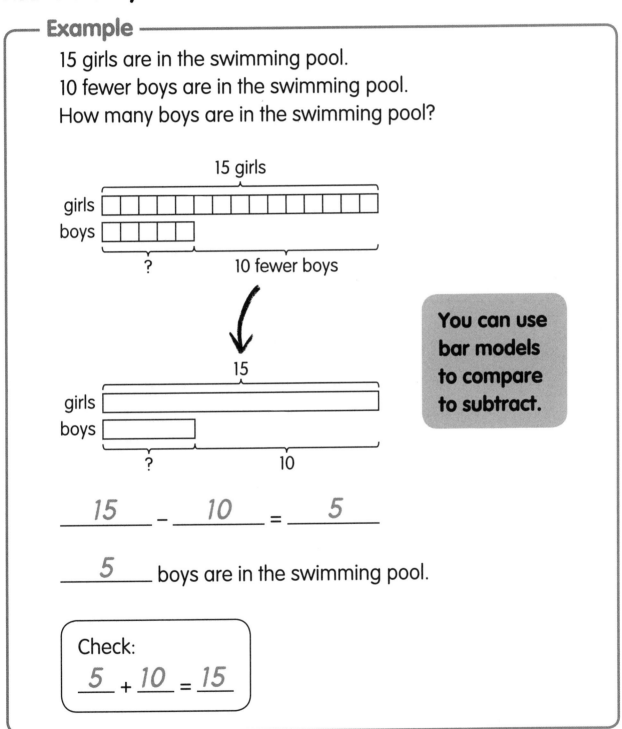

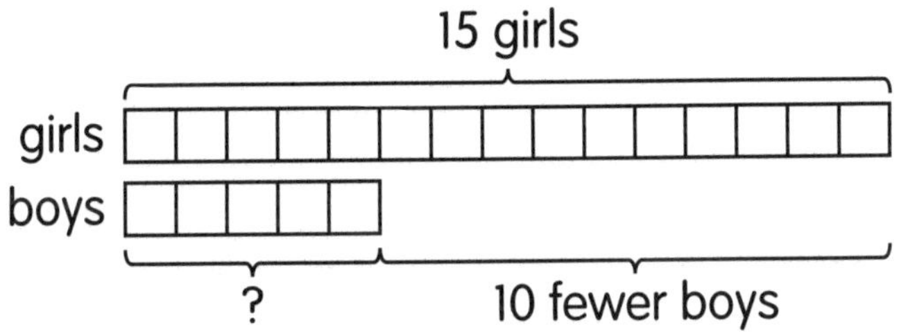

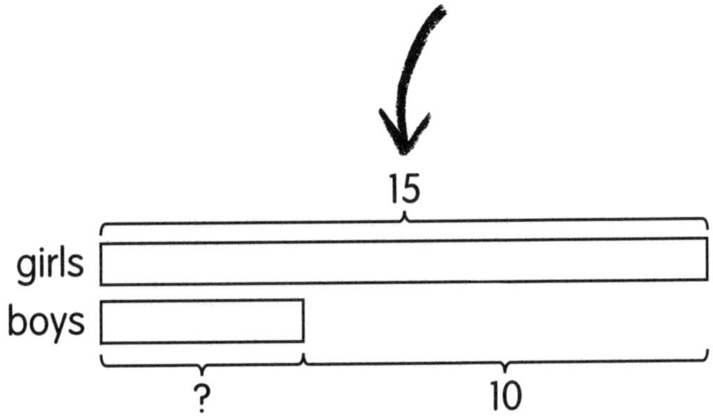

You can use bar models to compare to subtract.

15 – 10 = 5

5 boys are in the swimming pool.

Check:
5 + 10 = 15

Name: ______________________ Date: ______________

3. Ling has 13 bracelets.
Gabi has 5 fewer bracelets than Ling.
How many bracelets does Gabi have?

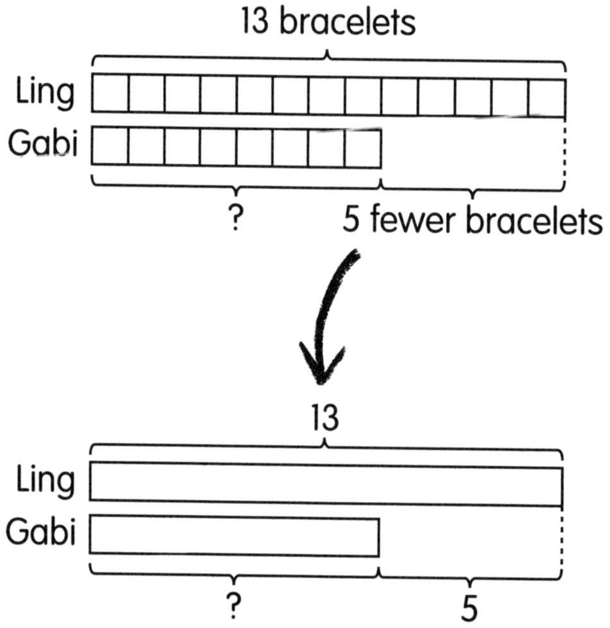

_______ – _______ = _______

Check:

____ + ____ = ____

Gabi has _______ bracelets.

4. A grocer has 380 strawberries.
She has 50 fewer peaches than strawberries.
How many peaches does she have?

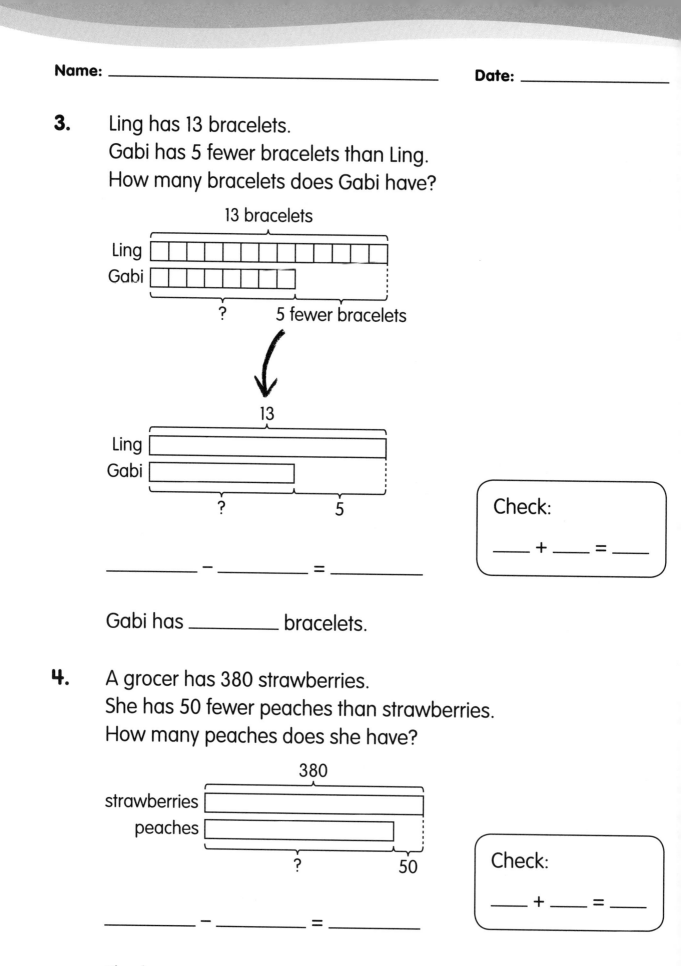

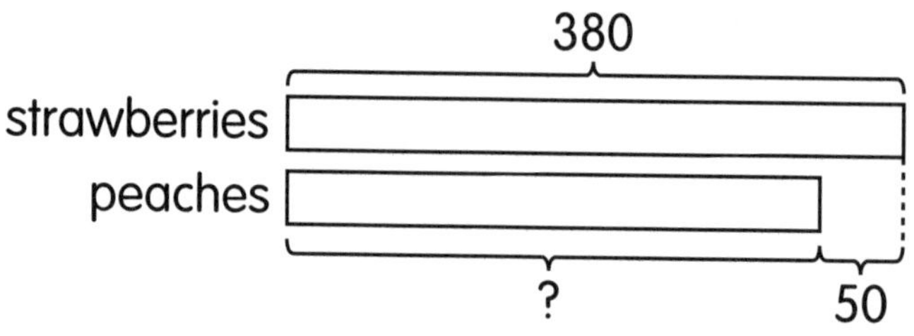

_______ – _______ = _______

Check:

____ + ____ = ____

She has _______ peaches.

Name: ____________________ Date: ____________

Worksheet 4 Real-World Problems: Two-Step Problems

Solve.
Use the bar models to help you.

Example

Ron has 8 apples and 4 pears.
He gives Ally some apples.
Now he has 5 apples and pears left.

a. How many apples and pears did Ron have at first?

b. How many apples did Ron give to Ally?

a.

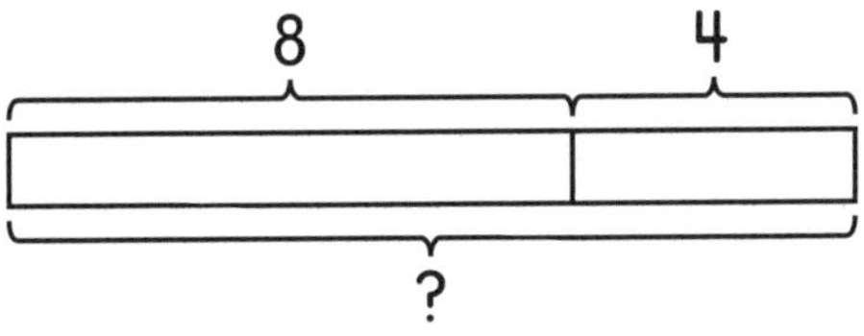

You can use bar models to solve two-step problems.

__8__ + __4__ = __12__

Ron had __12__ apples and pears at first.

b.

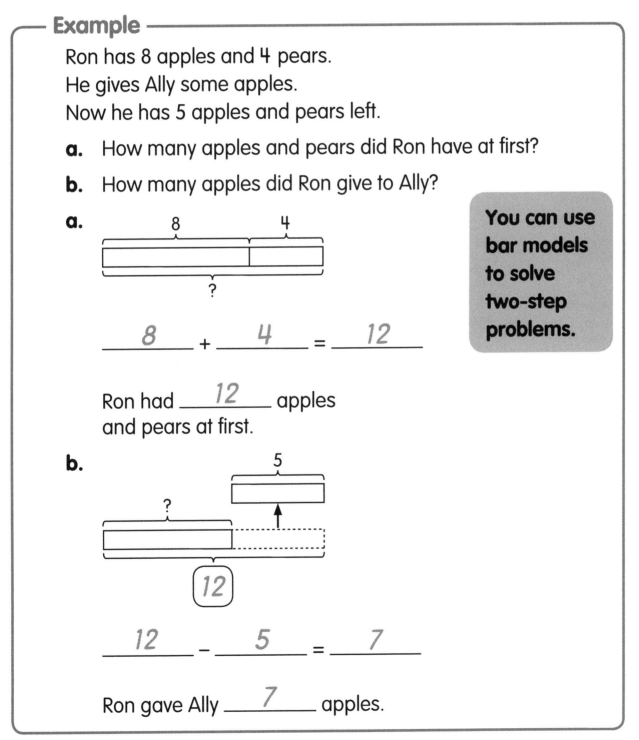

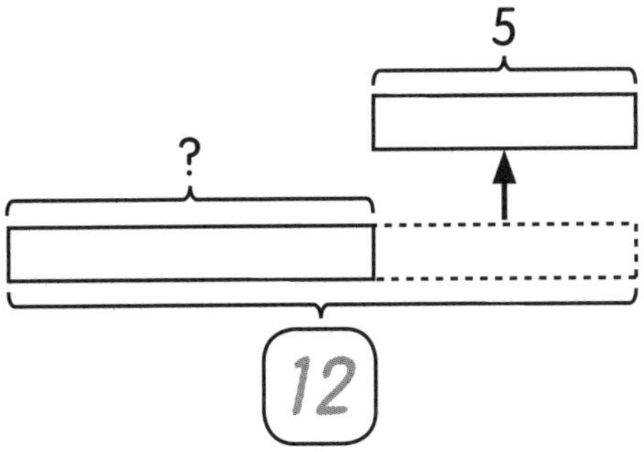

__12__ – __5__ = __7__

Ron gave Ally __7__ apples.

Name: ______________________________ Date: ______________

1. Mrs. Holley has 123 cookbooks and 277 reading books. Mr. Pearce gives her another 40 reading books.

   a. How many books did Mrs. Holley have at first?

   b. How many books does Mrs. Holley have now?

a.

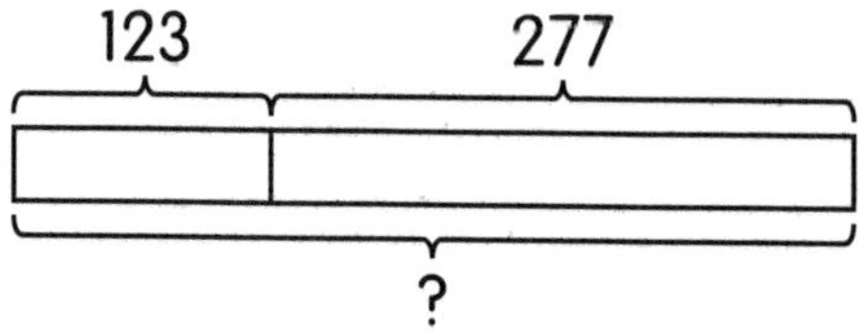

_______ + _______ = _______

Mrs. Holley had _______ books at first.

b.

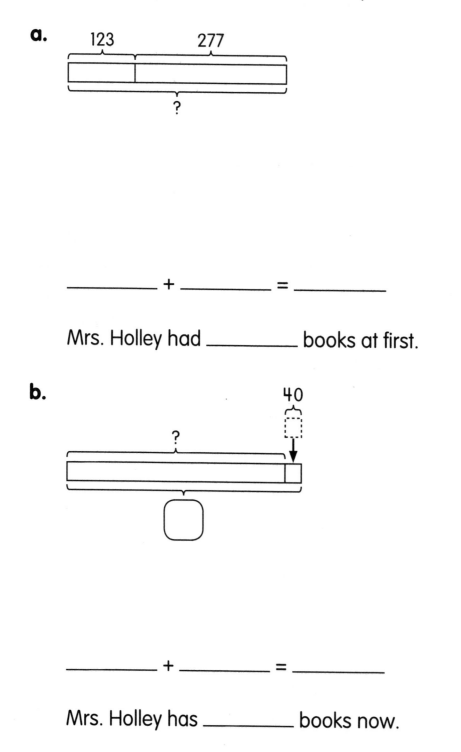

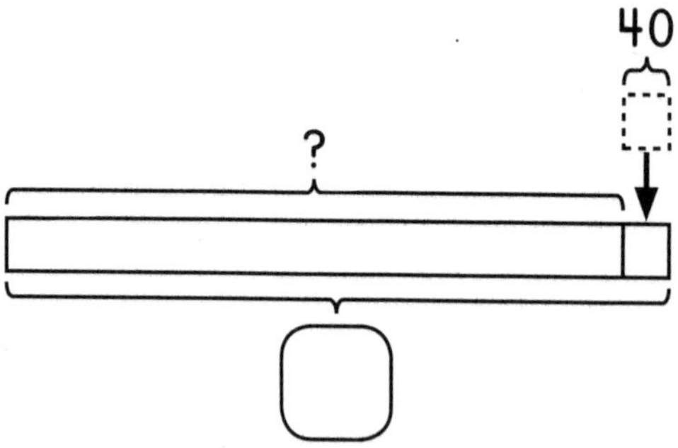

_______ + _______ = _______

Mrs. Holley has _______ books now.

Name: ______________________ Date: ______________

Solve.
Use the bar models to help you.

Example

A Science class has 8 girls.
There are 5 more boys than girls.

a. How many boys are in the class?

b. How many children are in the class?

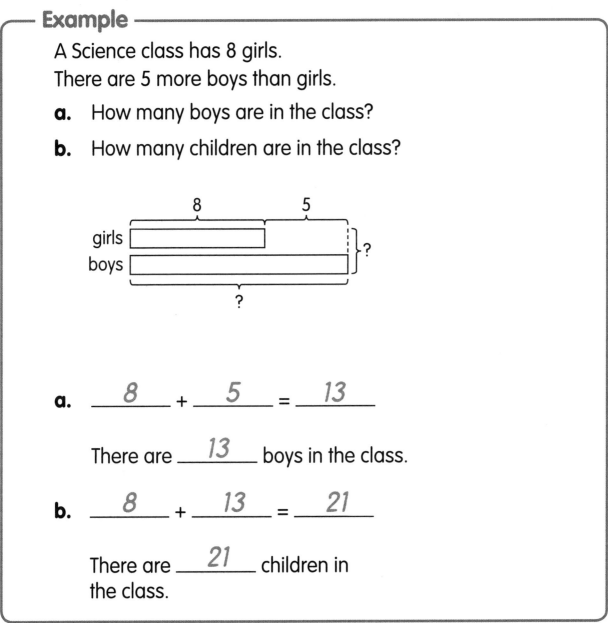

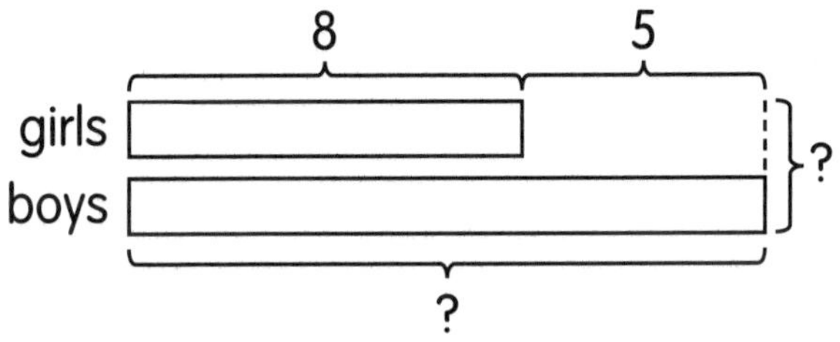

a. 8 + 5 = 13

There are 13 boys in the class.

b. 8 + 13 = 21

There are 21 children in the class.

Name: ______________________ Date: ______________

2. Mr. Jackson drives 195 miles.
Mr. Garcia drives 65 miles fewer than Mr. Jackson.

a. How many miles does Mr. Garcia drive?

b. How many miles do they drive in all?

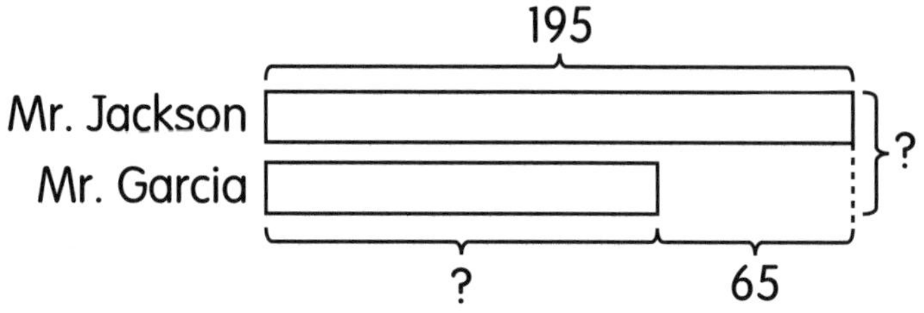

a. ________ − ________ = ________

Mr. Garcia drives ________ miles.

b. ________ + ________ = ________

They drive ________ miles in all.

3. Jesse has 160 magnets.
Benny has 40 magnets more than Jesse.

a. How many magnets does Benny have?

b. How many magnets do they have in all?

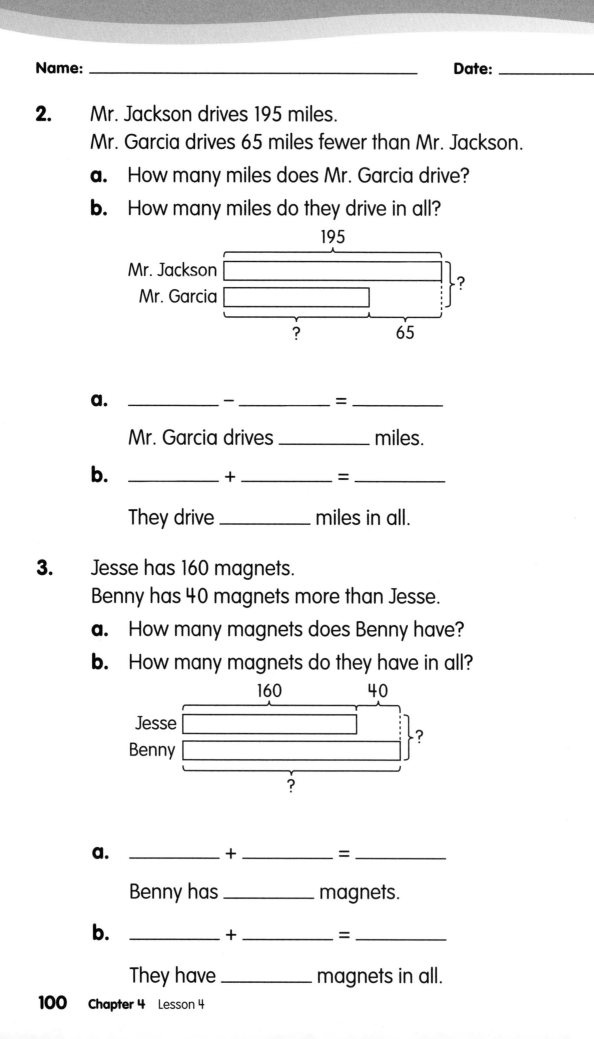

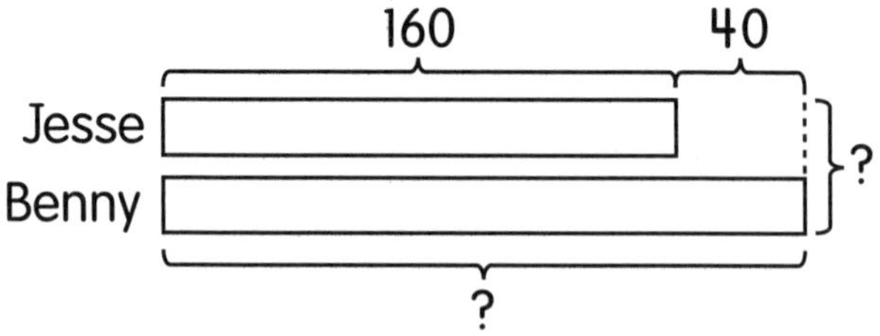

a. ________ + ________ = ________

Benny has ________ magnets.

b. ________ + ________ = ________

They have ________ magnets in all.

Name: ____________________ Date: ____________

CHAPTER 5 Multiplication and Division

Worksheet 1 How to Multiply

Find the missing numbers.

1.

A ladybug has ______ legs.

______ + ______ + ______ = ______

3 ______ = ______

3 ladybugs have ______ legs.

2.

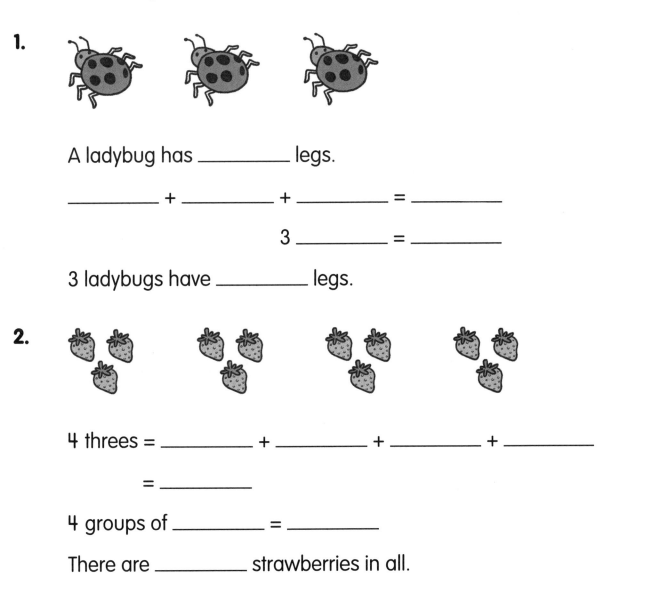

4 threes = ______ + ______ + ______ + ______

= ______

4 groups of ______ = ______

There are ______ strawberries in all.

Name: ____________________ Date: ____________

Find the missing numbers.

Example

group

There are 3 groups.

There are 3 ducks in each group.

Use **repeated addition** to find the number of ducks.

3 + 3 + 3 = 9

Multiply to find the number of ducks.

3 × 3 = 9

multiplication sentence

There are 9 ducks in all.

× is read as "times".
It means to multiply,
or to put all the equal groups together.

Name: ______________________ Date: ______________

3.

There are 2 groups.

There are ________ sheep in each group.

Use repeated addition to find the number of sheep.

________ + ________ = ________

Multiply to find the number of sheep.

2 × ________ = ________

There are ________ sheep in all.

Name: _______________ Date: _______________

4. 

There are ________ groups.

There are ________ ants in each group.

Use repeated addition to find the number of ants.

________ + ________ + ________ + ________ = ________

Multiply to find the number of ants.

4 × ________ = ________

There are ________ ants in all.

Name: ____________________ Date: ____________

Tell a multiplication story.

Example

There are 3 bowls of eggs.

Each bowl has ___4___ eggs.

$3 \times$ ___4___ = ___12___

There are ___12___ eggs.

5. 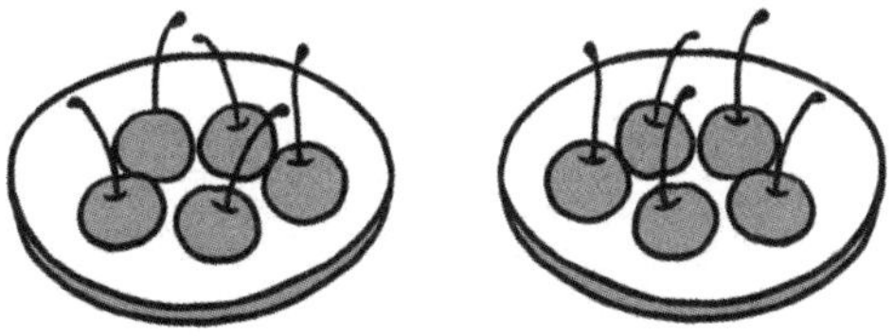

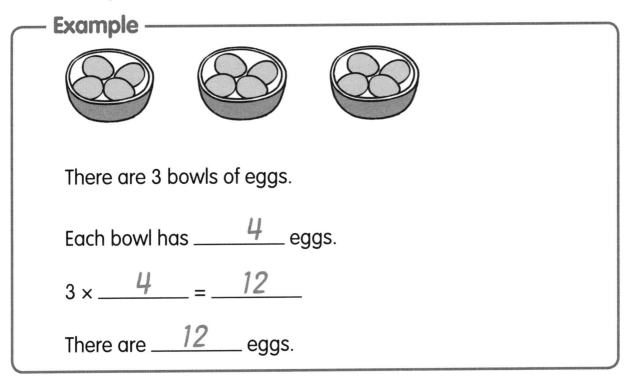

There are 2 plates of cherries.

Each plate has ________ cherries.

$2 \times$ ________ = ________

There are ________ cherries.

Name: ____________________ Date: ____________

6. 

There are 3 tanks of fish.

Each tank has ________ fish.

3 × ________ = ________

There are ________ fish.

Name: ______________________ Date: ______________

Worksheet 2 How to Divide

Circle equal groups. Then fill in the blank.

1.

Share 12 muffins equally among 4 children.

Each child gets ________ muffins.

2.

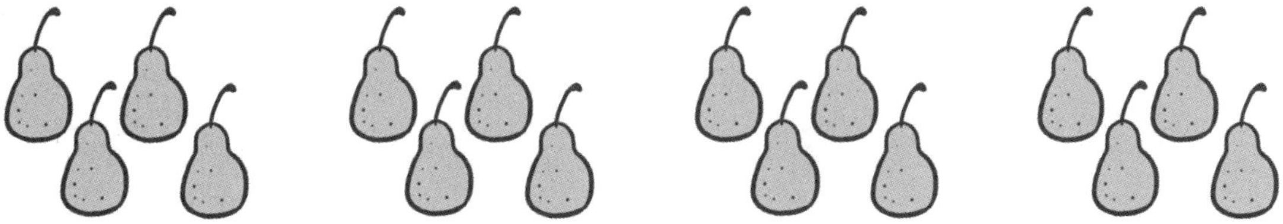

Share 16 pears equally among 4 baskets.

Each basket has ________ pears.

Name: ______________________ Date: ______________

3.

Put 6 tomatoes into groups of 2.

There are ________ groups of 2 tomatoes.

4.

Put 20 peaches into groups of 4.

There are ________ groups of 4 peaches.

Name: ______________________ Date: ______________

Find the missing numbers.

Example

Francis has 18 erasers.
He gives an equal number of erasers to each of his 3 sisters.
How many erasers does each sister get?

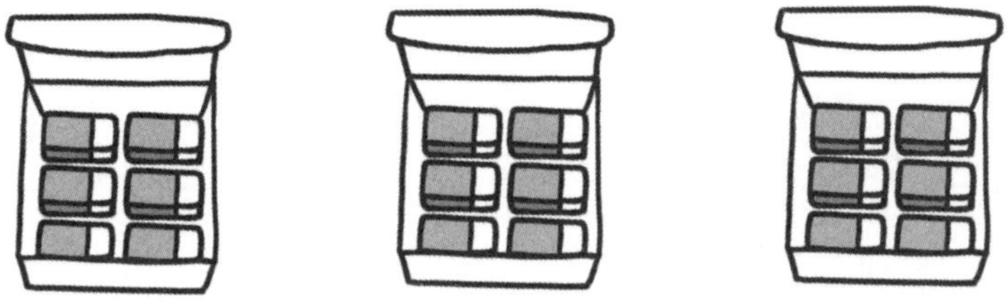

$18 \div 3 =$ 6 ← **division sentence**

Each sister gets 6 erasers.

÷ is read as "divided by", and stands for division.

5. Mrs. Perry has 15 marbles.
She gives an equal number of marbles to each of her 5 children.
How many marbles does each child get?

$15 \div 5 =$ ________

Each child gets ________ marbles.

Name: ______________________ Date: ______________

Solve.

Example

Brandi has 4 flowers.
She wants to give 2 flowers to each of her friends.
How many friends get flowers from her?
First, she gives 2 flowers to Pierre.

$4 - 2 = 2$
She has 2 flowers left.
Then, she gives 2 flowers to Jordan.

$2 - 2 = 0$
She has 0 flowers left.

Use **repeated subtraction** to find the number of friends.

$4 - 2 - 2 =$ ___0___

Divide to find the number of friends.

$4 \div 2 =$ ___2___

___2___ friends get flowers from her.

Name: ____________________ Date: ____________

6. Mandy has 4 toy cars.
She wants to give 2 toy cars to each of her friends.
How many friends get toy cars from her?
First, she gives 2 toy cars to Jack.

4 – 2 = 2
She has 2 toy cars left.
Then, she gives 2 toy cars to Sean.

2 – 2 = 0
She has 0 toy cars left.
Use repeated subtraction to find the number of friends.

4 – 2 – 2 = __________

Divide to find the number of friends.

4 ÷ 2 = __________

__________ friends get toy cars from her.

Name: ______________________ Date: ______________

7. Samuel has 12 crayons.
He wants to give 4 crayons to each of his cousins.
How many cousins get crayons from him?

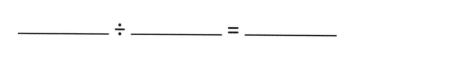

_______ – _______ – _______ – _______ = 0

_______ ÷ _______ = _______

_______ cousins get crayons from him.

Name: ______________________ Date: ____________

Worksheet 3 Real-World Problems: Multiplication and Division

Solve.

Example

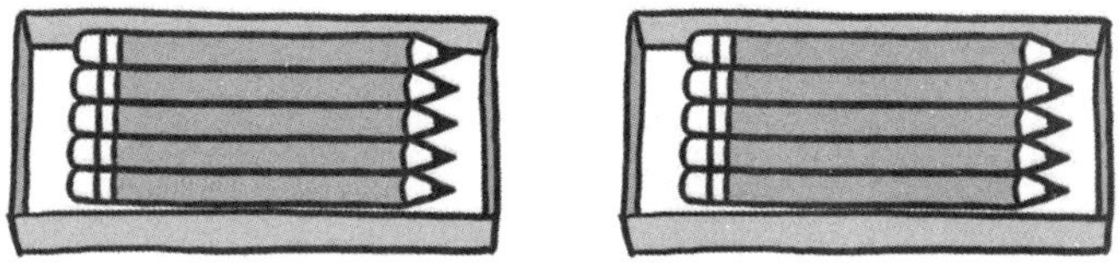

Fredrick has 2 pencil cases.
There are 5 pencils in each pencil case.
How many pencils does Fredrick have?

__2__ × __5__ = __10__

Fredrick has __10__ pencils.

1.

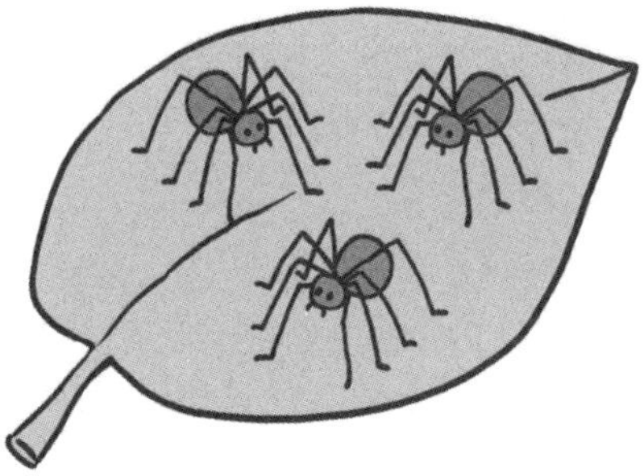

There are 3 spiders on a leaf.
There are 8 legs on each spider.
How many legs are there in all?

______ × ______ = ______

There are ______ legs in all.

Name: ______________________ Date: ______________

Solve.

Example

The teacher has 8 balloons.
He divides them equally among 4 children.
How many balloons does each child get?

__8__ ÷ __4__ = __2__

Each child gets __2__ balloons.

2.

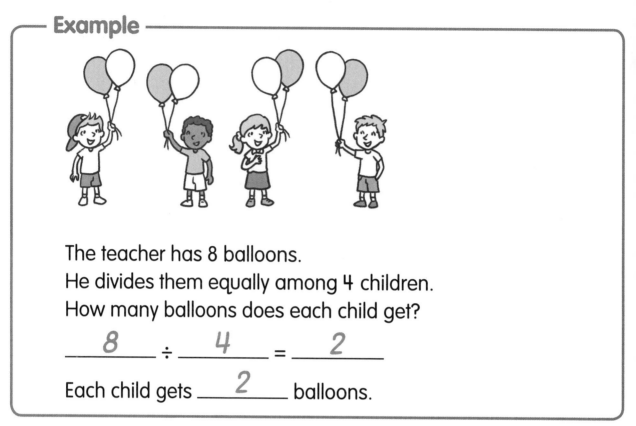

Maria has 20 apricots.
She puts 5 apricots in each glass jar.
How many glass jars are there?

______ ÷ ______ = ______

There are ______ glass jars.

Name: ________________ Date: ________________

CHAPTER 6 Multiplication Tables of 2, 5, and 10

Worksheet 1 Multiplying 2: Skip-Counting

Find the missing numbers in the number pattern.

1. 2, 4, 6, ________, ________, ________, ________

I add ________ to get the next number.

Find the missing numbers.

2.

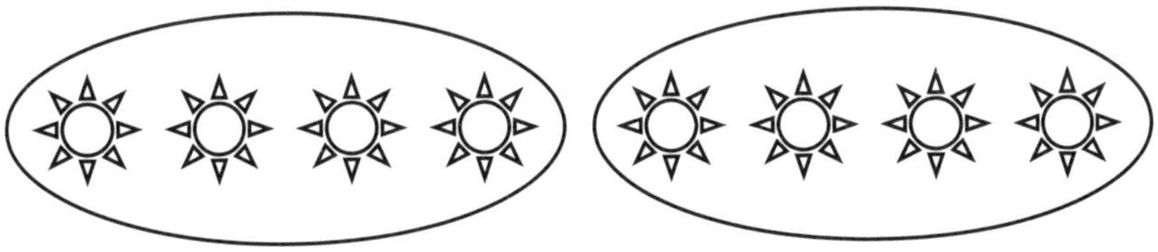

2 fours is ________ groups of ________.

Use skip-counting to find the missing numbers.

Example

Each child has 2 hands.

0 → 2 → 4 → 6 → 8

2, 4, __6__, __8__

4 × 2 = __8__

There are __8__ hands in all.

Name: ______________________ Date: ______________

3. Each butterfly has 2 wings.

0 → 2 → 4 → 6

2, ________, ________

$3 \times 2 =$ ________

There are ________ wings in all.

4. There are 5 boys.
Each boy has 2 baseball cards.
How many baseball cards do they have in all?

2, ________, ________, ________, ________

$5 \times 2 =$ ________

They have ________ baseball cards in all.

5. Molly and Sara eat 2 pancakes each.
How many pancakes do they eat in all?

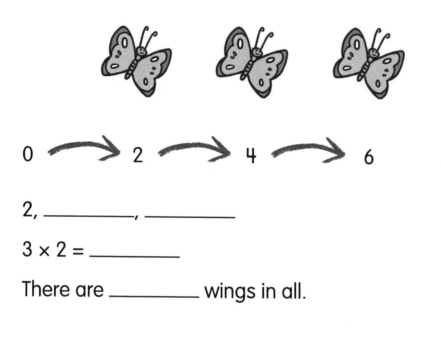

$2 \times$ ________ $=$ ________

They eat ________ pancakes in all.

Name: _______________________ Date: _______________

6. There are 6 children.
Each child holds 2 balloons.
How many balloons do they hold in all?

They hold ________ balloons in all.

7. Isabelle uses 2 pieces of bread to make a sandwich.
She makes 10 sandwiches.
How many pieces of bread does Isabelle use?

Isabelle uses ________ pieces of bread.

Name: ______________________ Date: ______________

8. Mrs. Clark has 8 pots.
Each pot has 2 handles.
How many handles are there in all?

There are ________ handles in all.

9. Benny runs two times around the track every day.
How many times does he run around the track in 6 days?

Benny runs ________ times around the track in 6 days.

Name: ______________________ Date: ____________

Worksheet 2 Multiplying 2: Using Dot Paper

Use dot paper to solve.

Example

Each squirrel has 2 acorns.
How many acorns do the 2 squirrels have in all?

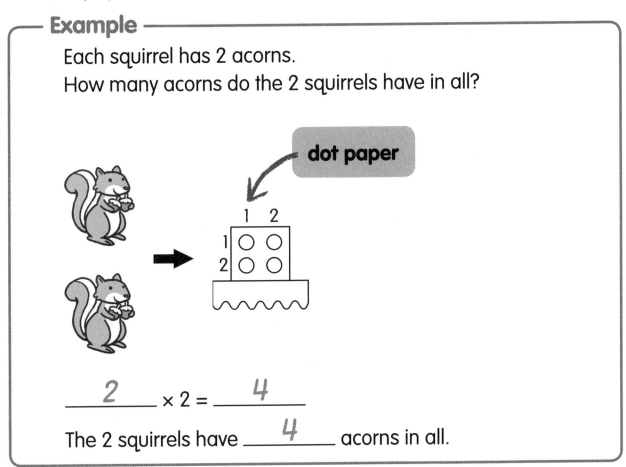

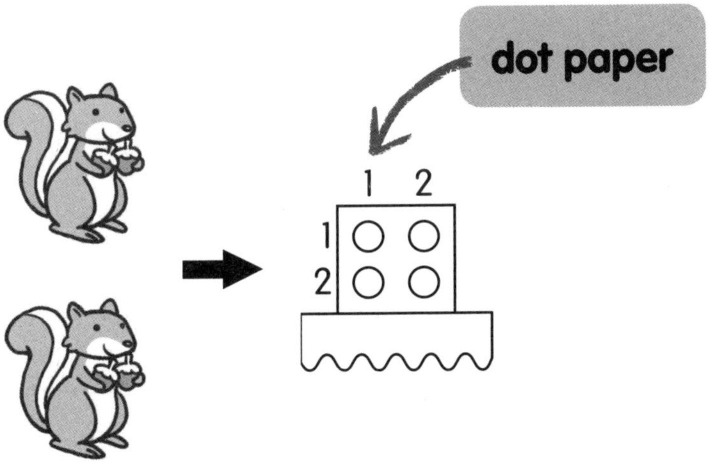

__2__ × 2 = __4__

The 2 squirrels have __4__ acorns in all.

Name: ______________________ Date: ______________

1. Each keychain has 2 keys on it.
How many keys do the 3 keychains have in all?

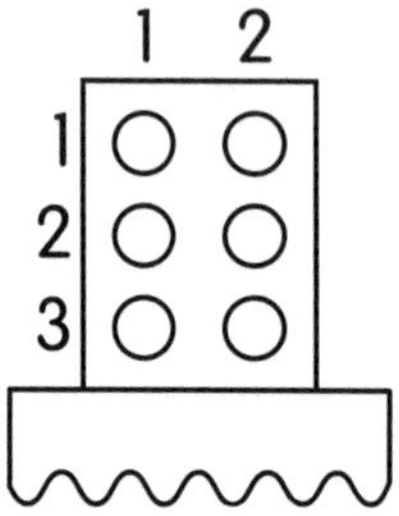

______ × 2 = ______

The 3 keychains have ______ keys in all.

2. Andre, Bart, Cedric, and Dorothy each have \$2.
How much money do they have in all?

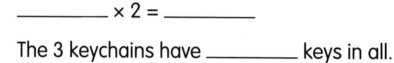

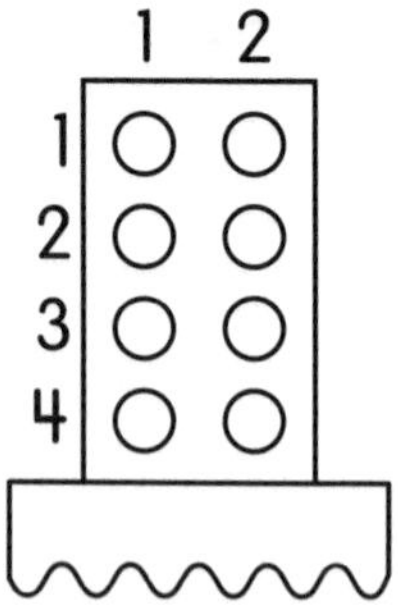

______ × \$______ = \$______

They have \$______ in all.

Name: ______________________ Date: ______________

3. Sharon buys 2 pencils for each of her 8 cousins.
How many pencils does Sharon buy in all?

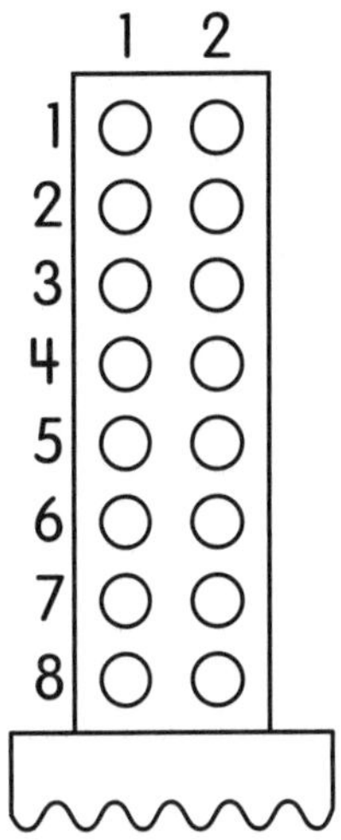

_______ × _______ = _______

Sharon buys _______ pencils in all.

Name: ______________________ Date: ______________

Use facts you know to find the missing numbers.

Example

6 × 2 = ?

Start with 5 groups of 2.

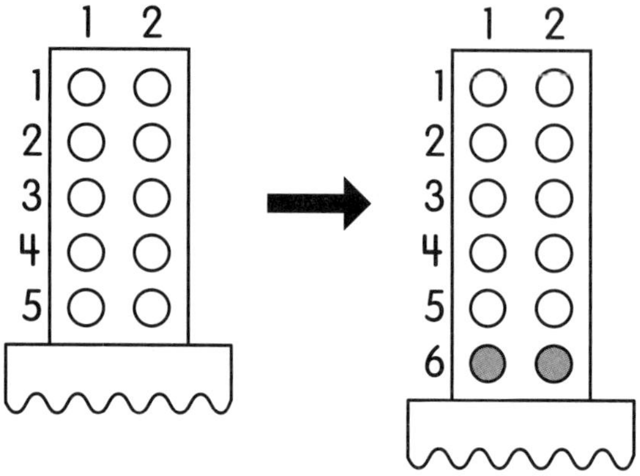

6 groups of 2 is the same as adding 1 group of 2 to 5 groups of 2.

5 × 2 = 10

6 × 2 = 5 groups of 2 + __1__ group of 2

= 10 + __2__

= __12__

4. 7 × 2 = ?

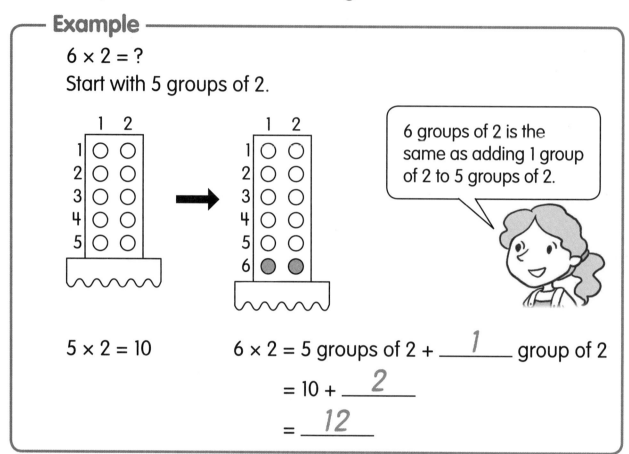

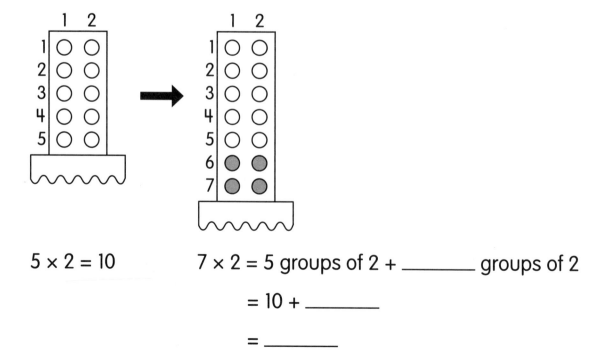

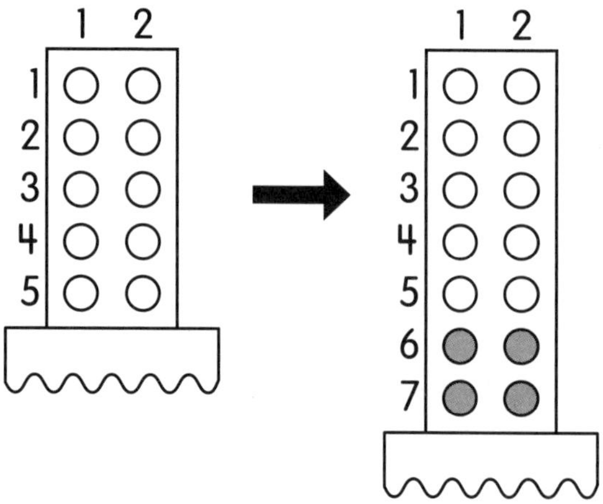

5 × 2 = 10

7 × 2 = 5 groups of 2 + ______ groups of 2

= 10 + ______

= ______

Name: ____________________ Date: ____________

Use facts you know to find the missing numbers.

Example

9 × 2 = ?

Start with 10 groups of 2.

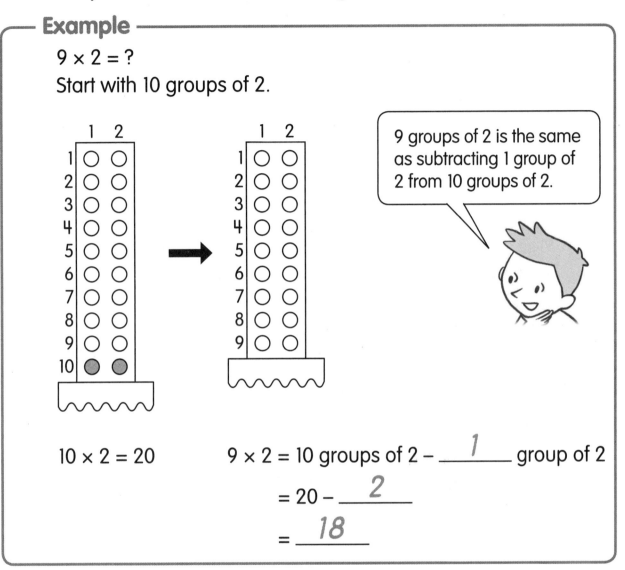

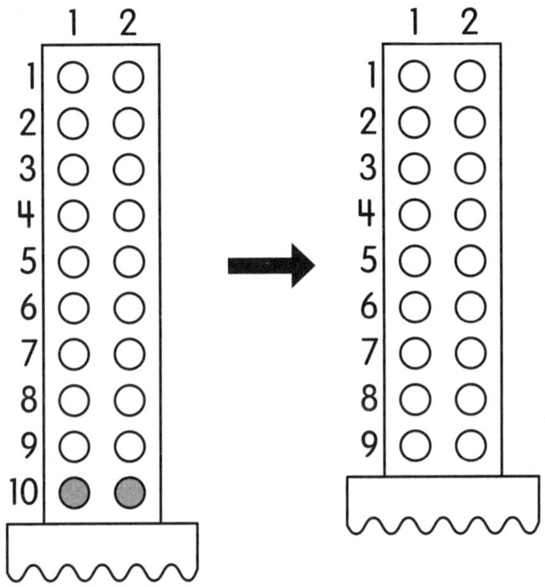

9 groups of 2 is the same as subtracting 1 group of 2 from 10 groups of 2.

10 × 2 = 20

9 × 2 = 10 groups of 2 – __1__ group of 2

= 20 – __2__

= __18__

Name: ______________________ Date: ______________

5. $8 \times 2 = ?$

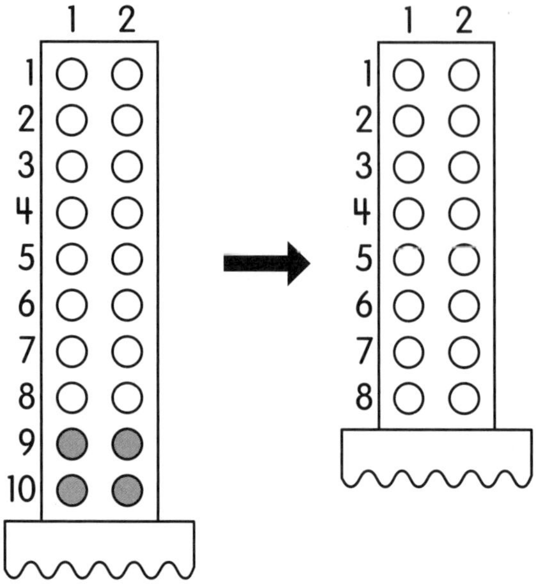

$10 \times 2 = 20$

$8 \times 2 =$ 10 groups of 2 – ________ groups of 2

$= 20 -$ ________

$=$ ________

Multiplication Table of 2
$1 \times 2 = 2$
$2 \times 2 = 4$
$3 \times 2 = 6$
$4 \times 2 = 8$
$5 \times 2 = 10$
$6 \times 2 = 12$
$7 \times 2 = 14$
$8 \times 2 = 16$
$9 \times 2 = 18$
$10 \times 2 = 20$

Name: ______________________ Date: ______________

Use dot paper to find the missing numbers.

Example

$6 \times 2 =$ 12 $2 \times 6 =$ 12

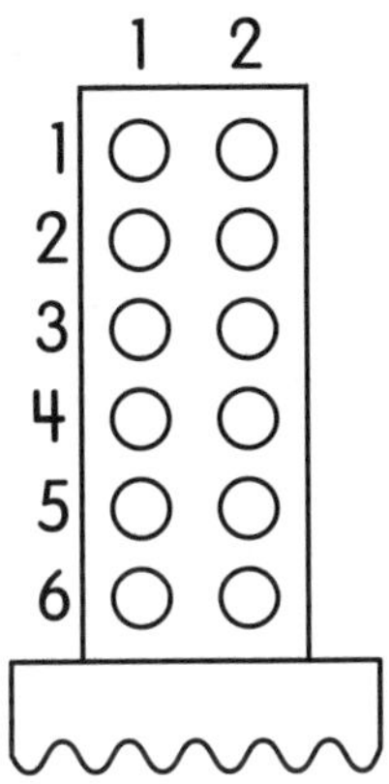

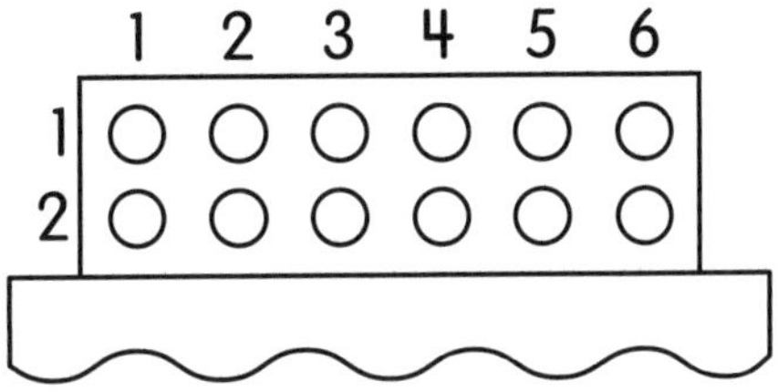

6. $8 \times 2 =$ ______ $2 \times 8 =$ ______

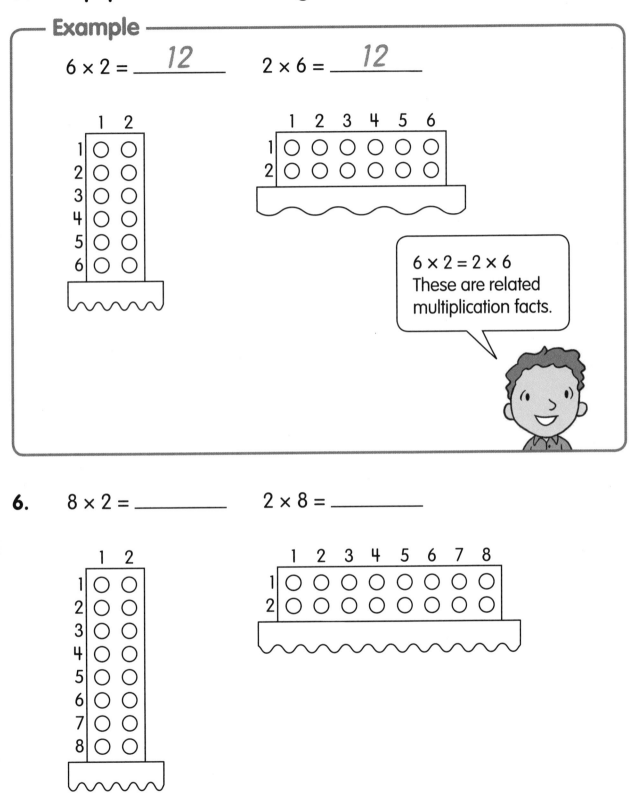

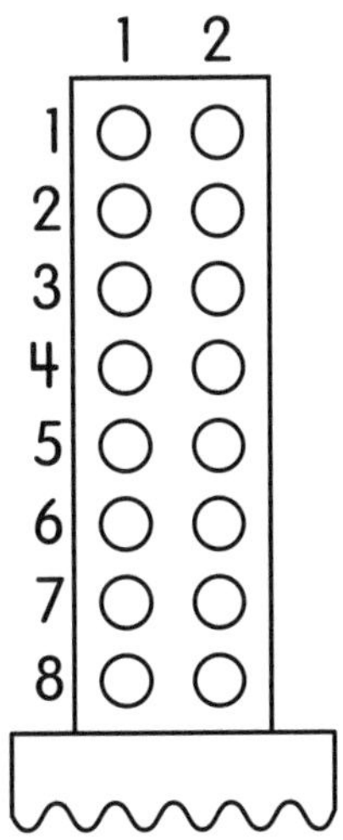

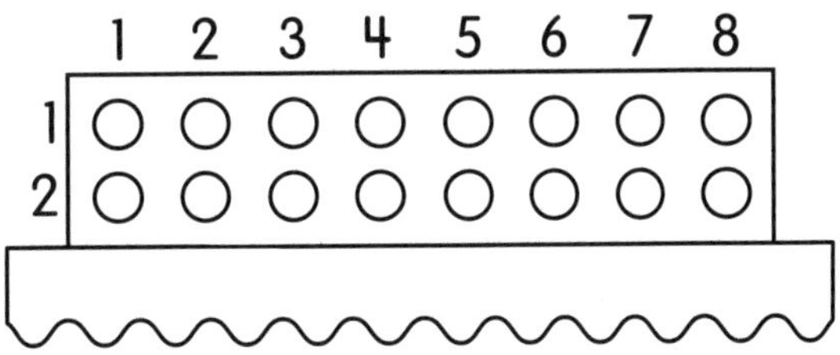

Name: ______________________ Date: ____________

Use dot paper to find the missing numbers.

7. $9 \times 2 =$ ______ $2 \times 9 =$ ______

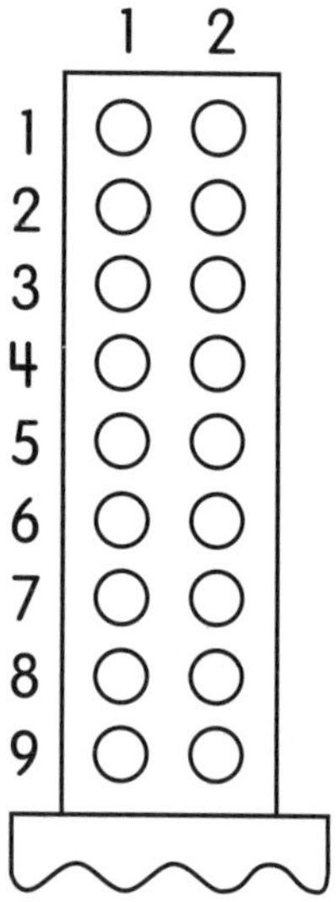

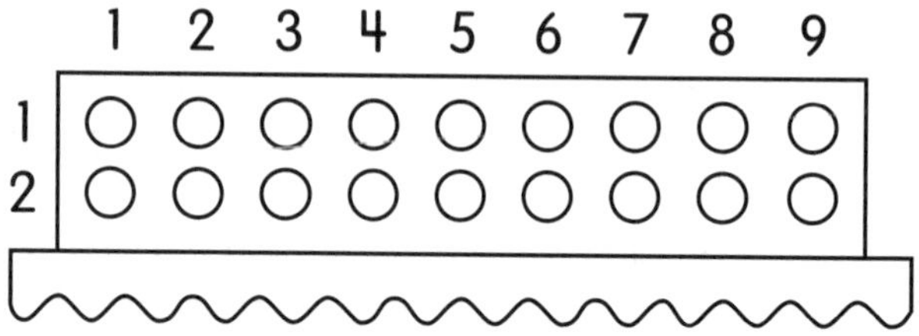

Name: ______________________ Date: ______________

Worksheet 3 Multiplying 5: Skip-Counting

Find the missing numbers in the number pattern.

1. 5, 10, 15, ________, ________, ________, ________

I add ________ to get the next number.

Find the missing numbers.

2.

2 fives is ________ groups of ________.

Use skip-counting to find the missing numbers.

Example

1 finger stands for 5.

5 → 10 → 15 → 20 → 25

5, 10, 15, 20, 25

$5 \times 5 =$ 25

The 5 fingers stand for 25.

Name: ______________________ Date: ______________

3. Barry has 3 bags.
Each bag has 5 bagels.
How many bagels does Barry have in all?

5, ________, ________

________ × 5 = ________

Barry has ________ bagels in all.

4. Mrs. Johnson sells 5 crayons in a box.
She sells 6 boxes of crayons.
How many crayons does Mrs. Johnson sell?

________ × 5 = ________

She sells ________ crayons.

5. A farmer has 5 cows in a barn.
She has 8 barns.
How many cows does she have in all?

________ × ________ = ________

She has ________ cows in all.

Name: ______________________ Date: ______________

Worksheet 4 Multiplying 5: Using Dot Paper

Use dot paper to find the missing numbers.

Example

Paula has 5 strings.
There are 5 beads on each string.
How many beads does Paula have in all?

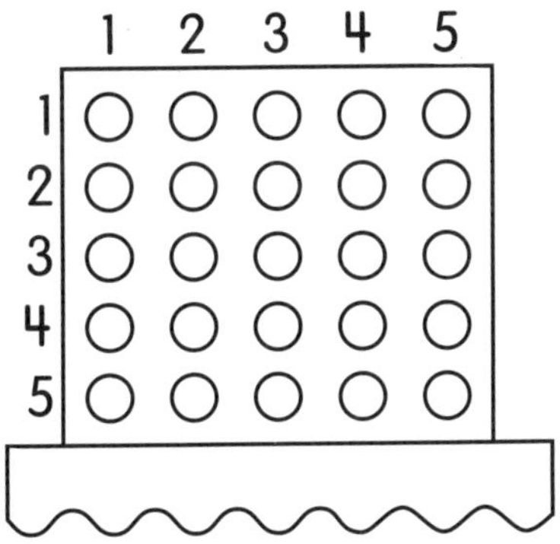

Paula has ___25___ beads in all.

1. Jasmine has 4 boxes.
Each box has 5 erasers.
How many erasers does Jasmine have in all?

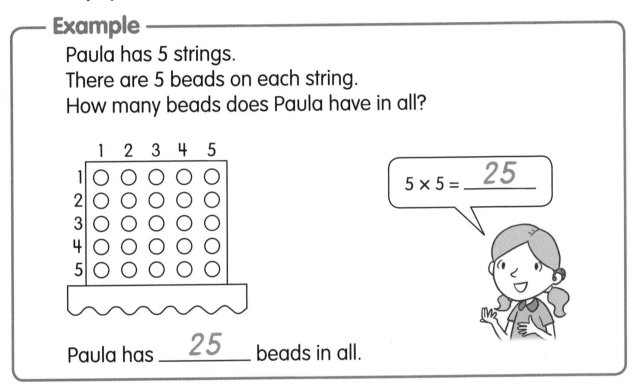

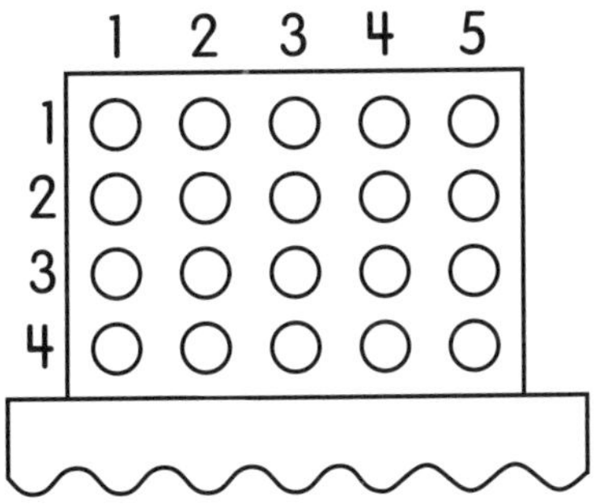

Jasmine has __________ erasers in all.

Name: ______________________ Date: ____________

Use short cuts to find the missing numbers.

Example

$2 \times 5 = ?$

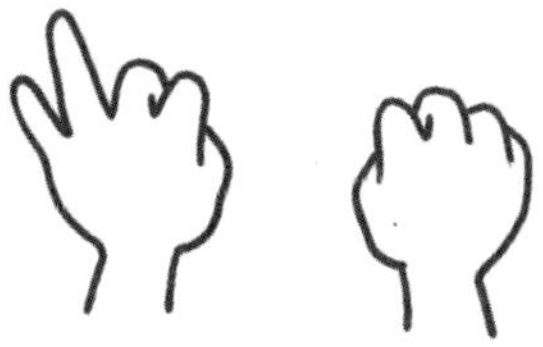

One finger stands for 5.
Two fingers stand for 10.

$2 \times 5 =$ 10

2. $5 \times 5 = ?$

$5 \times 5 =$ ______

3. $9 \times 5 = ?$

$9 \times 5 =$ ______

Name: ______________________ Date: ______________

Multiplication Table of 5
$1 \times 5 = 5$
$2 \times 5 = 10$
$3 \times 5 = 15$
$4 \times 5 = 20$
$5 \times 5 = 25$
$6 \times 5 = 30$
$7 \times 5 = 35$
$8 \times 5 = 40$
$9 \times 5 = 45$
$10 \times 5 = 50$

Use dot paper to find the missing numbers.

Example

$\underline{3} \times \underline{5} = \underline{15}$ $\underline{5} \times \underline{3} = \underline{15}$

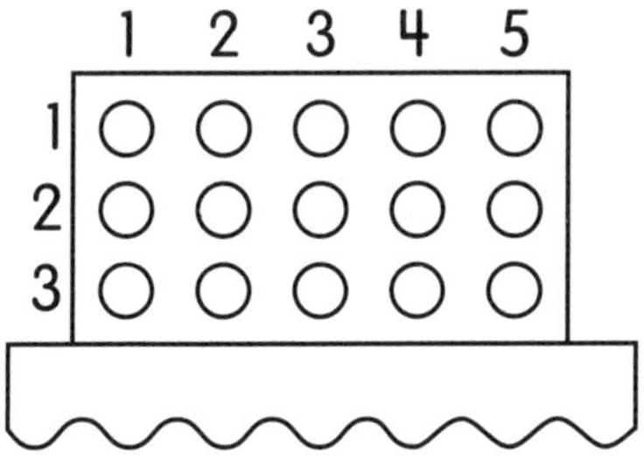

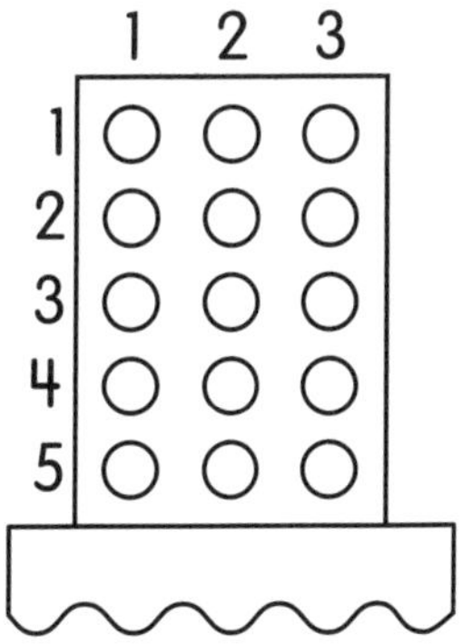

4. _____ × _____ = _____ _____ × _____ = _____

	1	2	3	4	5
1	○	○	○	○	○
2	○	○	○	○	○
3	○	○	○	○	○
4	○	○	○	○	○
5	○	○	○	○	○
6	○	○	○	○	○

	1	2	3	4	5	6
1	○	○	○	○	○	○
2	○	○	○	○	○	○
3	○	○	○	○	○	○
4	○	○	○	○	○	○
5	○	○	○	○	○	○

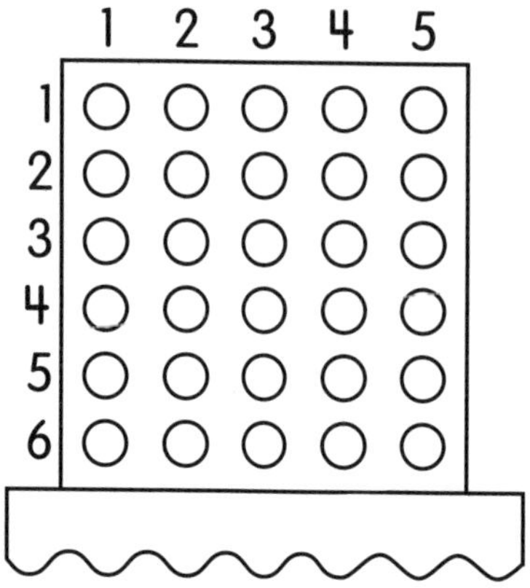

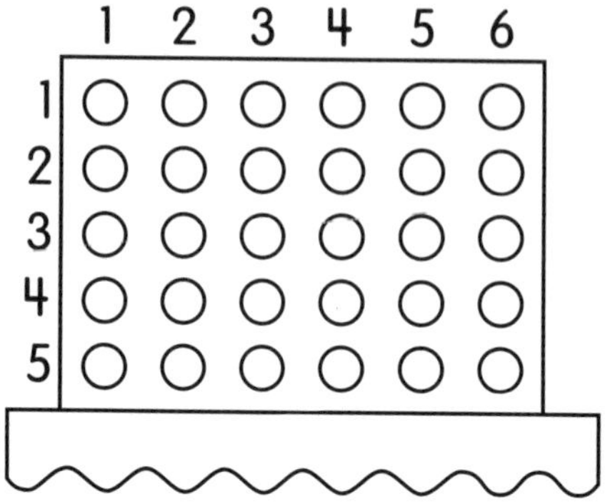

5. _____ × _____ = _____ _____ × _____ = _____

	1	2	3	4	5
1	○	○	○	○	○
2	○	○	○	○	○
3	○	○	○	○	○
4	○	○	○	○	○
5	○	○	○	○	○
6	○	○	○	○	○
7	○	○	○	○	○
8	○	○	○	○	○
9	○	○	○	○	○
10	○	○	○	○	○

	1	2	3	4	5	6	7	8	9	10
1	○	○	○	○	○	○	○	○	○	○
2	○	○	○	○	○	○	○	○	○	○
3	○	○	○	○	○	○	○	○	○	○
4	○	○	○	○	○	○	○	○	○	○
5	○	○	○	○	○	○	○	○	○	○

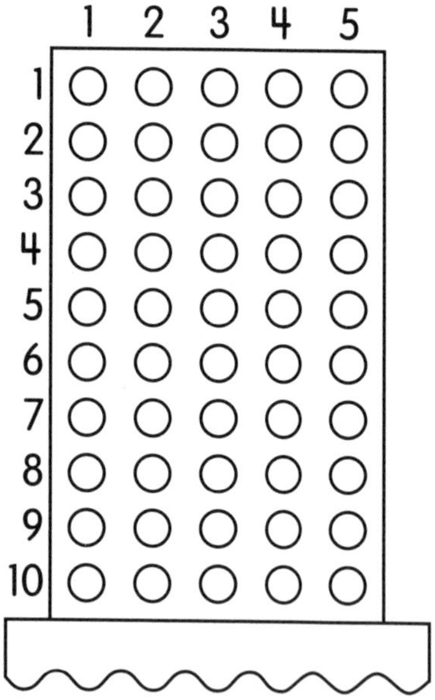

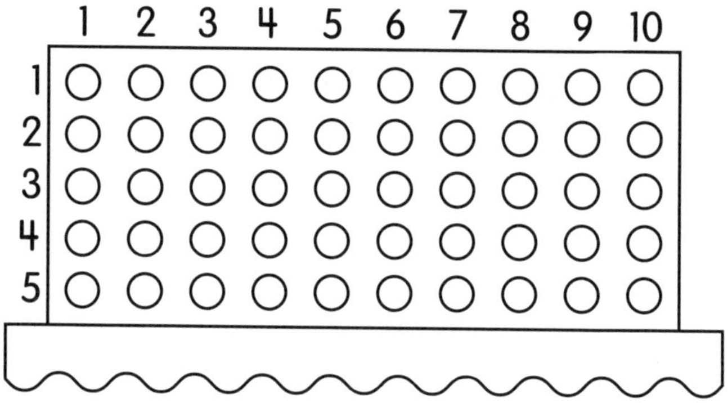

Name: ____________________ Date: ____________

Worksheet 5 Multiplying 10: Skip-Counting and Using Dot Paper

Find the missing numbers in the number pattern.

1. 10, 20, 30, ______, ______, ______, ______

I add ______ to get the next number.

Find the missing numbers.

2.

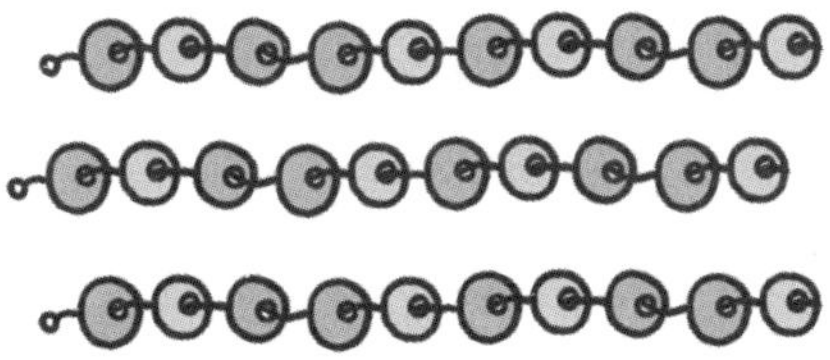

3 tens is ______ groups of ______.

Use skip-counting to find the missing numbers.

Example

1 finger stands for 10.

10, 20, 30, 40, 50

$5 \times 10 =$ 50

The 5 fingers stand for 50.

Name: ______________________ Date: ____________

3. There are 7 bags.
Each bag has 10 marbles.
How many marbles are there in all?

10, 20, 30, ________, ________, ________, ________

________ × 10 = ________

There are ________ marbles in all.

4. Jeanette has 5 glass bottles.
Each glass bottle has 10 coins.
How many coins are there in all?

________ × 10 = ________

There are ________ coins in all.

5. Pauline puts 10 books on each shelf.
Her bookcase has 4 shelves.
How many books does Pauline have in all?

________ × ________ = ________

Pauline has ________ books in all.

Name: ______________________ Date: ______________

Multiplication Table of 10
$1 \times 10 = 10$
$2 \times 10 = 20$
$3 \times 10 = 30$
$4 \times 10 = 40$
$5 \times 10 = 50$
$6 \times 10 = 60$
$7 \times 10 = 70$
$8 \times 10 = 80$
$9 \times 10 = 90$
$10 \times 10 = 100$

Use dot paper to find the missing numbers.

Example

$\underline{5} \times \underline{10} = \underline{50}$ $\underline{10} \times \underline{5} = \underline{50}$

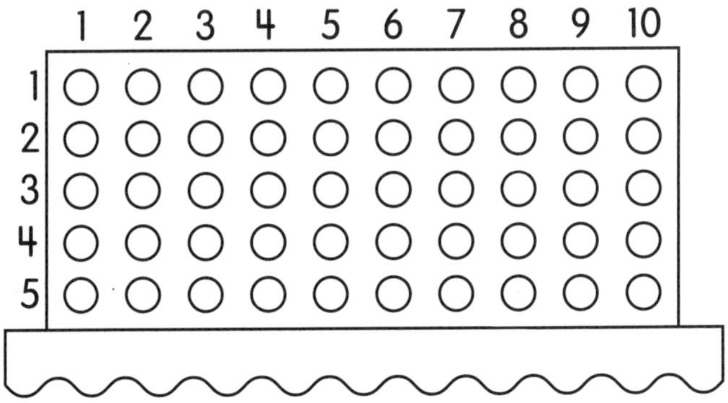

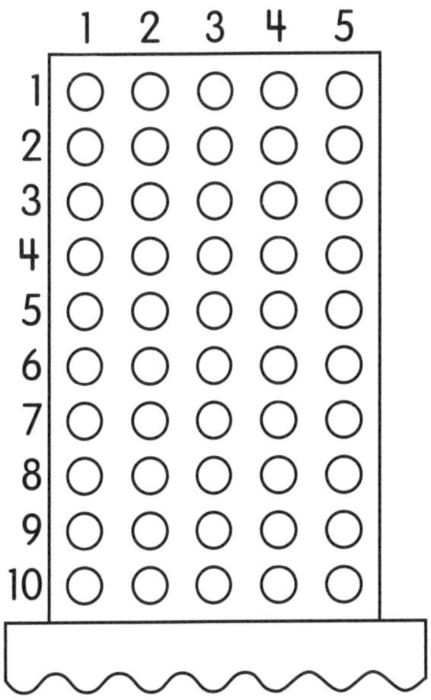

5 × 10 = 10 × 5
These are related multiplication facts.

6. _____ × _____ = _____ _____ × _____ = _____

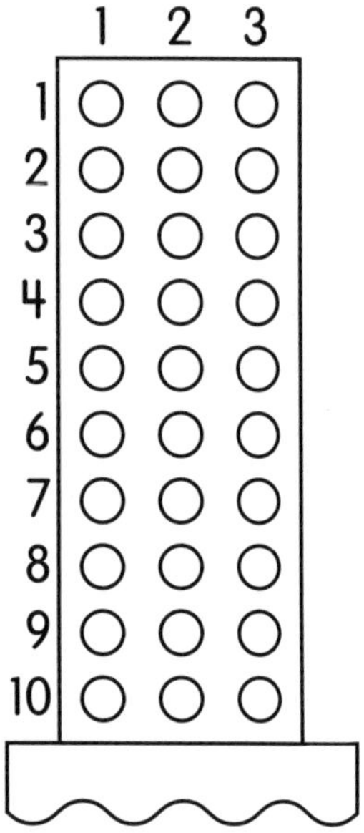

```
   1  2  3
1  ○  ○  ○
2  ○  ○  ○
3  ○  ○  ○
4  ○  ○  ○
5  ○  ○  ○
6  ○  ○  ○
7  ○  ○  ○
8  ○  ○  ○
9  ○  ○  ○
10 ○  ○  ○
```

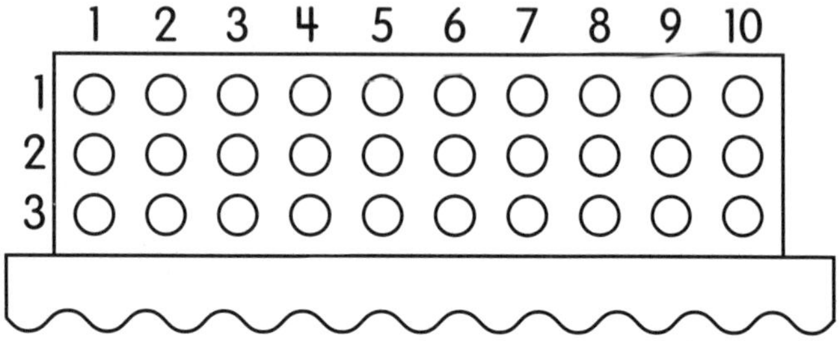

```
   1  2  3  4  5  6  7  8  9  10
1  ○  ○  ○  ○  ○  ○  ○  ○  ○  ○
2  ○  ○  ○  ○  ○  ○  ○  ○  ○  ○
3  ○  ○  ○  ○  ○  ○  ○  ○  ○  ○
```

7. _____ × _____ = _____ _____ × _____ = _____

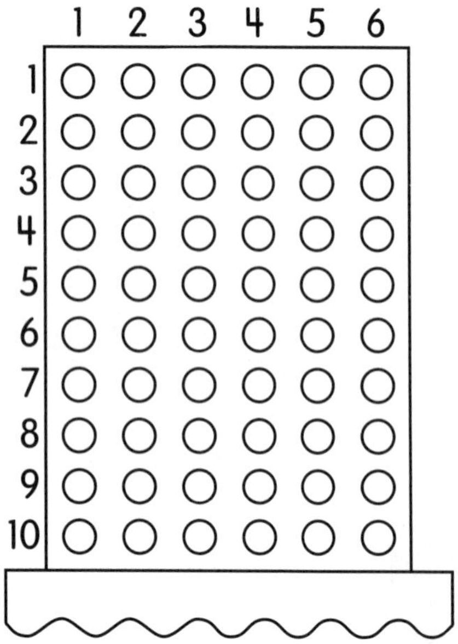

```
   1  2  3  4  5  6
1  ○  ○  ○  ○  ○  ○
2  ○  ○  ○  ○  ○  ○
3  ○  ○  ○  ○  ○  ○
4  ○  ○  ○  ○  ○  ○
5  ○  ○  ○  ○  ○  ○
6  ○  ○  ○  ○  ○  ○
7  ○  ○  ○  ○  ○  ○
8  ○  ○  ○  ○  ○  ○
9  ○  ○  ○  ○  ○  ○
10 ○  ○  ○  ○  ○  ○
```

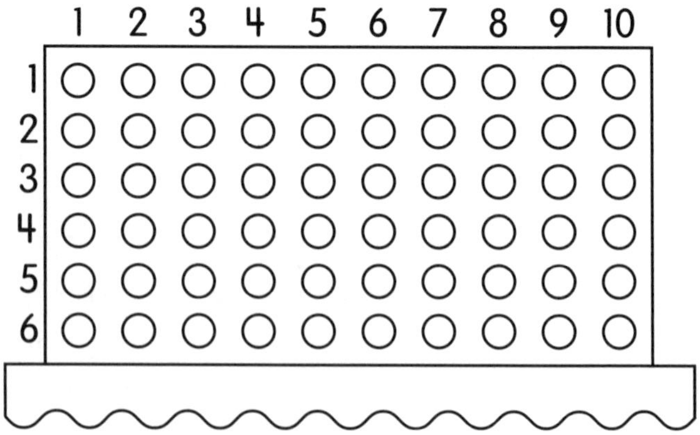

```
   1  2  3  4  5  6  7  8  9  10
1  ○  ○  ○  ○  ○  ○  ○  ○  ○  ○
2  ○  ○  ○  ○  ○  ○  ○  ○  ○  ○
3  ○  ○  ○  ○  ○  ○  ○  ○  ○  ○
4  ○  ○  ○  ○  ○  ○  ○  ○  ○  ○
5  ○  ○  ○  ○  ○  ○  ○  ○  ○  ○
6  ○  ○  ○  ○  ○  ○  ○  ○  ○  ○
```

Name: ______________________ Date: ______________

Worksheet 6 Odd and Even Numbers

Circle groups of 2.
Then write the number.

1. 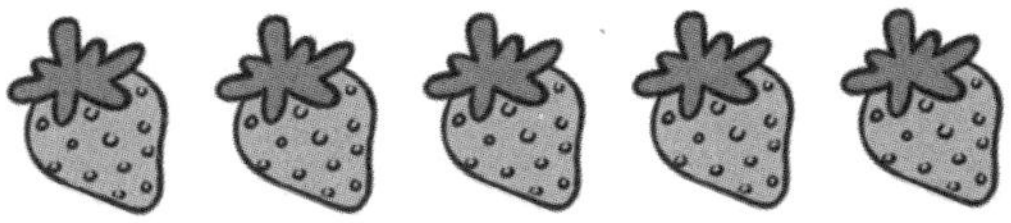

There is ________  left.

2. 

There are ________  left.

Solve.

3. Jack wrote the numbers 42, 43, 44.
The teacher says that 44 is an even number.
Is the next number odd or even?

The next number is ________.

Name: ______________________ Date: ______________

4. Jill wrote the numbers 77, 78, 79.
The teacher says that 79 is and odd number.
Is the next number odd or even?

The next number is ________.

Draw triangles to show the numbers.
Then write *odd* or *even*.

5. 9

9 is an ________ number.

6. 12

12 is an ________ number.

Name: ______________________________ Date: ______________

Draw objects to show the following statements.
Then fill in the blanks with *odd* or *even*.

7. Two equal groups of 3

The number of objects is ________.

8. Two equal groups of 10

The number of objects is ________.

Name: ______________________ Date: ____________

Count the fruit.
Then write *odd* or *even*.

9.

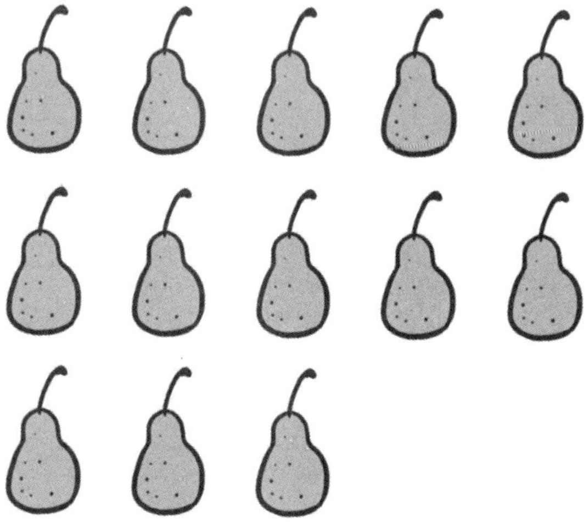

The number of pears is ________.

10.

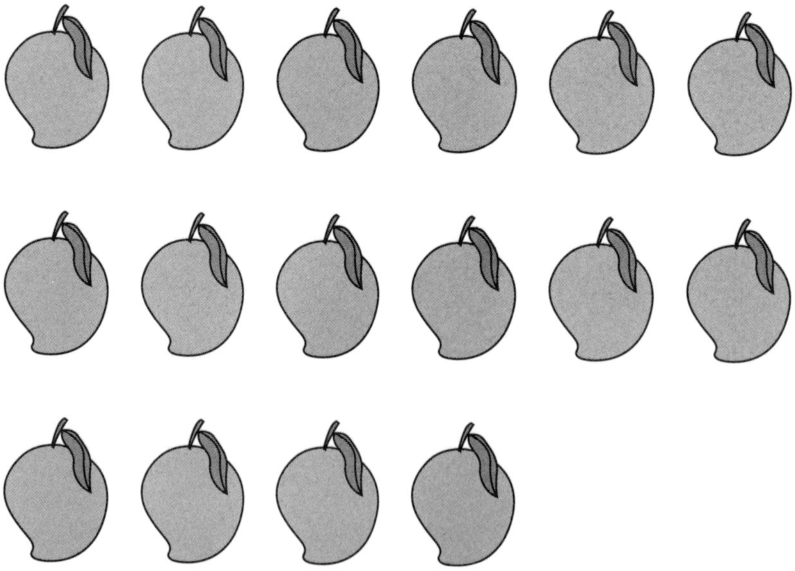

The number of mangoes is ________.

Name: ______________________ Date: ______________

Chapter 7 Metric Measurement of Length

Worksheet 1 Measuring in Meters

Find the missing numbers.

1  stands for 1 unit.

1.

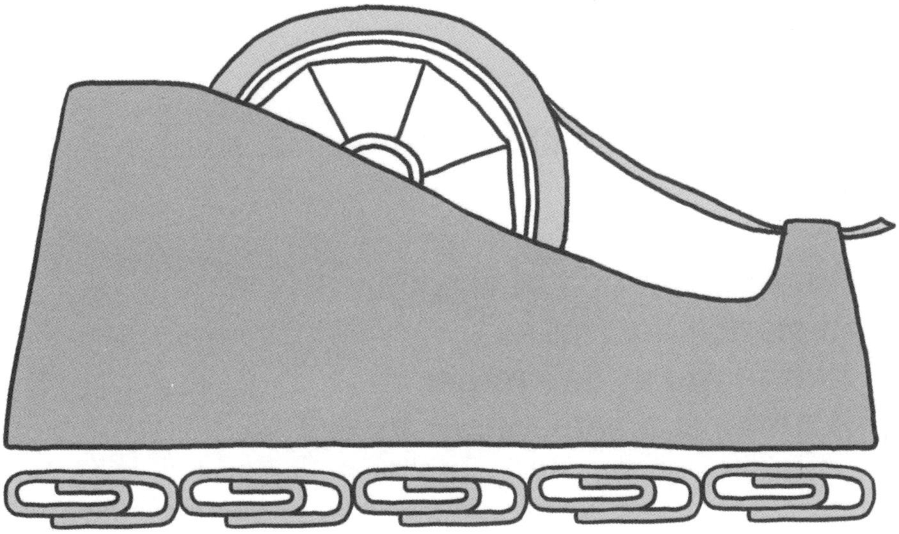

The tape dispenser is about ________ units long.

2.

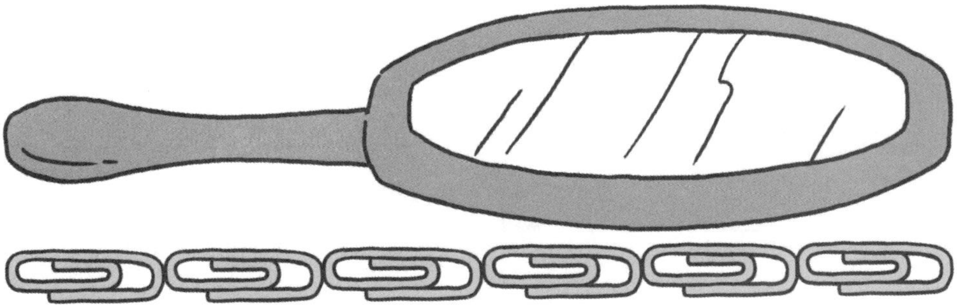

The mirror is about ________ units long.

Name: ______________________ Date: ______________

Look at the drawings.
Then answer the questions.

Example

The length of the chest is ___1___ meter.

A meter is a unit of length.
m stands for "meter".
Read 1 m as "one meter".
A meter is a little longer than 3 feet.

3.

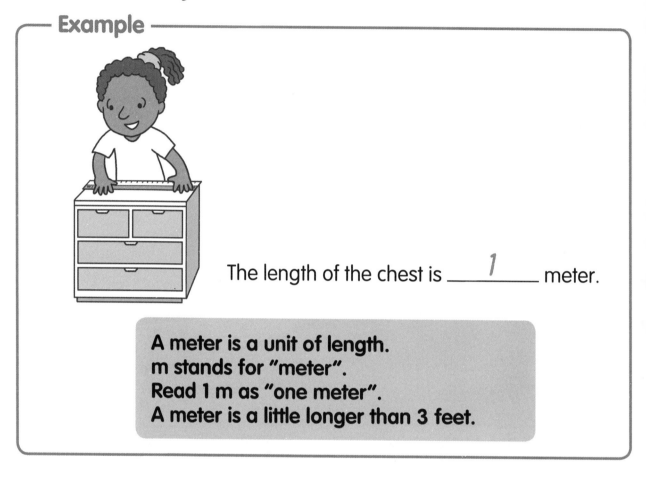

The length of the desk is __________ meters.

Name: ______________________ Date: ______________

Look at the drawings.
Then fill in the blanks with *more* or *less*.

Example

The length of the sketchpad is ___less___ than 1 meter.

4.

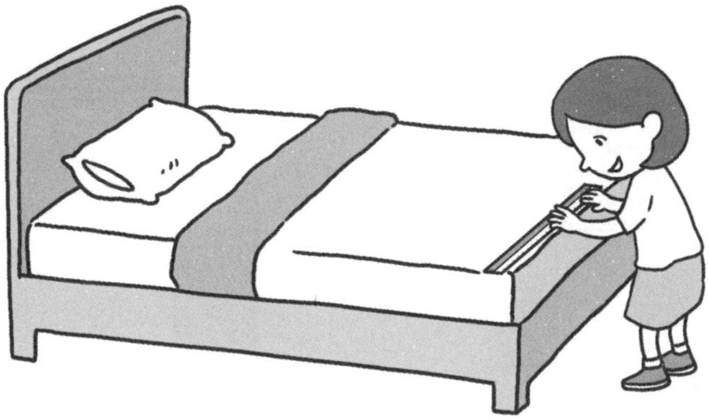

The width of the bed is ______________ than 1 meter.

5.

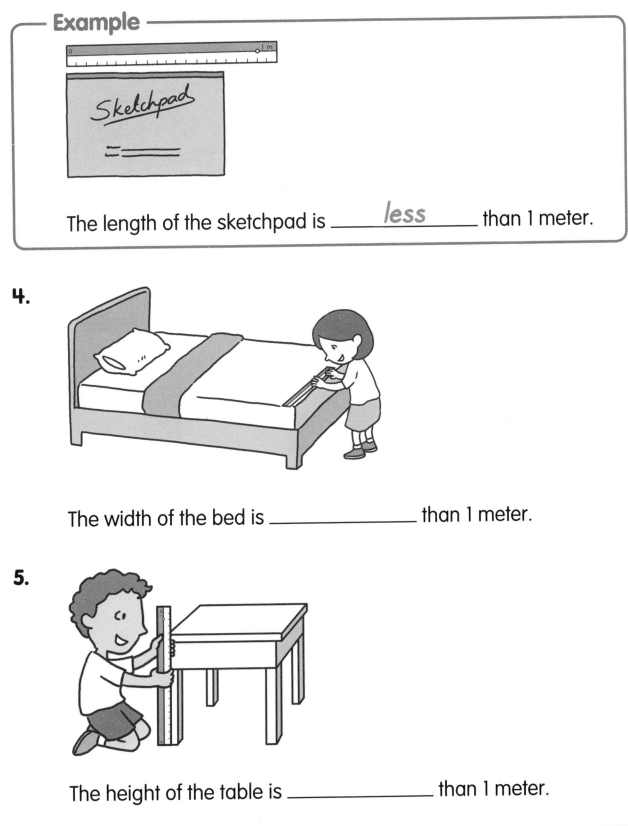

The height of the table is ______________ than 1 meter.

Name: ____________________ Date: ____________

Look at the drawings.
Circle the items that are longer than 1 meter in real life.

6.

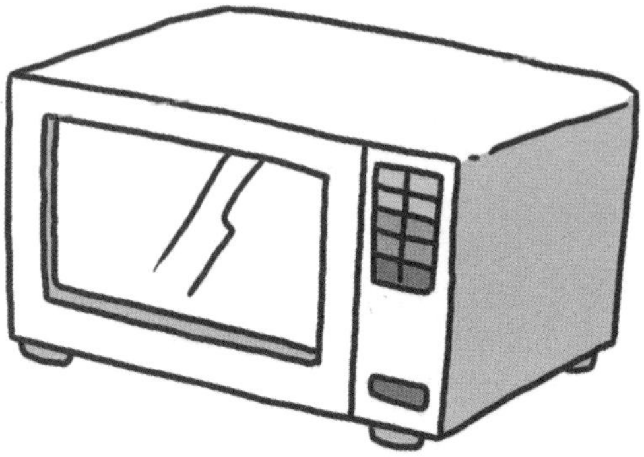

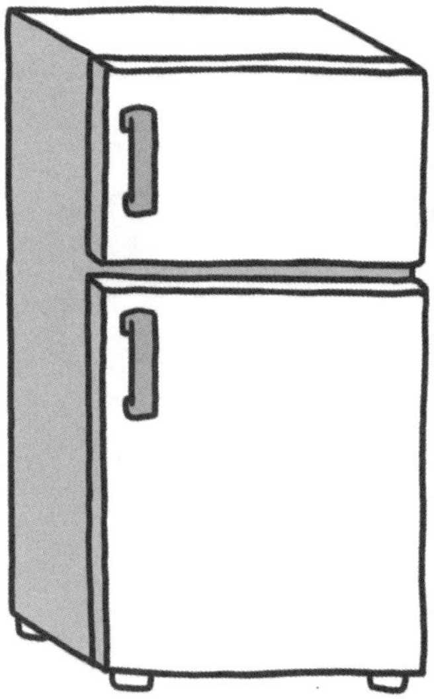

Name: ______________________ Date: ______________

Worksheet 2 Comparing Lengths in Meters

Write *True* or *False*.

Example

Shannon is taller than Melanie. True

1. Melanie is the tallest. ______________

2. Helen is shorter than Shannon. ______________

3. Helen is the shortest. ______________

Name: ____________________ Date: ____________

Write *True* or *False*.

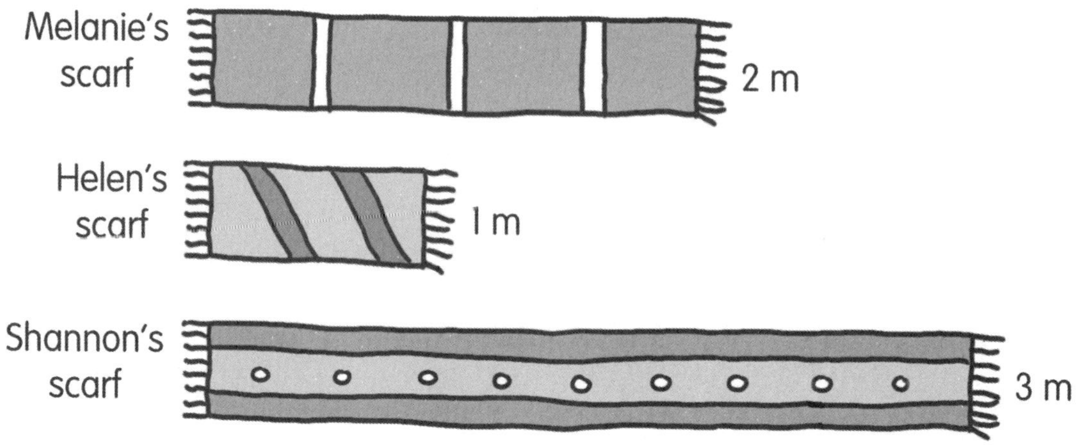

Example

Helen's scarf is longer than Shannon's scarf. *False*

4. Melanie's scarf is the longest. ____________

5. Helen's scarf is the shortest. ____________

6. Helen's scarf is longer than Melanie's scarf. ____________

7. Melanie's scarf is 1 meter longer than Helen's scarf. ____________

8. Helen's scarf is 2 meters shorter than Shannon's scarf. ____________

Name: ______________________________ Date: ______________

Worksheet 3 Measuring in Centimeters

Look at the drawings.
Then answer the questions.

Example

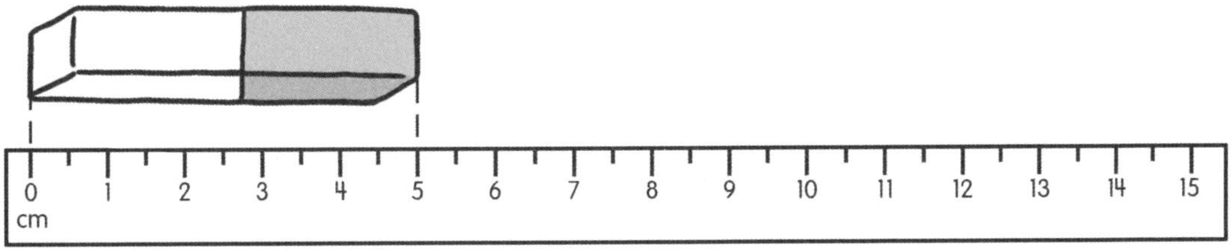

The length of the eraser is ___5___ centimeters.

A centimeter is a unit of length.
cm stands for centimeter.
Read 1 cm as "one centimeter".
A centimeter is used to measure shorter lengths.

1.

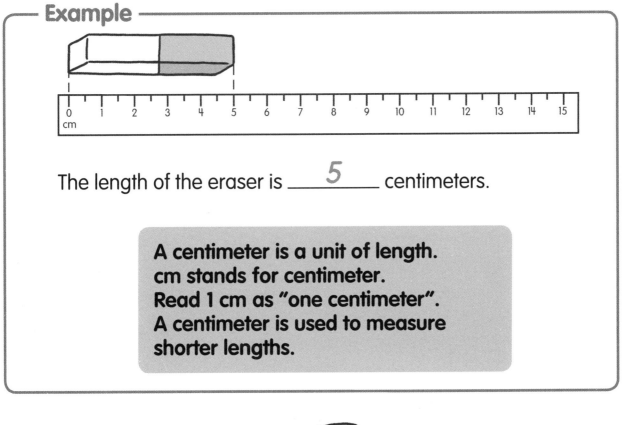

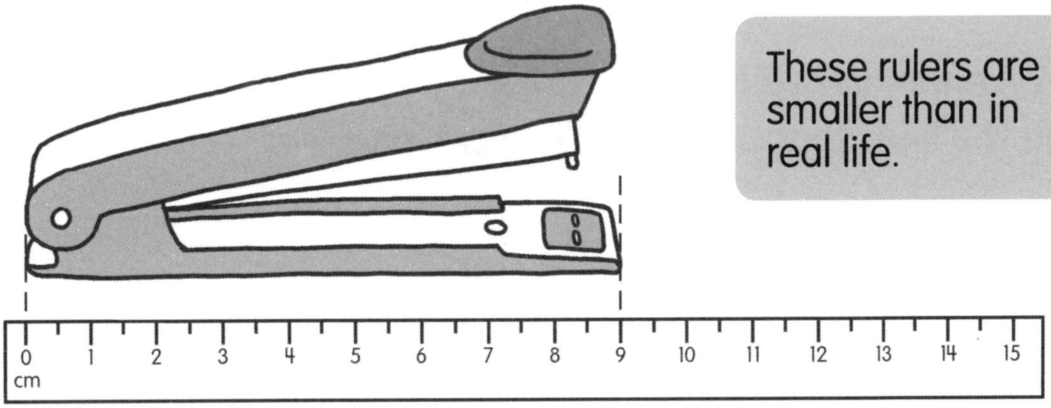

These rulers are smaller than in real life.

The length of the stapler is ________ centimeters.

Name: ______________________ Date: ______________

Look at the curve below.
Place a string along the curve.
Cut a piece of string as long as the curve.
Then place the string on a ruler to find its length in centimeters.

2. 

Place the string above the zero mark on a centimeter ruler to find its length.

Curve A is __________ centimeters long.

Use a centimeter ruler to measure.
Circle the lines that are 4 centimeters long.

3. 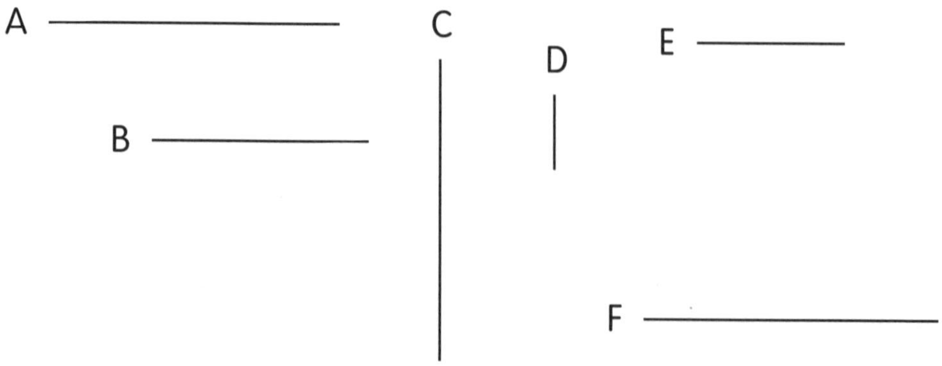

Name: _______________________________ Date: _______________

Use your centimeter ruler to draw.

4. A line that is 3 centimeters long

5. A line that is 7 centimeters long

6. A line that is 11 centimeters long

Name: ______________________ Date: ______________

Find the missing numbers.

Example

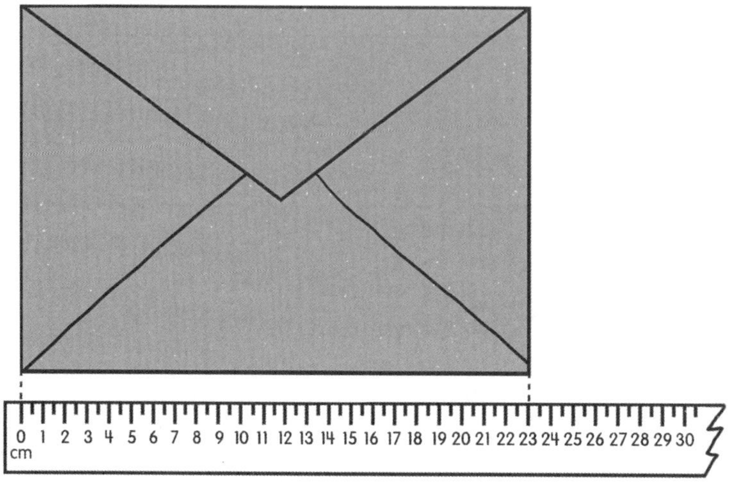

The length of the envelope is __23__ centimeters.

7.

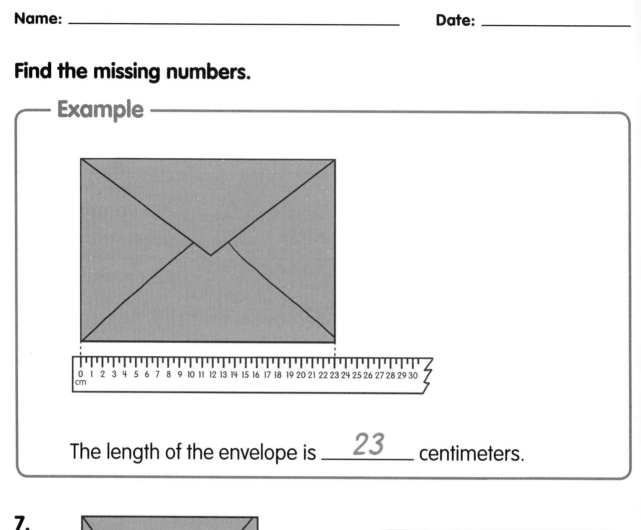

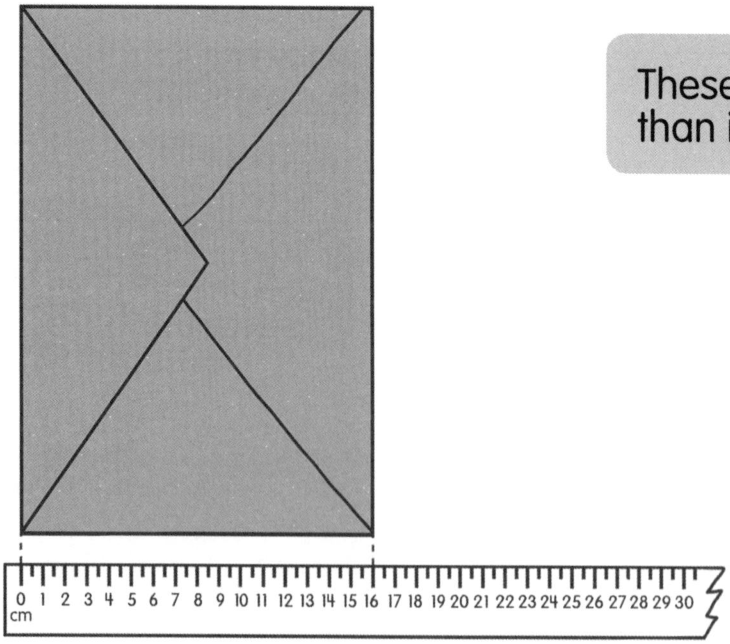

These rulers are smaller than in real life.

The width of the envelope is ________ centimeters.

Name: ______________________ Date: ______________

Find the missing numbers.

Example

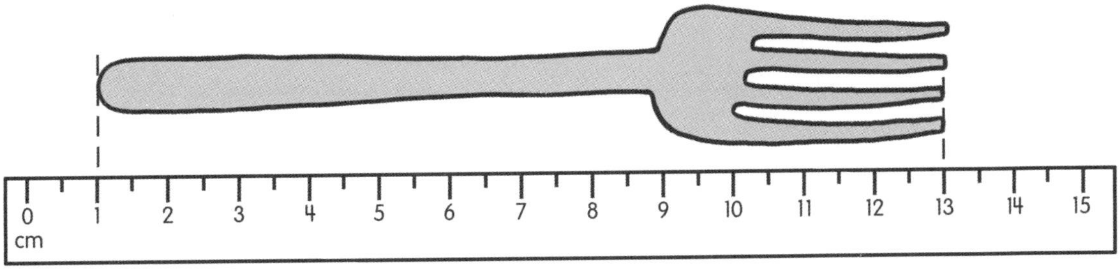

The fork is not above the zero mark of the ruler. How can I find its length?
You can subtract to find the length of the fork. 13 – 1 = 12

The length of the fork is 12 centimeters.

8.

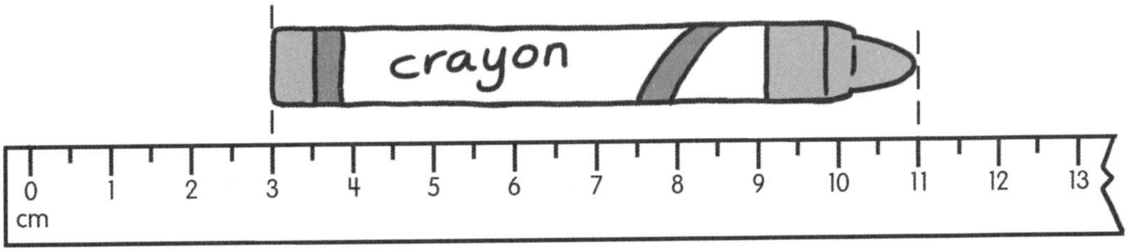

The crayon is ________ centimeters long.

Name: ______________________ Date: ______________

9.

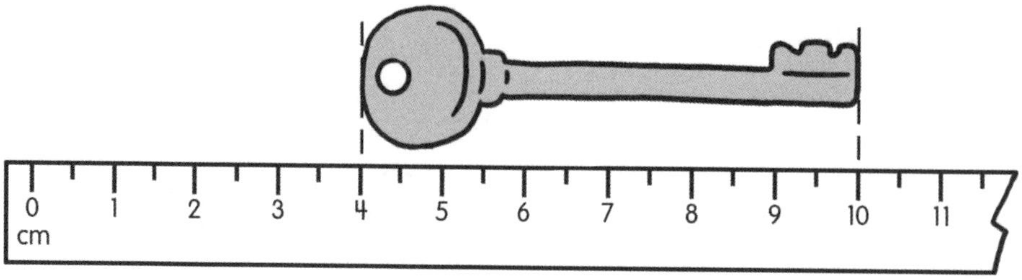

The key is ________ centimeters long.

10.

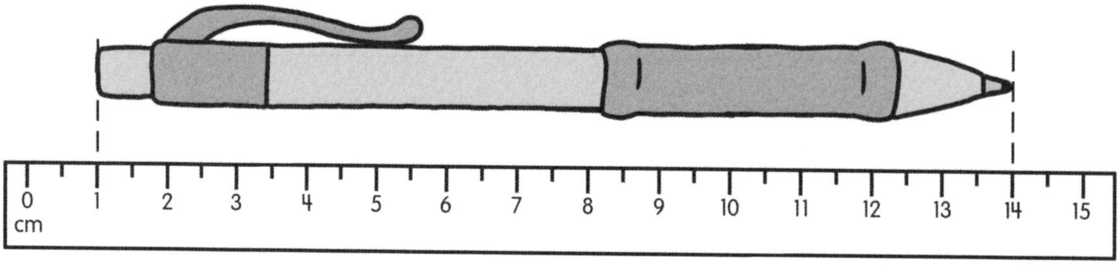

The pen is ________ centimeters long.

Name: ______________________ Date: ______________

Worksheet 4 Comparing Lengths in Centimeters

Find the missing numbers.

Example

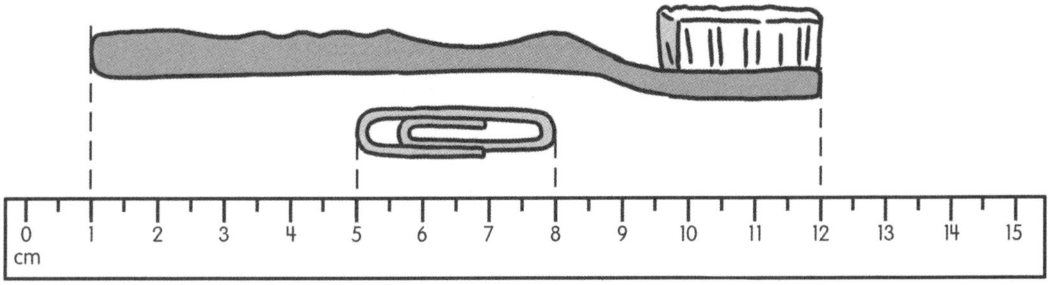

The toothbrush is ___11___ centimeters long.

The paper clip is ___3___ centimeters long.

The ___toothbrush___ is longer than the ___paper clip___.

1.

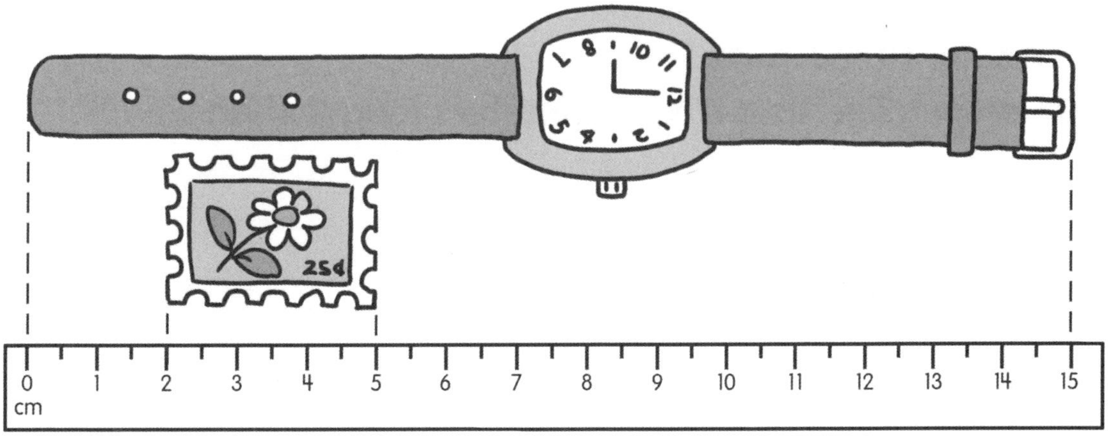

The watch is __________ centimeters long.

The stamp is __________ centimeters long.

The ______________ is shorter than the ______________.

Name: ______________________ Date: ______________

2.

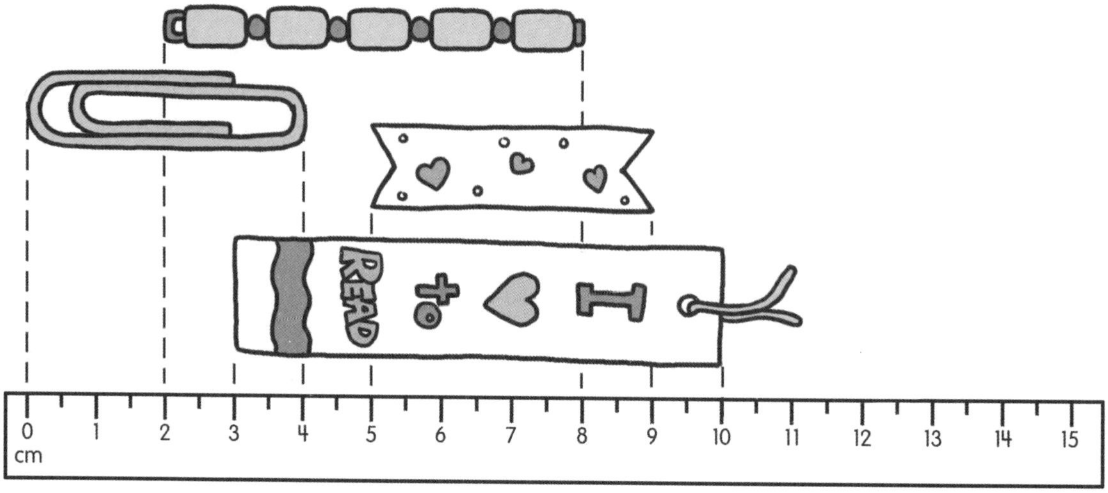

a. The length of the bookmark is ________ centimeters.

b. The longest item is the ____________.

c. The ____________ is longer than the bracelet.

d. The ________ and the ________ have the same length.

Use a ruler to measure Line A.
Then draw a line that is 4 centimeters longer than Line A.

3. Line A ____________________

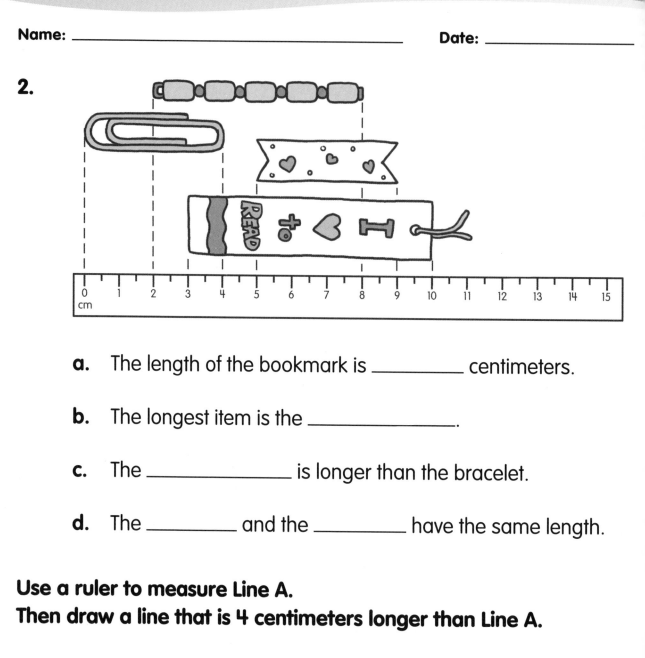

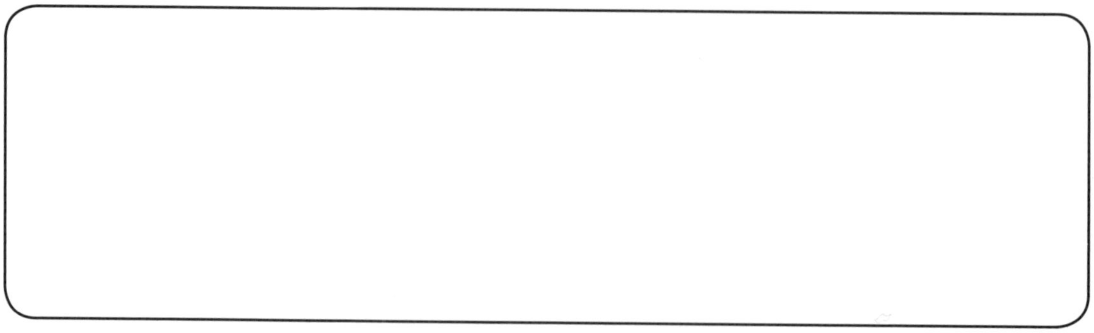

Name: ______________________ Date: ______________

Worksheet 5 Real-World Problems: Metric Length

Solve.
Use the bar models to help you.

Example

Nicole runs 550 meters.
Mina runs 425 meters.

a. How many meters do they run in all?

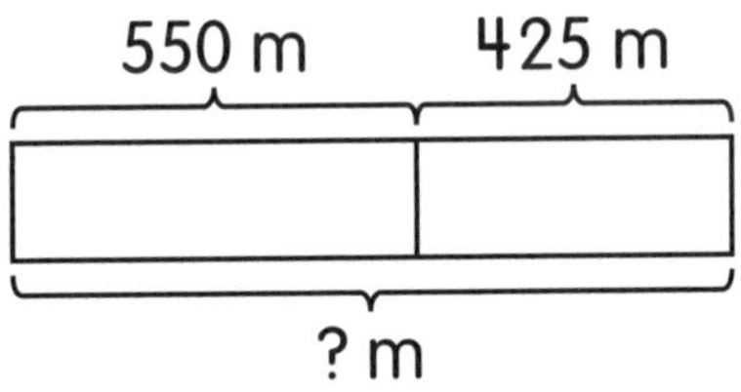

550 + 425 = 975

They run 975 meters in all.

b. How many meters farther than Mina does Nicole run?

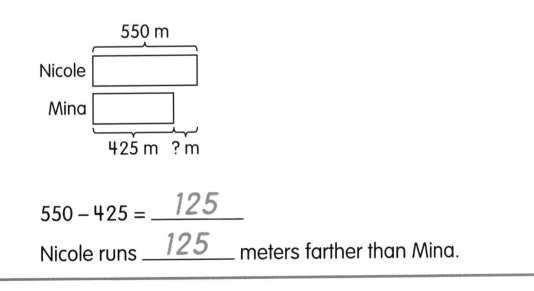

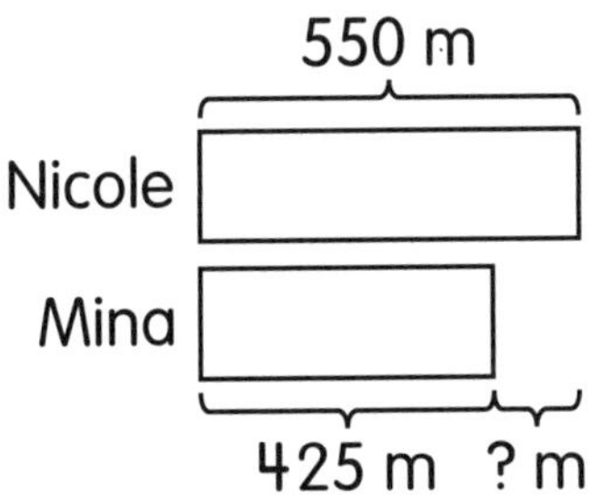

550 – 425 = 125

Nicole runs 125 meters farther than Mina.

Name: ______________________ Date: ______________

Solve.
Use the bar models to help you.

1. Harry bought a piece of cloth.
He cut off a piece of cloth 17 meters long.
He has 23 meters of cloth left.

a. How many meters of cloth did Harry buy?

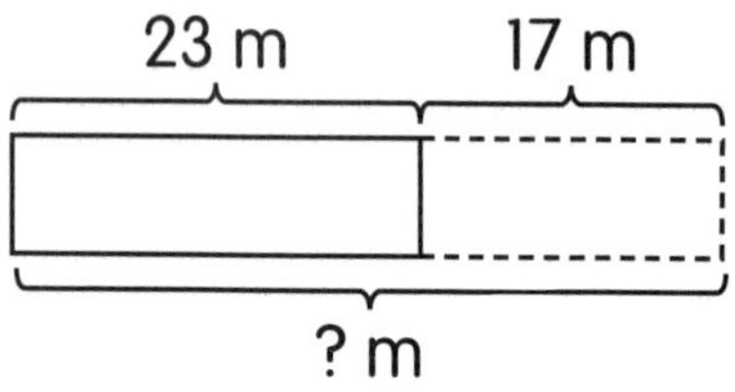

Harry bought ________ meters of cloth.

b. How much shorter is the piece of cloth that Harry cut off than the piece of cloth left?

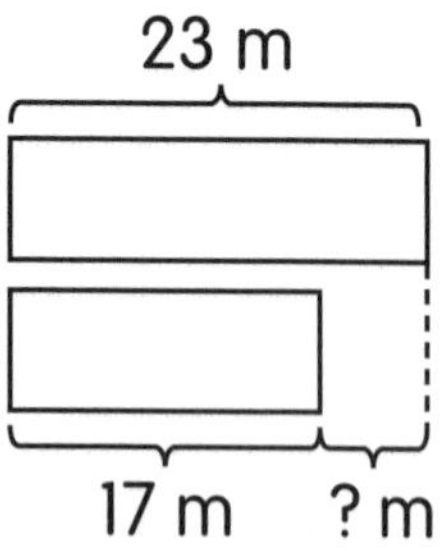

The piece of cloth that Harry cut off is ________ meters shorter.

Name: ______________________ Date: ______________

Example

The length of Liz's box is 30 centimeters.
The length of Jada's box is 12 centimeters less than the length of Liz's box.

a. What is the length of Jada's box?

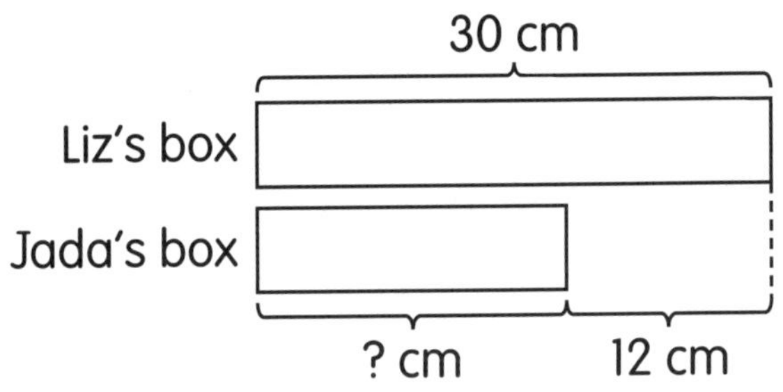

The length of Jada's box is ___18___ centimeters.

b. What is the total length of both their boxes?

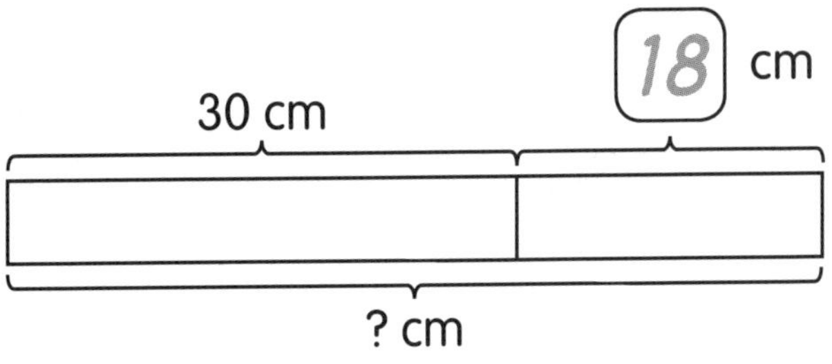

The total length of both their boxes is ___48___ centimeters.

Name: ______________________ Date: ____________

Solve.
Use the bar models to help you.

2. Breanne has a ribbon that is 13 centimeters long. Shirley has a ribbon that is 9 centimeters longer than Breanne's ribbon.

a. What is the length of Shirley's ribbon?

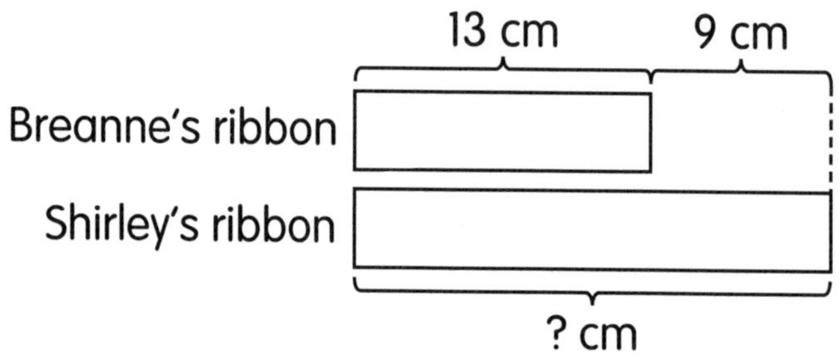

The length of Shirley's ribbon is ________ centimeters.

b. What is the total length of their ribbons?

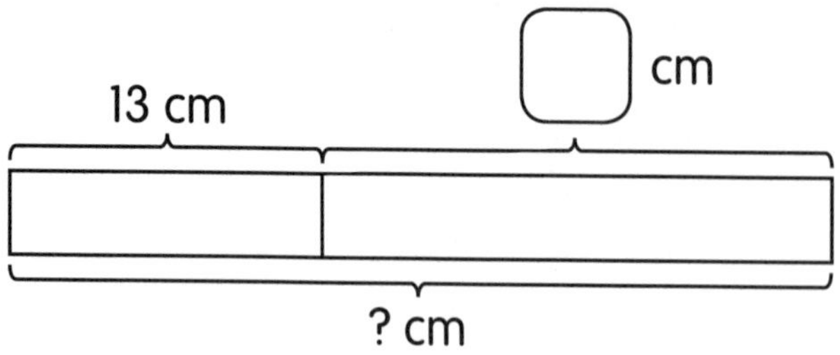

The total length of their ribbons is ________ centimeters.

Name: ______________________ Date: ______________

CHAPTER 8

Mass

Worksheet 1 Measuring in Kilograms

Find the mass of each object.

1 □ represents 1 unit.

1.

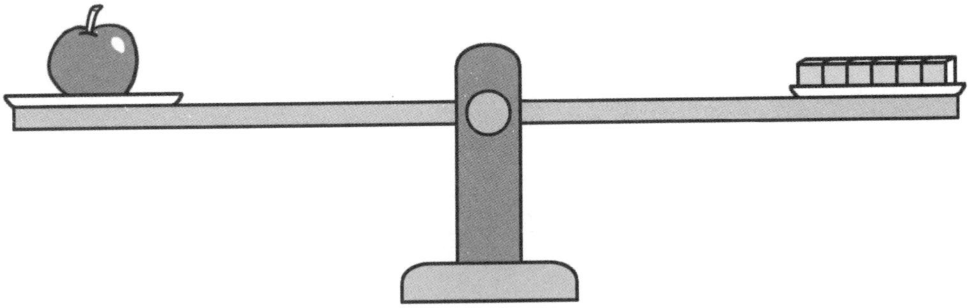

The mass of the apple is about ________ units.

2.

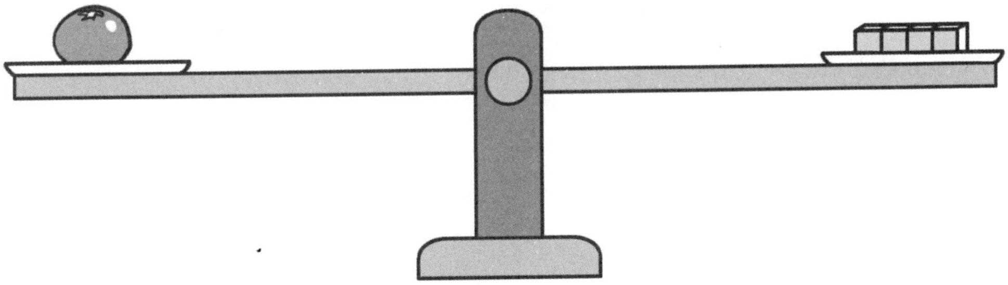

The mass of the tomato is about ________ units.

Name: ______________________ Date: ______________

Circle the correct answer.

Example

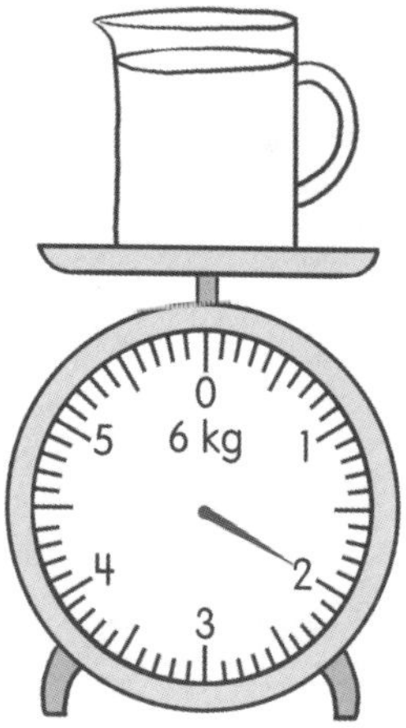

The jug of milk has a mass of ((2) / 3) kilograms.

The kilogram is a unit of mass.
kg stands for kilogram.
Read 1 kg as "one kilogram".
A kilogram is used to measure the mass of heavier objects.

3.

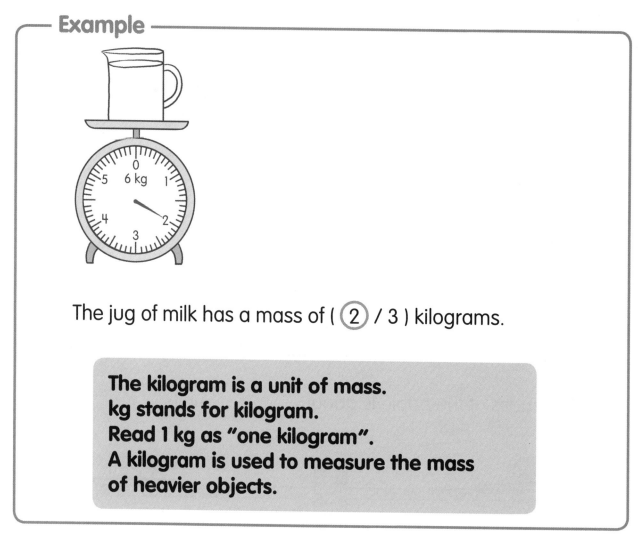

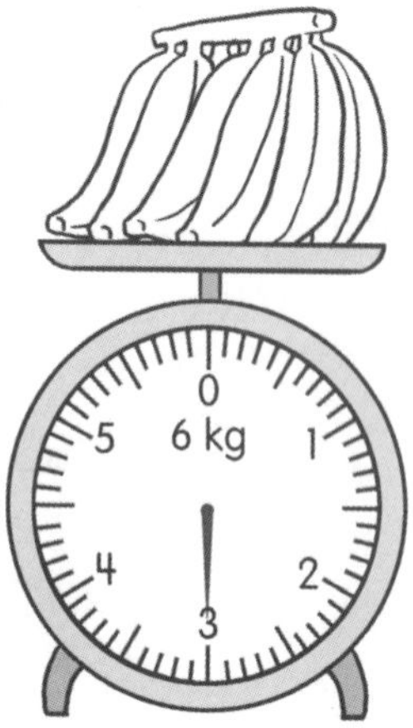

The bananas have a mass of (3 / 4) kilograms.

Name: ______________________ Date: ____________

Example

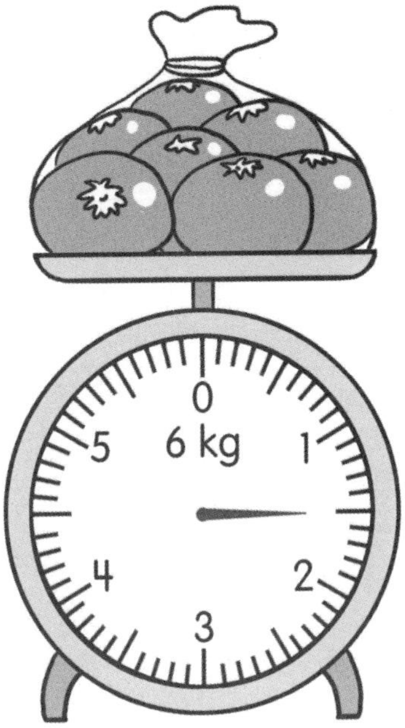

The mass of the bag of tomatoes is less than (1 / (2)) kilograms.

4.

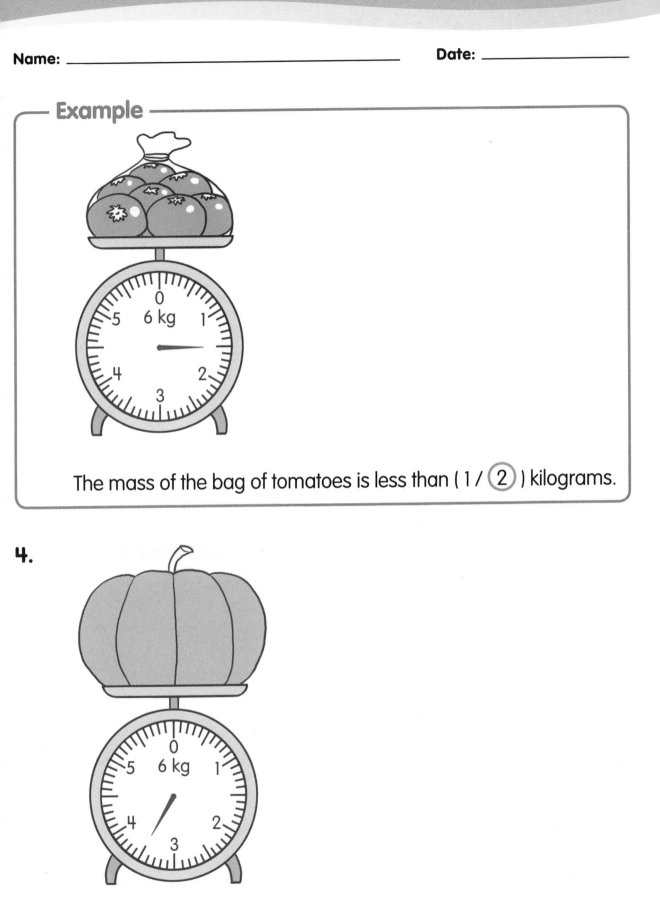

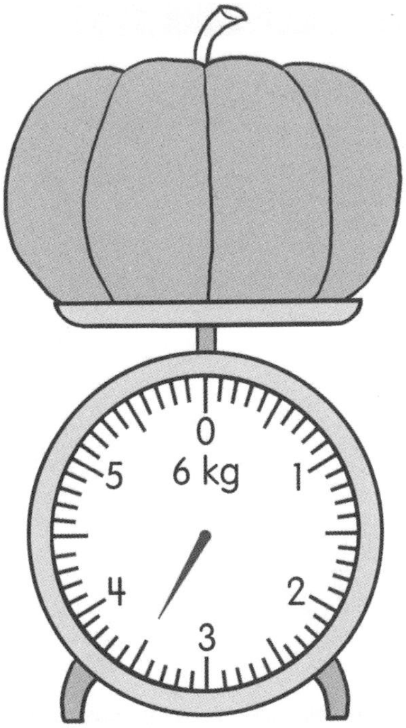

The mass of the pumpkin is less than (3 / 4) kilograms.

Name: ______________________ Date: ______________

Example

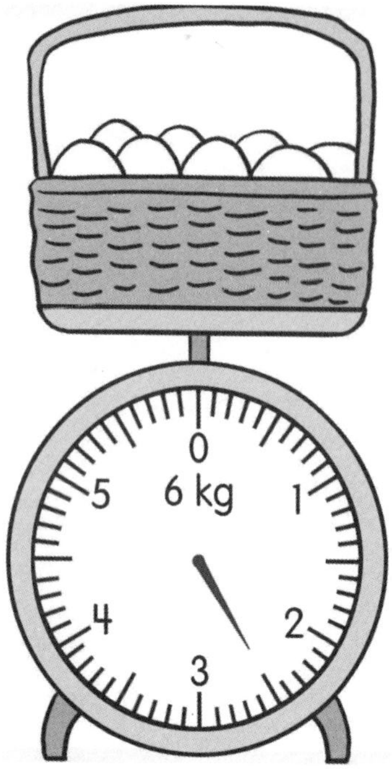

The mass of the basket of eggs is more than ((2) / 3) kilograms.

5.

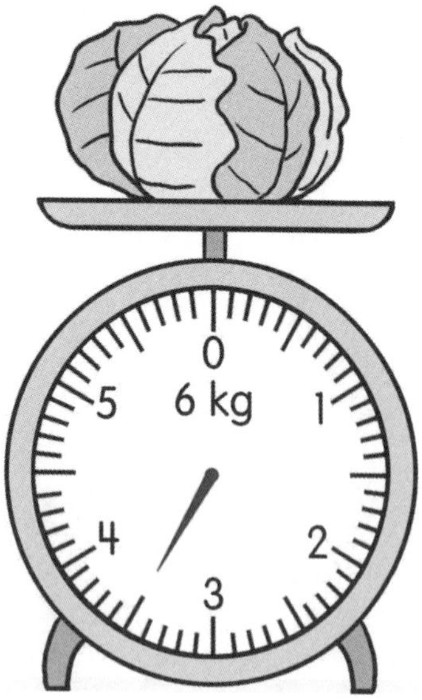

The mass of the cabbage is more than (3 / 4) kilograms.

Name: ______________________ Date: ______________

Find the mass of each object in kilograms.

Example

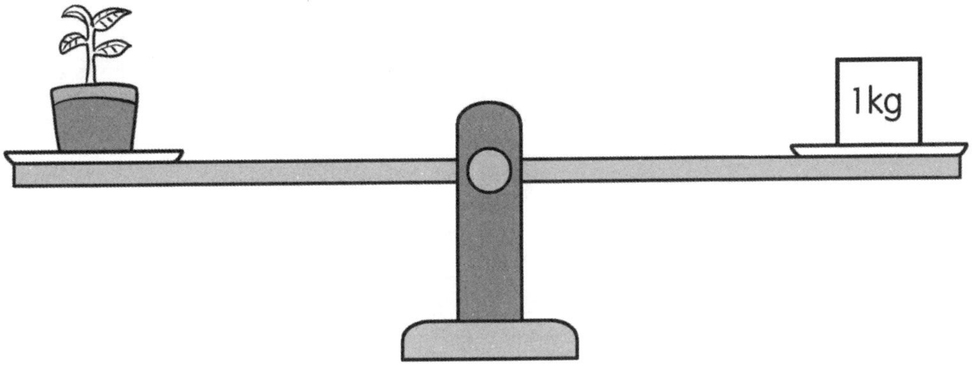

The mass of the plant is ___1___ kilogram.

6.

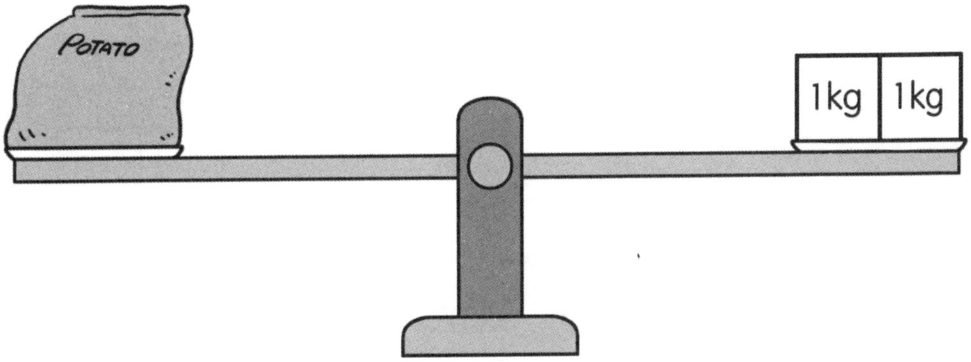

The mass of the bag of potatoes is ________ kilograms.

Name: ______________________ Date: ______________

Subtract to find the mass of each object in kilograms.

Example

2 – 1 = ___1___

The mass of the bag of grapes is ___1___ kilogram.

7.

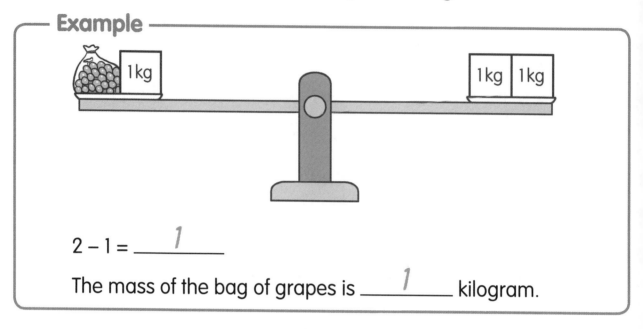

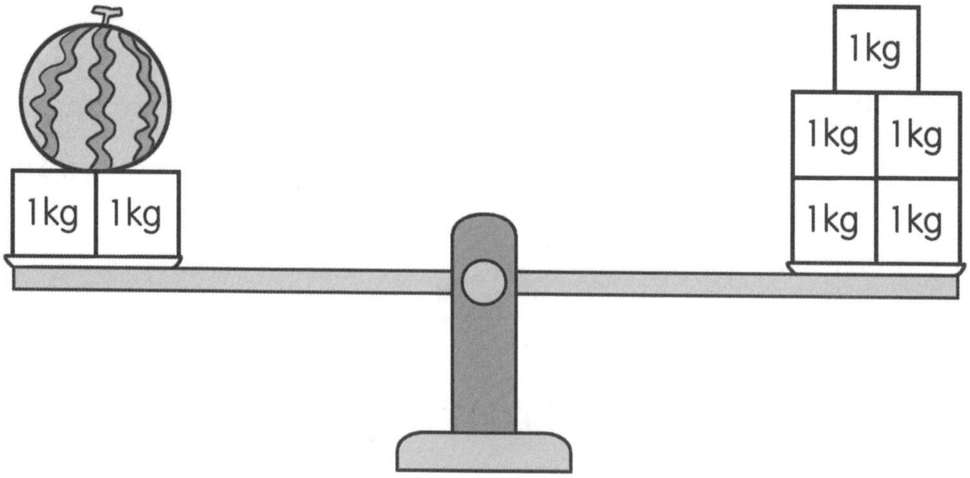

5 – 2 = ________

The mass of the watermelon is ________ kilograms.

Name: ______________________ Date: ______________

Worksheet 2 Comparing Masses in Kilograms

Look at the picture.
Write *heavier* or *lighter*.

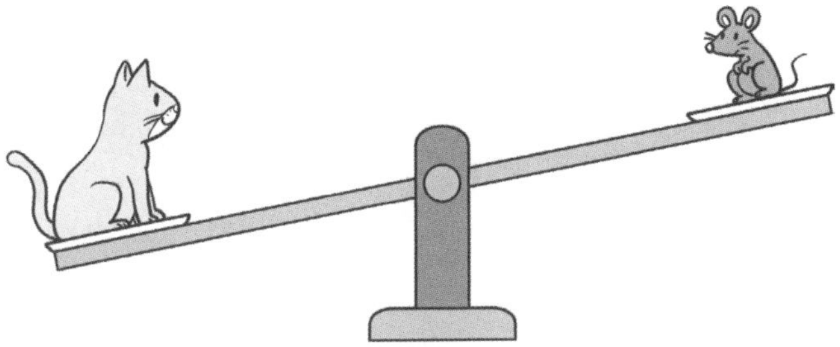

1. The mouse is ______________ than the cat.

2. The cat is ______________ than the mouse.

Write *True* or *False*.

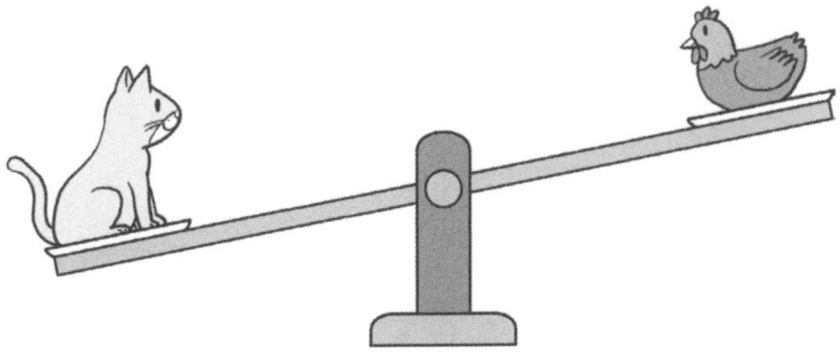

3. The cat is heavier than the hen. ______________

4. The cat is lighter than the hen. ______________

5. The cat is as heavy as the hen. ______________

6. The cat has the same weight as the hen. ______________

Name: ______________________ Date: ______________

Read the measuring scales to find the mass of each object. Then answer the questions.

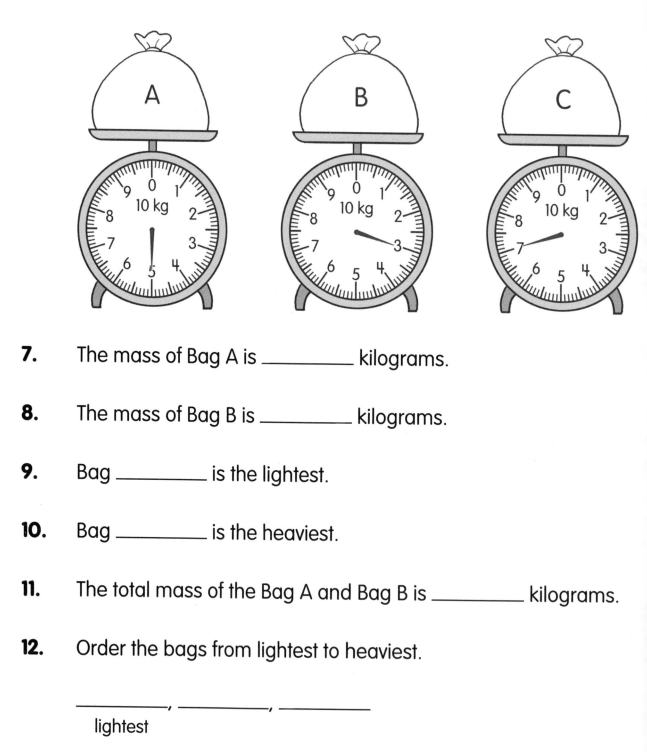

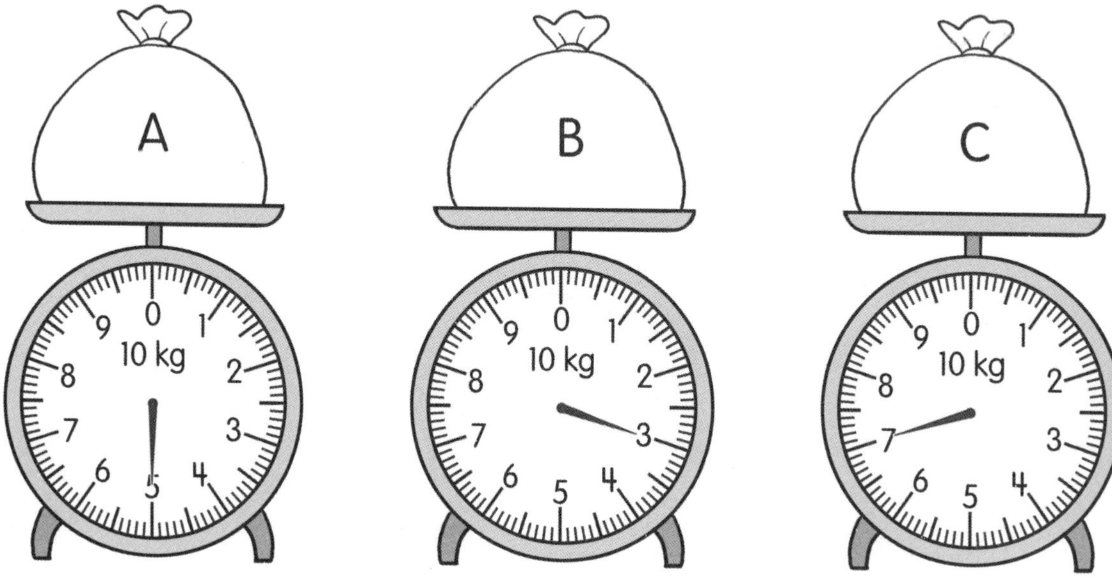

7. The mass of Bag A is ________ kilograms.

8. The mass of Bag B is ________ kilograms.

9. Bag ________ is the lightest.

10. Bag ________ is the heaviest.

11. The total mass of the Bag A and Bag B is ________ kilograms.

12. Order the bags from lightest to heaviest.

________, ________, ________

lightest

Name: ______________________ Date: ______________

Worksheet 3 Measuring in Grams

Find the mass of each object in grams.

Example

The mass of the shoe is __20__ grams.

The gram is a unit of mass.
g stands for gram.
Read 1 g as "one gram".
A gram is used to measure the mass of lighter objects.

1.

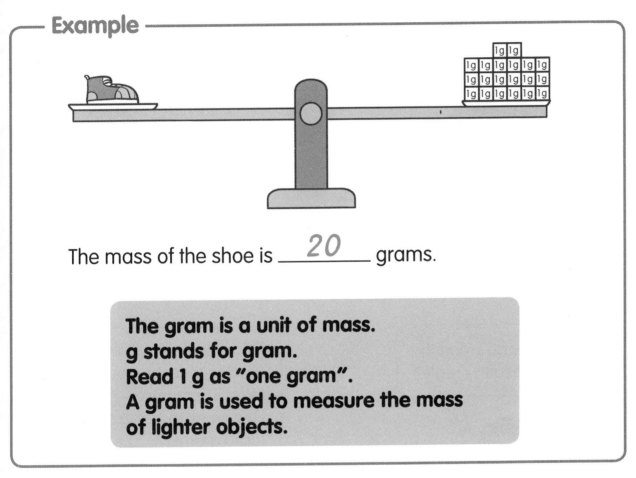

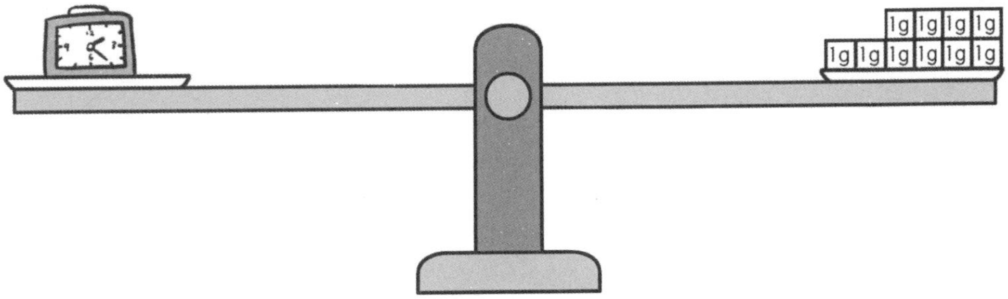

The mass of the clock is ________ grams.

Name: ____________________ Date: ____________

Read the scale to find the mass of each object.

Example

The mass of the bag of lemons is <u>300</u> grams.

Name: ______________________ Date: ______________

2.

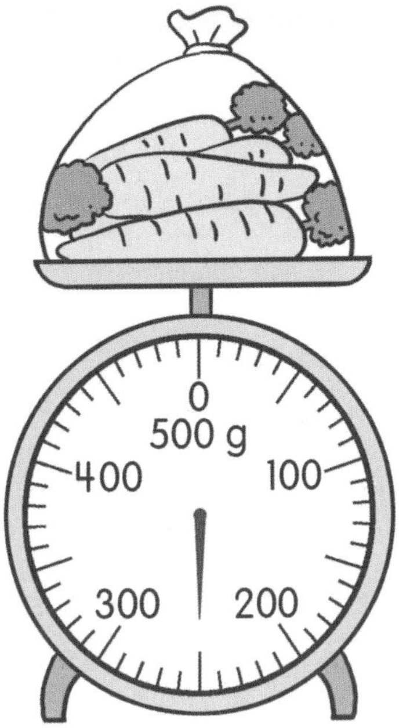

The mass of the bag of carrots is ________ grams.

3.

The mass of the puppy is ________ grams.

Name: ______________________ **Date:** ______________

4.

The mass of the teddy bear is ________ grams.

5.

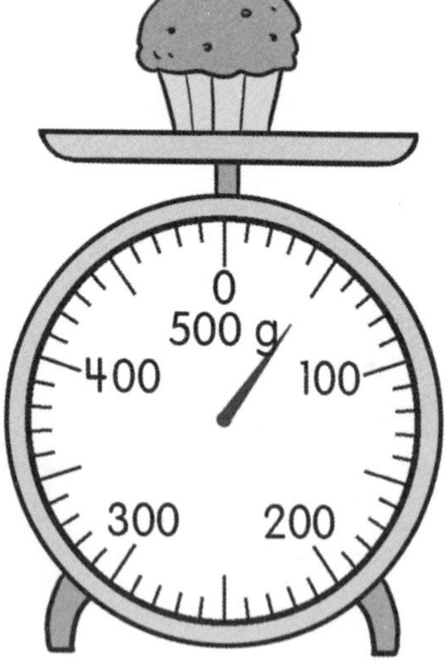

The mass of the muffin is ________ grams.

Name: ______________________ Date: ______________

Worksheet 4 Comparing Masses in Grams

Look at the pictures.
Then answer the questions.

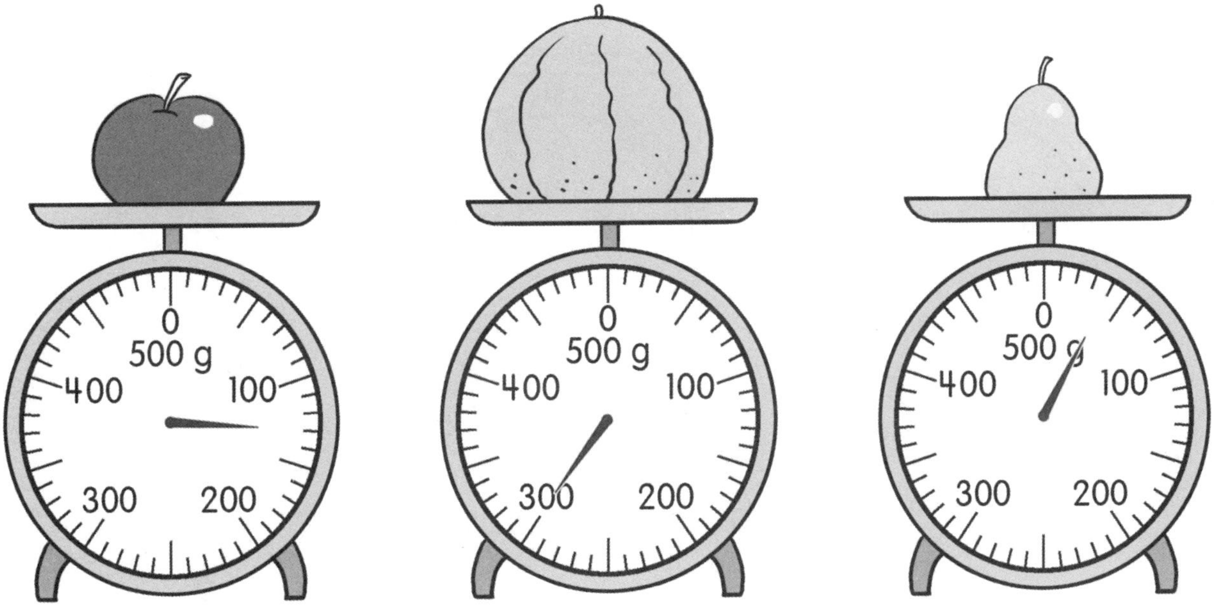

Example

The mass of the apple is 130 grams.

1. The mass of the melon is ________ grams.

2. The mass of the pear is ________ grams.

3. The ______________ is the lightest.

4. The ______________ is the heaviest.

5. The total mass of the fruits is ________ grams.

Name: ______________________ Date: ____________

Look at the pictures.
Then answer the questions.

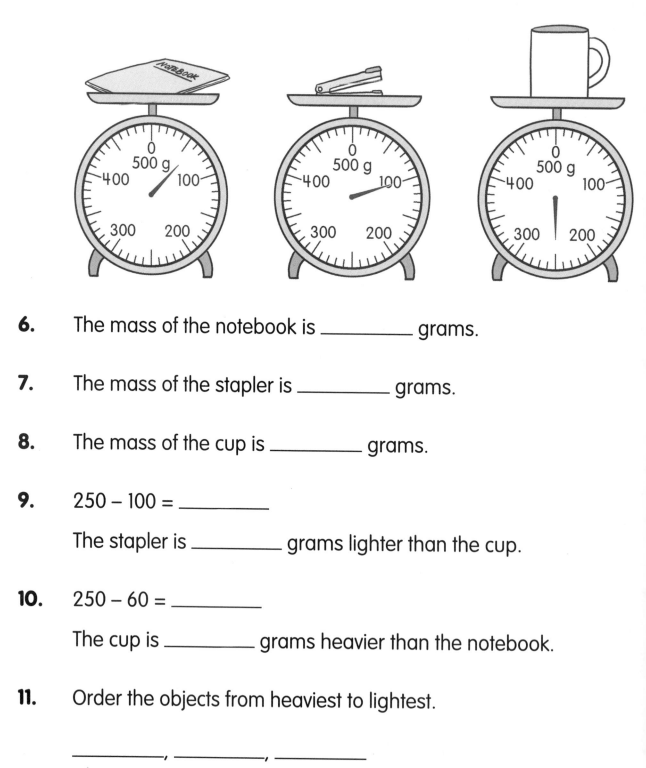

6. The mass of the notebook is ________ grams.

7. The mass of the stapler is ________ grams.

8. The mass of the cup is ________ grams.

9. 250 – 100 = ________

The stapler is ________ grams lighter than the cup.

10. 250 – 60 = ________

The cup is ________ grams heavier than the notebook.

11. Order the objects from heaviest to lightest.

________, ________, ________
heaviest

Name: ____________________ Date: ____________

Worksheet 5 Real-World Problems: Mass

Solve.
Use the bar models to help you.

Example

Joseph and his suitcase weigh 94 kilograms in all.
Joseph weighs 67 kilograms.
What is the mass of the suitcase?

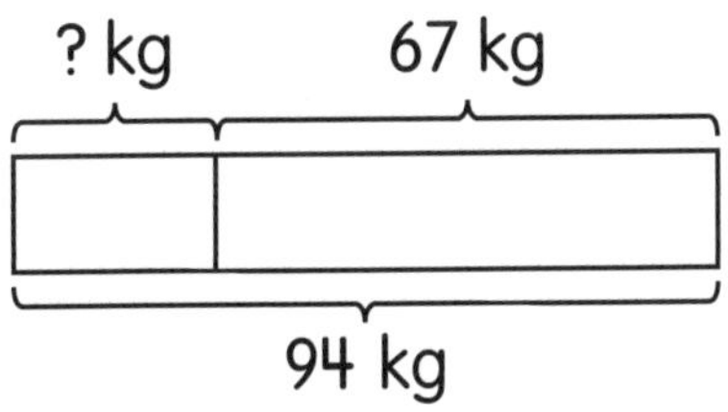

94 − 67 = 27

The suitcase weighs 27 kilograms.

1. A grocer has 45 kilograms of onions.
He sells 16 kilograms of onions.
How many kilograms of onions does he have left?

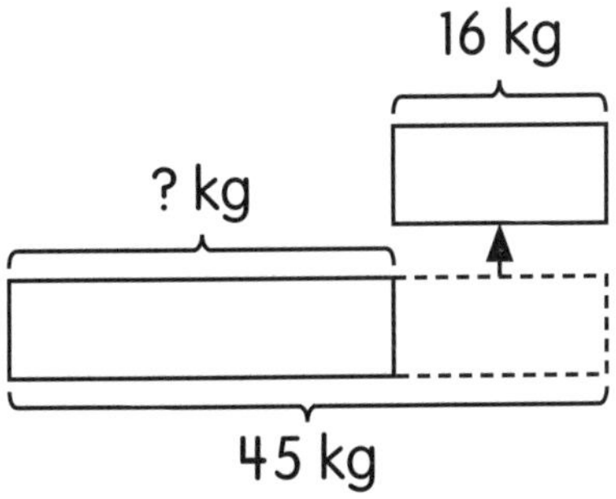

He has ________ kilograms of onions left.

Name: ______________________ Date: ______________

Example

A box full of toy trains is 26 kilograms lighter than a box full of books.
The mass of the box of toy trains is 8 kilograms.
Find the total mass of the two boxes.

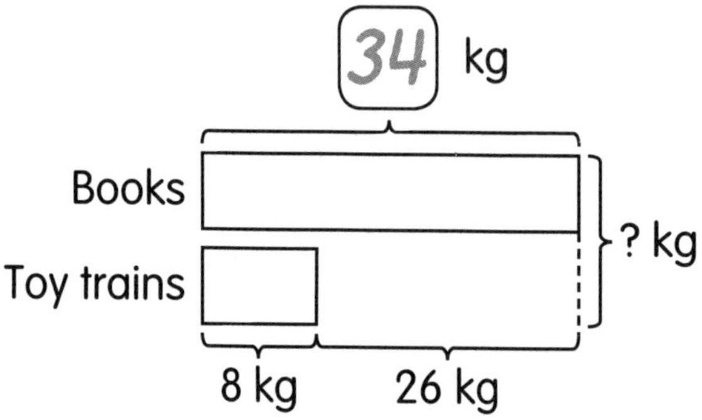

The total mass of the two boxes is 42 kilograms.

2. Sarah has a mass of 48 kilograms.
She is 12 kilograms lighter than Ricky.
What is the total mass of Ricky and Sarah?

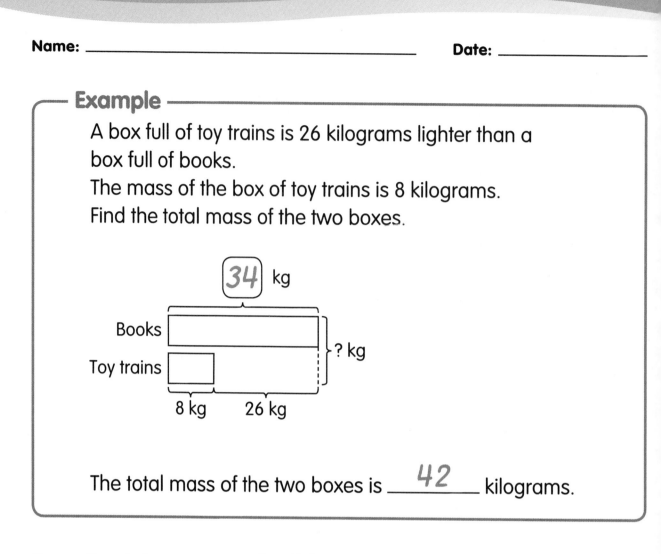

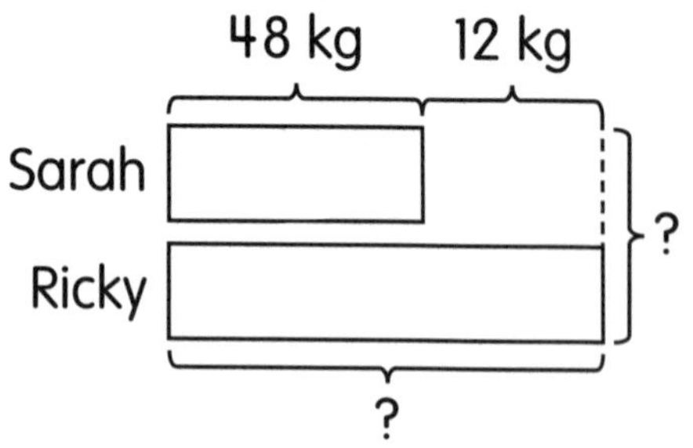

The total mass of Ricky and Sarah is __________ kilograms.

Name: ______________________ Date: ______________

Solve.
Draw bar models to help you.

3. A restaurant bought 140 kilograms of meat.
The chef cooked 45 kilograms of meat in the afternoon.
How many kilograms of meat were left?

__________ kilograms of meat were left.

4. The mass of a box of potatoes is 950 grams.
The mass of the potatoes is 700 grams.
What is the mass of the box?

The mass of the box is __________ grams.

Name: ______________________ Date: ______________

5. The mass of a table is 16 kilograms.
The mass of a chair is 12 kilograms less than the mass of the table.
What is the total mass of the table and the chair?

The total mass of the table and the chair is ________ kilograms.

6. Duncan's toy box is 140 grams heavier than Pete's toy box.
The mass of Duncan's toy box is 500 grams.
What is the total mass of the two toy boxes.

The total mass of the two toy boxes is ________ grams.

Name: ____________________ Date: ____________

Chapter 9 Volume

Worksheet 1 Getting to Know Volume

Fill in the blanks.

Bottle A, B, C, and D are the same size.

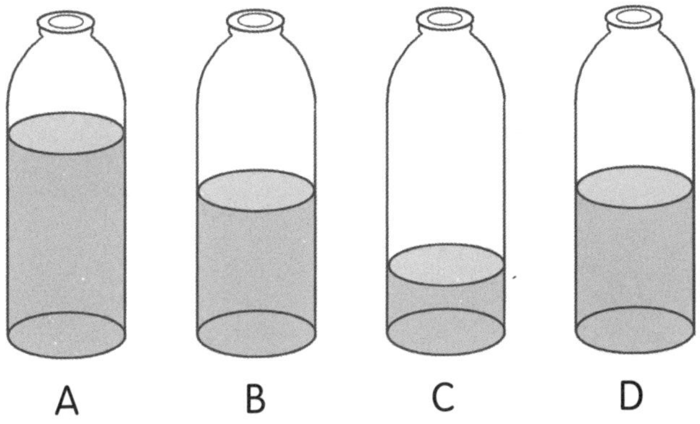

The amount of water is called the **volume** of water.

Example

Bottle __D__ contains as much water as Bottle B.

The volume of water in Bottle __A__ is more than the volume of water in Bottle D.

The volume of water in Bottle __C__ is less than the volume of water in Bottle B.

Bottle __A__ has the greatest amount of water.

Bottle __C__ has the least amount of water.

Name: ______________________ Date: ______________

1. The two bowls are the same size.
Circle the bowl that contains more water.

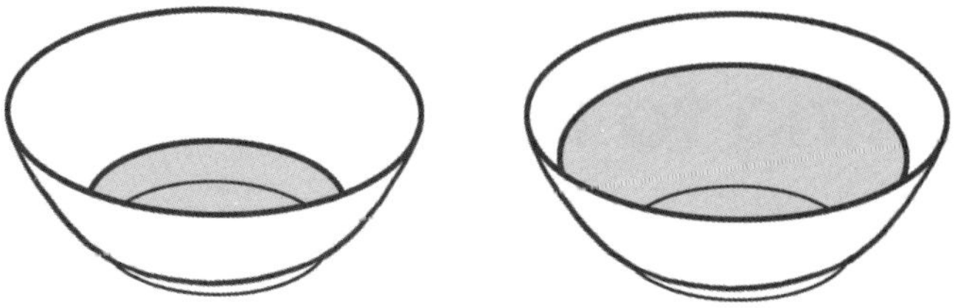

2. The two jugs are the same size.
Circle the jug that contains less water.

3. The three bottles are the same size.
Order Bottles A, B, and C.
Begin with the container that has the greatest amount of water.

__________, __________, __________
greatest

Name: ____________________ Date: ____________

Find the missing letters or numbers.

Jonas fills glasses of the same size with all the water from Container A, Container B, and Container C.

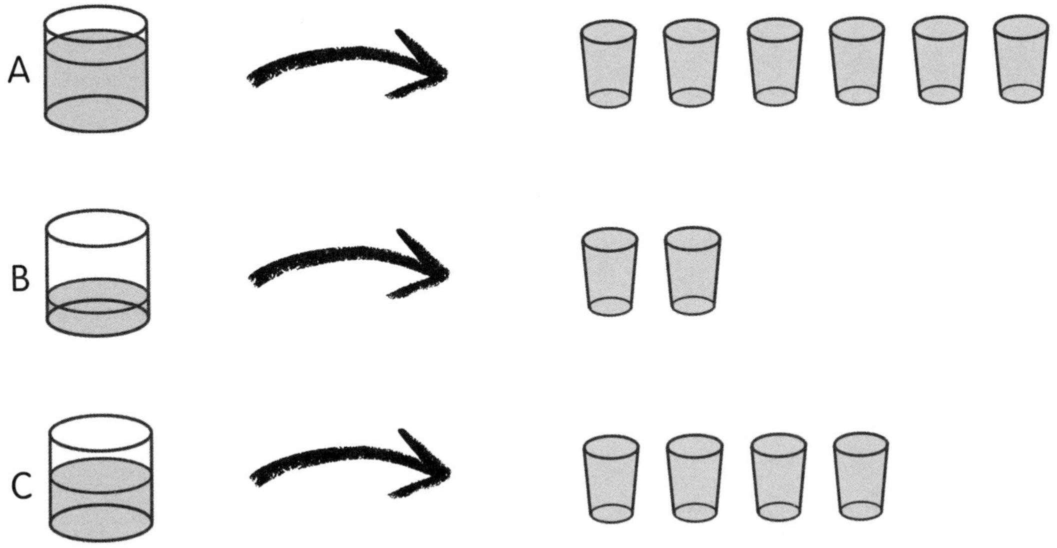

Example

Container ___B___ contains the least amount of water.

4. Container ________ contains more water than Container C.

5. Container A contains ________ more glasses of water than Container B.

6. Container C contains ________ fewer glasses of water than Container A.

7. Order Containers A, B, and C.
Begin with the container that has the greatest amount of water.

________, ________, ________
greatest

Name: ____________________ Date: ____________

Find the missing letters or numbers.

Susanna fills glasses of the same size with all the water from Jug A, Jug B, and Jug C.

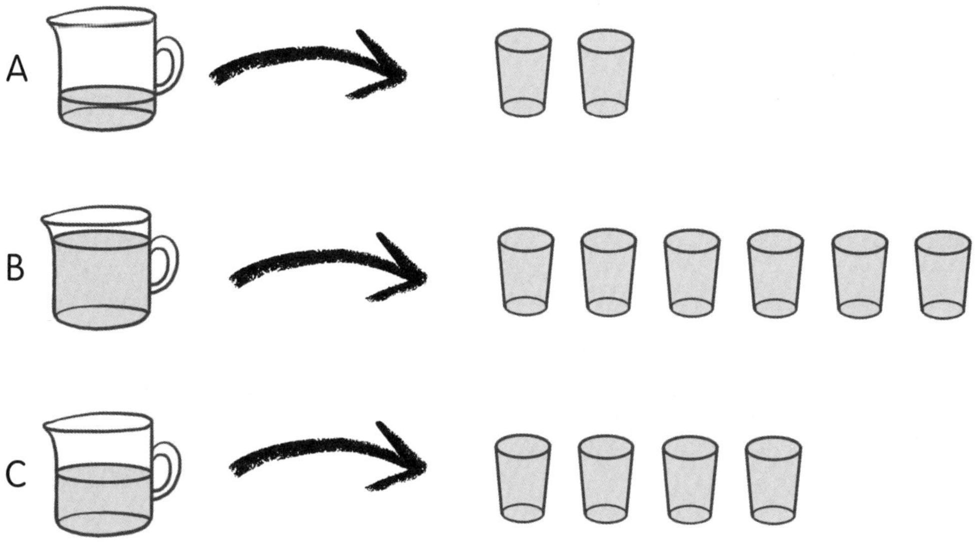

8. Jug ________ contains the greatest amount of water.

9. Jug ________ contains more water than Jug C.

10. Jug A contains ________ fewer glasses of water than Jug B.

11. Jug C contains ________ more glasses of water than Jug A.

12. Order Jugs A, B, and C.
Begin with the jug that has the least amount of water.

________, ________, ________
least

Name: ____________________ Date: ____________

Worksheet 2 Measuring in Liters

Circle the container that holds more than 1 liter of water.

Example

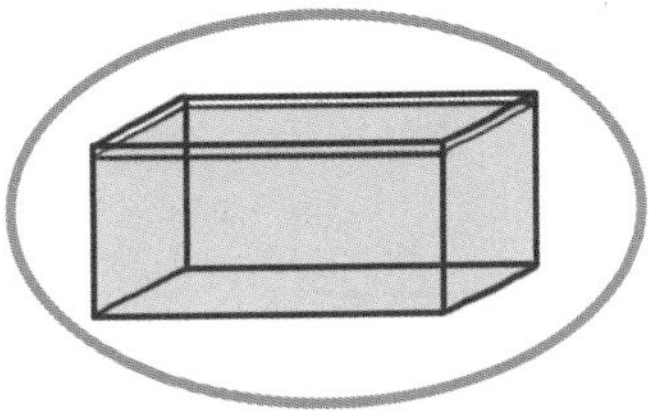

The liter is a unit of volume.
L stands for liter.
Read 1 L as "1 liter".
A liter is used to measure volume.

1.

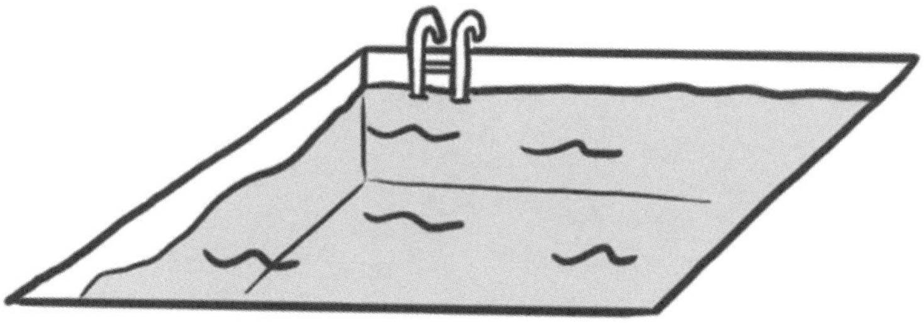

2.

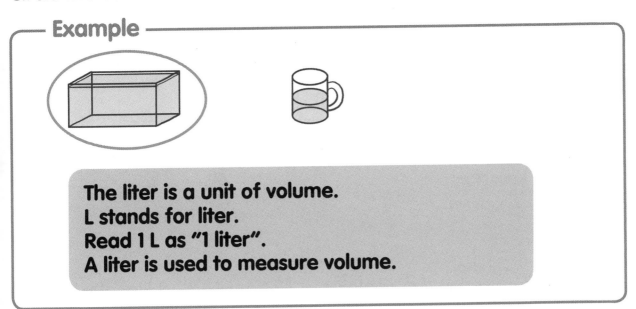

Name: ______________________ Date: ______________

Use *more than* or *less than* to complete each sentence.

Example

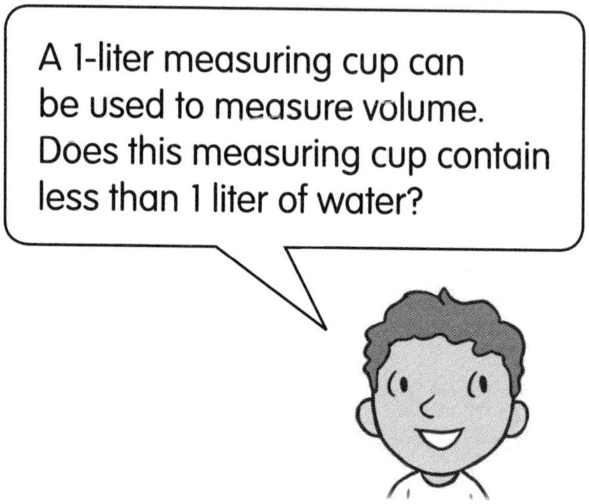

A 1-liter measuring cup can be used to measure volume. Does this measuring cup contain less than 1 liter of water?

This measuring cup contains ___less than___ 1 liter of water.

3.

This measuring cup contains ______________ 1 liter of water.

Name: ____________________ Date: ____________

Find the volume of water in each container.

4. 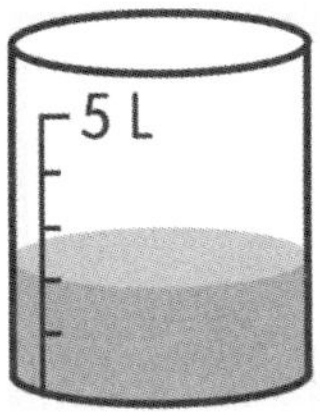

Volume of water = ________ liters

5. 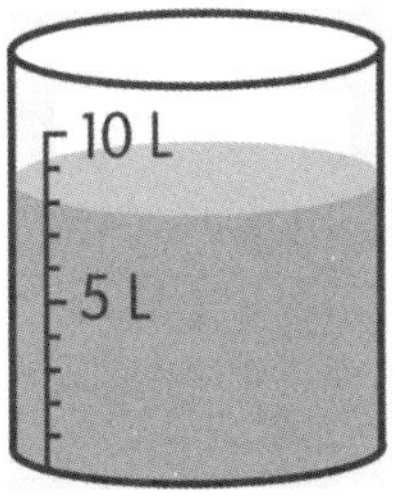

Volume of water = ________ liters

Look at the pictures.
Then fill in the blanks.

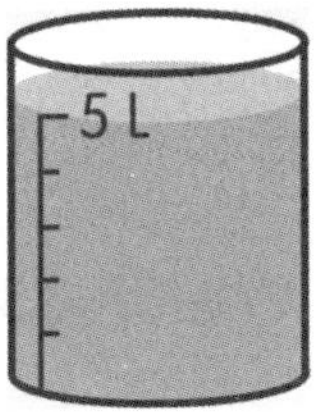

A

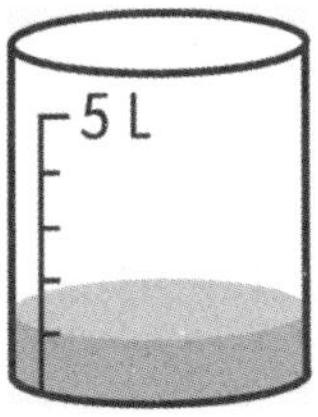

B

6. Container A contains ________ liters of water.

7. Container B contains ________ liter of water.

8. Container A contains ________ more liters of water than Container B.

9. Container B contains ________ fewer liters of water than Container A.

Name: ______________________________ Date: ______________

Look at the pictures.
Then find the missing numbers and letters.

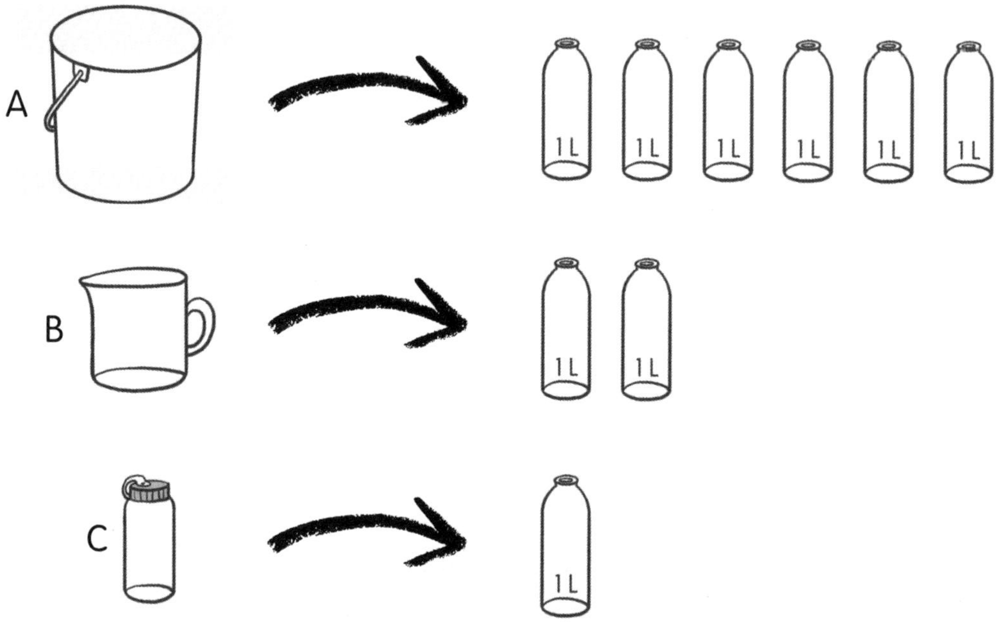

10. Container B has __________ liters of water.

11. Container __________ has the greatest amount of water.

12. Container __________ contains two times as much water as Container C.

13. Container A has __________ liters of water more than Container B.

14. Order the containers.
Begin with the container that has the least amount of water.

__________, __________, __________
least

Name: ______________________ Date: ______________

Worksheet 3 Real-World Problems: Volume

Solve.

Use the bar models to help you.

Example

A bucket contains 15 liters of water.
Jocky uses 9 liters to water the plants.
How much water is left in the bucket?

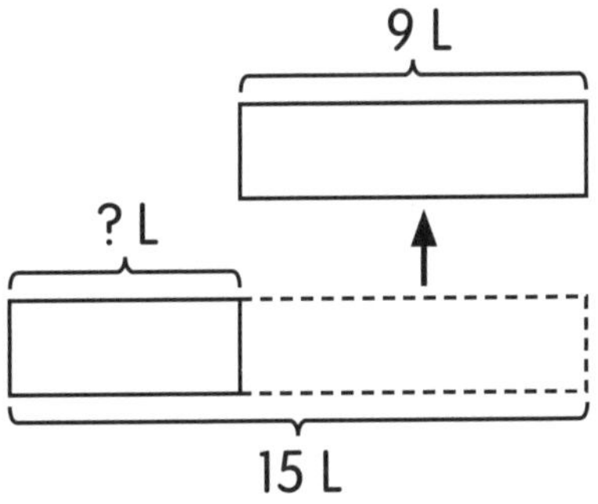

15 – 9 = 6

6 liters of water are left in the bucket.

1. Jennifer mixes apple juice and carrot juice in a jug.
The jug contains 7 liters of apple juice.
It also contains 3 liters of carrot juice.
How much juice is in the jug in all?

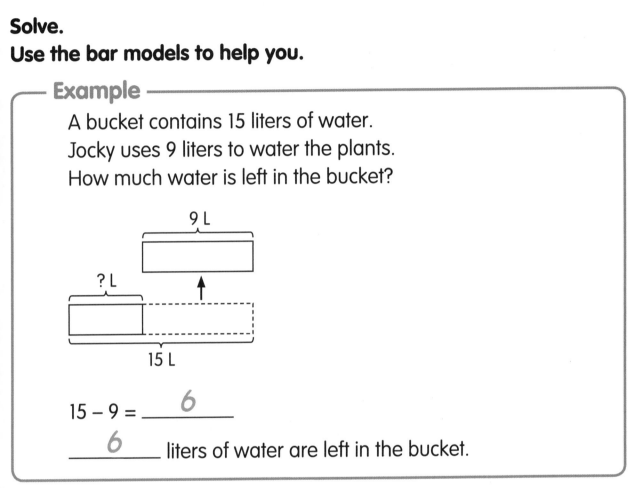

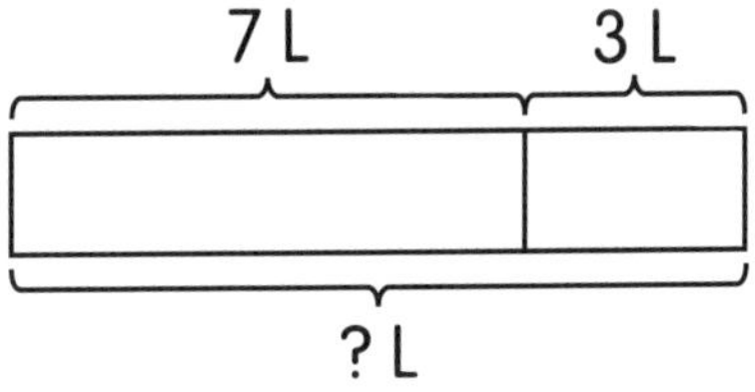

The volume of juice in the jug is ________ liters.

Name: ______________________ Date: ______________

Example

Tank A contains 36 liters of water.
Tank B contains 9 liters of water less than Tank A.
What is the volume of water in both tanks in all?

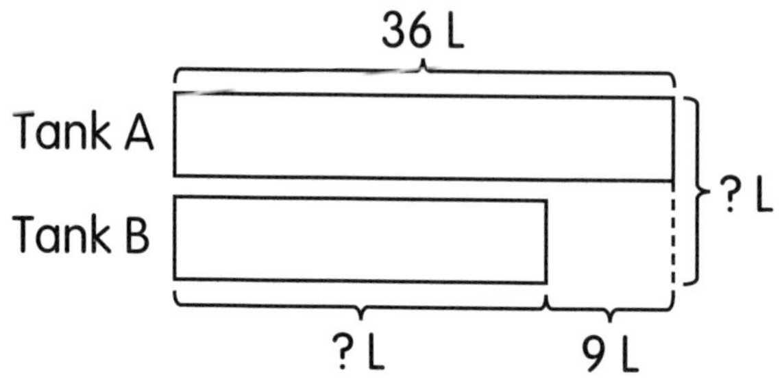

36 – 9 = 27

Tank B contains 27 liters of water.

36 + 27 = 63

The volume of water in both tanks is 63 liters in all.

2. Diana's water tank contains 24 liters more water than Faye's water tank.
Faye's water tank contains 87 liters of water.
How much water do both tanks contain in all?

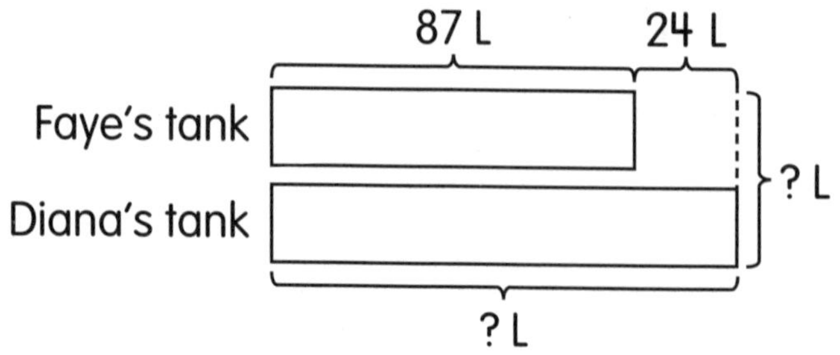

The volume of water in both tanks is ________ liters.

Name: ______________________ Date: ______________

Solve.
Draw bar models to help you.

3. Sophia collects 14 liters of rainwater in July.
She collects 8 liters of rainwater in August.
How much rainwater does she collect in all?

She collects ________ liters of rainwater in all.

4. A water tank contains 30 liters of water.
Mrs. Renata uses 8 liters of water for drinking.
How much water is left in the tank?

________ liters of water are left in the tank.

Name: ______________________ Date: ______________

5. A fish tank contains 7 liters of water.
Tommy pours out 2 liters of water from the tank.
He pours another 4 liters of sea water into the tank.
What is the volume of water in the tank now?

The volume of water in the tank now is ________ liters.

6. A company uses 45 liters of water on Monday.
It uses 14 fewer liters of water on Tuesday.
How much water does the company use on both days?

The company uses ________ liters of water on both days.

Answers

Chapter 1

Worksheet 1

1. 56
   fifty-six
2. 28, 29, 30, 31, 32, 33
3. 22, 32, 42, 52, 62, 72
4. 6, 2, 3; 623
5. 9, 7, 4; 974
6.

991	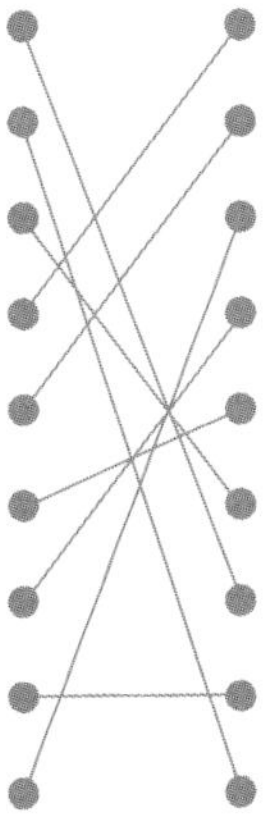	four hundred sixty-two
686		one hundred twenty-nine
214		seven hundred thirty-five
462		three hundred fifty-seven
129		eight hundred forty-three
843		two hundred fourteen
357		nine hundred ninety-one
578		five hundred seventy-eight
735		six hundred eighty-six

7. seven hundred fifty-nine
8. eight hundred forty-five
9. three hundred seventy-two
10. 368, 369, 370, 371, 372
11. 821, 822, 823, 824, 825
12. 249, 259, 269, 279, 289
13. 716, 726, 736, 746, 756
14. 125, 225, 325, 425, 525
15. 356, 456, 556, 656, 756
16. 459, 460, 461, 462, 463
17. 800, 799, 798, 797, 796
18. 973, 972, 971, 970, 969
19. 120, 130, 140, 150, 160
20. 650, 640, 630, 620, 610
21. 433, 423, 413, 403, 393
22. 100, 200, 300, 400, 500
23. 740, 640, 540, 440, 340
24. 534, 434, 334, 234, 134

Worksheet 2

1. 6, 5
   60 and 5 make 65.
   65 is 60 and 5.
   60 + 5 = 65
2.

55	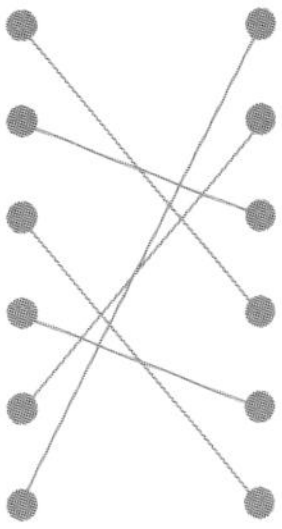	eighty-nine
92		seventy-one
68		ninety-two
47		fifty-five
71		forty-seven
89		sixty-eight

3. 2 hundreds 8 tens 1 ones; 200, 80, 1
4. 627 = 6 hundreds 2 tens 7 ones
   627 = 600 + 20 + 7
5. 835 = 8 hundreds 3 tens 5 ones
   835 = 800 + 30 + 5
6. 904 = 9 hundreds 0 tens 4 ones
   904 = 900 + 0 + 4
7. hundreds, tens, ones
8. ones, hundreds, tens
9. 850
10. 907
11. 400, 10, and 3 make 413.
    413 is the standard form of 413.
    four hundred thirteen is the word form of 413.
    400 + 10 + 3 is the expanded form of 413.
12. 5, 0, 7; 507; five hundred seven; 500 + 7

Worksheet 3

1. 46 13
2. 55 62
3. 69 94
4. 78 87
5. greater than
6. less than
7. greater than
8. less than
9. 8 hundreds is greater than 6 hundreds.
   825 is greater than 699.
   825 > 699
   6 hundreds is less than 8 hundreds.
   699 is less than 825.
   699 < 825
10. 8 tens is greater than 7 tens.
    580 is greater than 579.
    580 > 579
    7 tens is less than 8 tens.
    579 is less than 580.
    579 < 580
11. 628 374

12. 789 798
13. 506 503
14. 475 469
15. 299 198
16. less than
17. greater than
18. less than
19. greater than
20. less than

Worksheet 4

1. 68, 69, 70, 71, 72, 73
2. 84, 83, 82, 81, 80, 79
3. 237, 291, 680
4. 403, 409, 498
5. 358, 448, 458
6. 204, 264
7. 143, 643
8. 404, 405, 406, 407, 408, 409
9. 589, 590, 591, 592, 593, 594
10. 110, 120, 130, 140, 150, 160
11. 290, 300, 310, 320, 330, 340
12. 200, 300, 400, 500, 600, 700
13. 291, 391, 491, 591, 691, 791

Chapter 2

Worksheet 1

1. 2 + 8 = 10
2. 3 + 7 = 10
3. 4 + 6 = 10
4. 1 + 9 = 10
5. 10 = 3 + 7
6. 10 = 5 + 5
7. 7 + 5 = 7 + 3 + 2 = 12
8. 9 + 6 = 9 + 2 + 4 = 15
9. 7 + 4 = 11
10. 8 + 5 = 13
11. 9 + 7 = 16
12. 6 + 6 = 12
13. 7 + 5 = 2 + 5 + 5 = 12
14. 6 + 6 = 5 + 1 + 5 + 1 = 12
15. 6 + 8 = 14
16. 7 + 1 = 11
17. 8 + 7 = 15
18. 9 + 6 = 15
19. 6 = 10 – 4
20. 7 = 10 – 3
21. 9 = 10 – 1
22. 8 = 10 – 2
23. 11 – 6 = 5
24. 12 – 7 = 5
25. 13 – 8 = 5
26. 15 – 9 = 6
27. 14 – 5 = 9
28. 12 – 9 = 3

Worksheet 2

1. 3 ones + 4 ones = 7 ones
   5 tens + 0 tens = 5 tens
   So, 53 + 4 = 57.
2. 9, 1, 3
   So, 312 + 7 = 319.
3. 4, 7, 2
   271 + 3 = 274
4. 636
5. 559
6. 459
7. 236
8. 140 + 8 = 148
   Joy has 148 beads now.
9. 5, 6, 1
   So, 143 + 22 = 165.
10. 287
11. 869
12. 583
13. 679
14. 144 + 24 = 168
    Jorge has 168 magnets now.
15. 4, 9, 6
    So, 462 + 232 = 694.
16. 557
17. 935
18. 998
19. 798
20. 170 + 119 = 289
    The dressmaker has 289 spools of thread now.

Worksheet 3

1. 5 ones + 9 ones = 14 ones
   14 ones = 1 ten 4 ones
   1 ten + 1 ten + 1 ten = 3 tens
   So, 15 + 19 = 34

2. 592
3. 3 ones + 9 ones = 12 ones
   = 1 ten 2 ones
   1 ten + 1 ten + 2 tens = 4 tens
   7 hundreds + 1 hundred = 8 hundreds
   713 + 129 = 842
4. 960
5. 695
6. 793
7. 280
8. 286 + 104 = 390
   Thom uses 390 bricks.
9. 459 + 105 = 564
   The school has 564 students now.

Worksheet 4

1. 545
2. 1 one + 8 ones = 9 ones
   4 tens + 6 tens = 10 tens
   = 1 hundred 0 tens
   1 hundred + 7 hundreds + 1 hundred
   = 9 hundreds
   741 + 168 = 909
3. 914
4. 317
5. 926
6. 657
7. 539
8. 776
9. 460 + 50 = 510
   510 men were at the baseball game.

Worksheet 5

1. 810
2. 7 ones + 8 ones = 15 ones
   = 1 ten 5 ones
   1 ten + 5 tens + 5 tens = 11 tens
   = 1 hundred 1 ten
   1 hundred + 1 hundred + 6 hundreds
   = 8 hundreds
   157 + 658 = 815
3. 520
4. 538
5. 500
6. 683
7. 821
8. 913
9. 217 + 95 = 312
   312 fish are in the pond now.

Chapter 3

Worksheet 1

1. 4 ones – 3 ones = 1 one
   3 tens – 1 ten = 2 tens
   So, 34 – 13 = 21.
2. 9 ones – 6 ones = 3 ones
   4 tens – 0 tens = 4 tens
   8 hundreds – 0 hundreds = 8 hundreds
   So, 849 – 6 = 843.
   843 + 6 = 849
3. 6 ones – 5 ones = 1 one
   8 tens – 0 tens = 8 tens
   4 hundreds – 0 hundreds = 4 hundreds
   486 – 5 = 481
4 837 – 2 = 835
5. 557 – 4 = 553
6. 854 – 4 = 850
7. 298 – 7 = 291
8. 146 – 4 = 142
   Jody has 142 eggs now.
9. 6 ones – 0 ones = 6 ones
   8 tens – 1 ten = 7 tens
   5 hundreds – 0 hundreds = 5 hundreds
   So, 586 – 10 = 576.
   576 + 10 = 586
10. 359 – 45 = 314
11. 128 – 25 = 103
12. 975 – 71 = 904
13. 255 – 12 = 243
14. 243 – 33 = 210
    Xavier has 210 bookmarks left.
15. 7 ones – 3 ones = 4 ones
    8 tens – 5 tens = 3 tens
    6 hundreds – 1 hundred = 5 hundreds
    So, 687 – 153 = 534
    534 + 153 = 687
16. 835 – 314 = 521
17. 467 – 156 = 311
18. 999 – 471 = 528
19. 574 – 161 = 413
20. 175 – 155 = 20
    She needs 20 more cloves of garlic.

Worksheet 2

1. 3 tens 3 ones = 2 tens 13 ones
   13 ones – 8 ones = 5 ones
   2 tens – 0 tens = 2 tens
   So, 33 – 8 = 25

2. 15 ones – 6 ones = 9 ones
1 ten – 1 ten = 0 tens
4 hundreds – 1 hundred = 3 hundreds
So, 425 – 116 = 309
309 + 116 = 425

3. 9 tens 2 ones = 8 tens 12 ones
12 ones – 6 ones = 6 ones
8 tens – 2 tens = 6 tens
7 hundreds – 4 hundreds = 3 hundreds
792 – 426 = 366

4. 543 – 224 = 319

5. 992 – 784 = 208

6. 460 – 115 = 345
Stella has 345 straws left.

7. 355 – 109 = 246
Pauline has 246 coins left.

Worksheet 3

1. 3 ones – 2 ones = 1 one
8 hundreds 2 tens = 7 hundreds 12 tens
12 tens – 4 tens = 8 tens
7 hundreds – 1 hundred = 6 hundreds
So, 823 – 142 = 681
681 + 142 = 823

2. 9 ones – 2 ones = 7 ones
4 hundreds 1 ten = 3 hundreds 11 tens
11 tens – 3 tens = 8 tens
3 hundreds – 1 hundred = 2 hundreds
419 – 132 = 287

3. 192

4. 451

5. 132

6. 93

7. 42

8. 556

9. 450 – 190 = 260
Mr. Rivers drives 260 miles.

Worksheet 4

1. 5 tens 1 one = 4 tens 11 ones
11 ones – 4 ones = 7 ones
7 hundreds 4 tens = 6 hundreds 14 tens
14 tens – 9 tens = 5 tens
6 hundreds – 5 hundreds = 1 hundred
So, 751 – 594 = 157
157 + 594 = 751

2. 8 tens 5 ones = 7 tens 15 ones
15 ones – 7 ones = 8 ones
7 hundreds 7 tens = 6 hundreds 17 tens
17 tens – 9 tens = 8 tens
6 hundreds – 2 hundreds = 4 hundreds
785 – 297 = 488

3. 445

4. 74

5. 57

6. 439

7. 557

8. 359

9. 120 – 35 = 85
85 apples are not rotten.

Worksheet 5

1. 1 hundred = 10 tens
10 tens = 9 tens 10 ones
10 ones – 5 ones = 5 ones
9 tens – 4 tens = 5 tens
0 hundreds – 0 hundreds = 0 hundreds
So, 100 – 45 = 55.

2. 9 hundreds = 8 hundreds 10 tens
10 tens = 9 tens 10 ones
10 ones – 1 one = 9 ones
9 tens – 6 tens = 3 tens
8 hundreds – 4 hundreds = 4 hundreds
900 – 461 = 439

3. 536

4. 72

5. 119

6. 158

7. 342

8. 231

9. 200 – 147 = 53
53 stamps are not U.S. stamps.

Chapter 4

Worksheet 1

1. 3 + 4 = 7
Kai has 7 ☐.

2. 9 – 5 = 4
Tonya has 4 more pens.

3. 15 + 2 = 17
They have 17 coins in all.
Check: 17 – 2 = 15
17 – 15 = 2

4. 40 + 60 = 100
They have 100 cherries in all.
Check: 100 – 40 = 60
100 – 60 = 40

5. 10 – 3 = 7
7 birds are left.
Check: 3 + 7 = 10

6. 450 – 315 = 135
135 Spanish books are in the library.
Check: 315 + 135 = 450

7. 107 + 44 = 151
They fold 151 paper cranes in all.

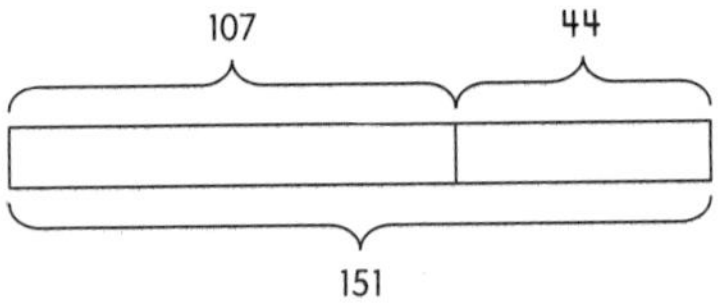

8. 145 + 35 = 180
Aiden has 180 trading cards now.

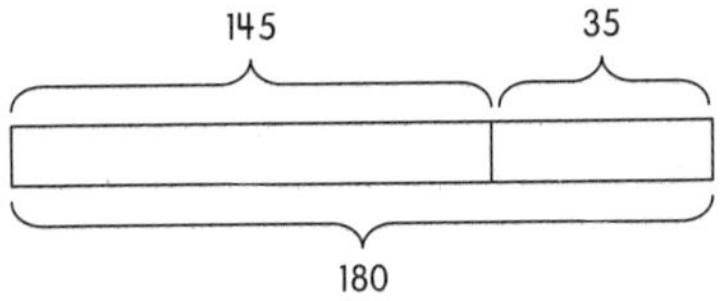

Worksheet 2

1. 5 + 6 = 11
11 books are on the bookshelf now.
Check: 11 – 5 = 6
11 – 6 = 5

2. 180 + 60 = 240
He has 240 red roses now.
Check: 240 – 180 = 60
240 – 60 = 180

3. 13 – 4 = 9
Peter has 9 baseball cards now.
Check: 9 + 4 = 13

4. 125 – 45 = 80
80 markers are left in the supply closet.
Check: 80 + 45 = 125

Worksheet 3

1. \$6 + \$6 = \$12
Jerome has \$12.
Check: 12 – 6 = 6

2. 372 + 148 = 520
Samuel has 520 sheep.
Check: 520 – 372 = 148
520 – 148 = 372

3. 13 – 5 = 8
Gabi has 8 bracelets.
Check: 8 + 5 = 13

4. 380 – 50 = 330
She has 330 peaches.
Check: 330 + 50 = 380

Worksheet 4

1. a. 123 + 277 = 400
Mrs. Holley had 400 books at first.
b. 400 + 40 = 440
Mrs. Holley has 440 books now.

2. a. 195 – 65 = 130
Mr. Garcia drives 130 miles.
b. 195 + 130 = 325
They drive 325 miles in all.

3. a. 160 + 40 = 200
Benny has 200 magnets.
b. 160 + 200 = 360
They have 360 magnets in all.

Chapter 5

Worksheet 1

1. A ladybug has 6 legs.
6 + 6 + 6 = 18
3 sixes = 18
3 ladybugs have 18 legs.

2. 4 threes = 3 + 3 + 3 + 3
= 12
4 groups of 3 = 12
There are 12 strawberries in all.

3. 4; 4 + 4 = 8; 2 × 4 = 8; 8
4. 4; 4; 4 + 4 + 4 + 4 = 16; 4 × 4 = 16; 16
5. 5; 2 × 5 = 10; 10
6. 3; 3 × 3 = 9; 9

Worksheet 2

1. Each child gets 3 muffins.
2. Each basket has 4 pears.
3. There are 3 groups of 2 tomatoes.
4. There are 5 groups of 4 peaches.
5. 15 ÷ 5 = 3; 3
6. 4 – 2 – 2 = 0; 4 ÷ 2 = 2; 2
7. 12 – 4 – 4 – 4 = 0
12 ÷ 4 = 3
3 cousins get crayons from him.

Worksheet 3

1. $3 \times 8 = 24$
   There are 24 legs in all.
2. $20 \div 5 = 4$
   There are 4 glass jars.

Chapter 6

Worksheet 1

1. 2, 4, 6, 8, 10, 12, 14
   I add 2 to get the next number.
2. 2 fours is 2 groups of 4.
3. 2, 4, 6
   $3 \times 2 = 6$
   There are 6 wings in all.
4. 2, 4, 6, 8, 10
   $5 \times 2 = 10$
   They have 10 baseball cards in all.
5. $2 \times 2 = 4$
   They eat 4 pancakes in all.
6. $6 \times 2 = 12$
   They hold 12 balloons in all.
7. $2 \times 10 = 20$
   Isabelle uses 20 pieces of bread.
8. $2 \times 8 = 16$
   There are 16 handles in all.
9. $2 \times 6 = 12$
   Benny runs 12 times around the track in 6 days.

Worksheet 2

1. $3 \times 2 = 6$
   The 3 keychains have 6 keys in all.
2. $4 \times \$2 = \$8$
   They have \$8 in all.
3. $8 \times 2 = 16$
   Sharon buys 16 pencils in all.
4. 2; 4; 14
5. 2; 4; 16
6. 16; 16
7. 18; 18

Worksheet 3

1. 5, 10, 15, 20, 25, 30, 35
   I add 5 to get the next number.
2. 2 fives is 2 groups of 5.
3. 5, 10, 15
   $3 \times 5 = 15$
   Barry has 15 bagels in all.
4. $6 \times 5 = 30$
   She sells 30 crayons.
5. $8 \times 5 = 40$
   She has 40 cows in all.

Worksheet 4

1. $4 \times 5 = 20$
   Jasmine has 20 erasers in all.
2. $5 \times 5 = 25$
3. $9 \times 5 = 45$
4. $6 \times 5 = 30$; $5 \times 6 = 30$
5. $10 \times 5 = 50$; $5 \times 10 = 50$

Worksheet 5

1. 10, 20, 30, 40, 50, 60, 70
   I add 10 to get the next number.
2. 3 tens is 3 groups of 10.
3. 10, 20, 30, 40, 50, 60, 70
   $7 \times 10 = 70$
   There are 70 marbles in all.
4. $5 \times 10 = 50$
   There are 50 coins in all.
5. $4 \times 10 = 40$
   Pauline has 40 books in all.
6. $10 \times 3 = 30$; $3 \times 10 = 30$
7. $10 \times 6 = 60$; $6 \times 10 = 60$

Worksheet 6

1. Circle 2 groups of 2.
   There is 1  left.
2. Circle 2 groups of 2.
   There are 0  left.
3. The next number is odd.
4. The next number is even.
5. Draw 9 triangles.
   9 is an odd number.
6. Draw 12 triangles.
   12 is an even number.
7. Draw 2 groups of 3 objects.
   The number of objects is even.
8. Draw 2 groups of 10 objects.
   The number of objects is even.
9. The number of pears is odd.
10. The number of mangoes is even.

Chapter 7

Worksheet 1

1. The tape dispenser is about 5 units long.
2. The mirror is about 6 units long.
3. The length of the desk is 2 meters.
4. The width of the bed is more than 1 meter.
5. The height of the table is less than 1 meter.
6. Circle bus, house, traffic light and the refrigerator.

Worksheet 2

1. False
2. True
3. True
4. False
5. True
6. False
7. True
8. True

Worksheet 3

1. The length of the stapler is 9 centimeters.
2. Curve A is 7 centimeters long.
3. Circle lines A, C, and F.
4. Draw a 3-centimeter line.
5. Draw a 7-centimeter line.
6. Draw a 11-centimeter line.
7. The width of the envelope is 16 centimeters.
8. The crayon is 8 centimeters long.
9. The key is 6 centimeters long.
10. The pen is 13 centimeters long.

Worksheet 4

1. The watch is 15 centimeters long.
   The stamp is 3 centimeters long.
   The stamp is shorter than the watch.
2. a. The length of the bookmark is 7 centimeters.
   b. The longest item is the bookmark.
   c. The bookmark is longer than the bracelet.
   d. The paperclip and the ribbon have the same length.
3. Draw a 10-centimeter line.

Worksheet 5

1. a. 17 + 23 = 40
   Harry bought 40 meters of cloth.
   b. 23 − 17 = 6
   The piece of cloth that Harry cut off is 6 meters shorter.
2. a. 13 + 9 = 22
   The length of Shirley's ribbon is 22 centimeters.
   b. 13 + 22 = 35
   The total length of their ribbons is 35 centimeters.

Chapter 8

Worksheet 1

1. The mass of the apple is about 6 units.
2. The mass of the tomato is about 4 units.
3. Circle 3.
4. Circle 4.
5. Circle 3.
6. The mass of the bag of potatoes is 2 kilograms.
7. 5 − 2 = 3
   The mass of the watermelon is 3 kilograms.

Worksheet 2

1. The mouse is lighter than the cat.
2. The cat is heavier than the mouse.
3. True
4. False
5. False
6. False
7. The mass of Bag A is 5 kilograms.
8. The mass of Bag B is 3 kilograms.
9. Bag B is the lightest.
10. Bag C is the heaviest.
11. The total mass of Bag A and Bag B is 8 kilograms.
12. Bag B, Bag A, Bag C

Worksheet 3

1. The mass of the clock is 10 grams.
2. The mass of the bag of carrots is 250 grams.
3. The mass of the puppy is 490 grams.
4. The mass of the teddy bear is 200 grams.
5. The mass of the muffin is 50 grams.

Worksheet 4

1. The mass of the melon is 300 grams.
2. The mass of the pear is 40 grams.
3. The pear is the lightest.
4. The melon is the heaviest.
5. The total mass of the fruits is 470 grams.
6. The mass of the notebook is 60 grams.
7. The mass of the stapler is 100 grams.
8. The mass of the cup is 250 grams.
9. 250 – 100 = 150
   The stapler is 150 grams lighter than the cup.
10. 250 – 60 = 190
    The cup is 190 grams heavier than the notebook.
11. cup, stapler, notebook

Worksheet 5

1. 45 – 16 = 29
   He has 29 kilograms of onions left.
2. 48 + 12 = 60
   48 + 60 = 108
   The total mass of Ricky and Sarah is 108 kilograms.
3. 140 – 45 = 95
   95 kilograms of meat were left.
4. 950 – 700 = 250
   The mass of the box is 250 grams.
5. 16 – 12 = 4
   4 + 16 = 20
   The total mass of the table and the chair is 20 kilograms.
6. 500 – 140 = 360
   360 + 500 = 860
   The total mass of the two toy boxes is 860 grams.

Chapter 9

Worksheet 1

1. Circle the bowl on the right.
2. Circle the jug on the left.
3. Bottle C, Bottle A, Bottle B
4. Container A contains more water than Container C.
5. Container A contains 4 more glasses of water than Container B.
6. Container C contains 2 fewer glasses of water than Container A.
7. Container A, Container C, Container B
8. Jug B contains the greatest amount of water.
9. Jug B contains more water than Jug C.
10. Jug A contains 4 fewer glasses of water than Jug B.
11. Jug C contains 2 more glasses of water than Jug A.
12. Jug A, Jug C, Jug B

Worksheet 2

1. Circle swimming pool.
2. Circle pail.
3. This measuring cup contains more than 1 liter of water.
4. 2
5. 8
6. Container A contains 5 liters of water.
7. Container B contains 1 liter of water.
8. Container A contains 4 more liters of water than Container B.
9. Container B contains 4 fewer liters of water than Container A.
10. Container B has 2 liters of water.
11. Container A has the greatest amount of water.
12. Container B contains two times as much water as Container C.
13. Container A has 4 liters of water more than Container B.
14. Container C, Container B, Container A

Worksheet 3

1. 7 + 3 = 10
   The volume of juice in the jug is 10 liters.
2. 87 + 24 = 111
   87 + 111 = 198
   The volume of water in both tanks is 198 liters.
3. 14 + 8 = 22
   She collects 22 liters of rainwater in all.
4. 30 – 8 = 22
   22 liters of water are left in the tank.
5. 7 – 2 = 5
   5 + 4 = 9
   The volume of water in the tank now is 9 liters.
6. 45 – 14 = 31
   31 + 45 = 76
   The company uses 76 liters of water on both days.